CAPITAL ACCOUNT REGIMES AND THE DEVELOPING COUNTRIES

Also by G. K. Helleiner

AGRICULTURAL PLANNING IN EAST AFRICA (*editor*)

A WORLD DIVIDED (*editor*)

FOR GOOD OR EVIL (*editor*)

FROM ADJUSTMENT TO DEVELOPMENT IN AFRICA (*editor with Giovanni Andrea Cornia*)

MANUFACTURING FOR EXPORT IN THE DEVELOPING WORLD (*editor*)

PEASANT AGRICULTURE, GOVERNMENT AND ECONOMIC GROWTH IN NIGERIA

POVERTY, PROSPERITY AND THE WORLD ECONOMY (*editor with S. Abrahamian, E. Bacha, R. Lawrence and P. Malan*)

THE IMF AND AFRICA (*editor*)

INTERNATIONAL ECONOMIC DISORDER

THE INTERNATIONAL MONETARY AND FINANCIAL SYSTEM (*editor*)

INTERNATIONAL TRADE AND ECONOMIC DEVELOPMENT

INTRA-FIRM TRADE AND THE DEVELOPING COUNTRIES

THE NEW GLOBAL ECONOMY AND THE DEVELOPING COUNTRIES

THE OTHER SIDE OF INTERNATIONAL DEVELOPMENT POLICY (*editor*)

TRADE POLICY AND INDUSTRIALIZATION IN TURBULENT TIMES (*editor*)

TRADE POLICY, INDUSTRIALIZATION AND DEVELOPMENT (*editor*)

Capital Account Regimes and the Developing Countries

Edited by

G. K. Helleiner
Professor of Economics
University of Toronto
Canada

in association with
UNITED NATIONS CONFERENCE
ON TRADE AND DEVELOPMENT

First edition 1998
Reprinted (with new preface) 1999

Published by
MACMILLAN PRESS LTD
Houndmills, Basingstoke, Hampshire RG21 6XS
and London
Companies and representatives
throughout the world

ISBN 0–333–72070–9 hardcover
ISBN 0–333–77835–9 paperback

A catalogue record for this book is available from the British Library.

This book is printed on paper suitable for recycling and made from fully managed and sustained forest sources.

10 9 8 7 6 5 4 3 2 1
08 07 06 05 04 03 02 01 00 99

Printed and bound in Great Britain by
Antony Rowe Ltd, Chippenham, Wiltshire

Published in the United States of America by
ST. MARTIN'S PRESS, INC.,
Scholarly and Reference Division
175 Fifth Avenue, New York, N.Y. 10010

ISBN 0–312–21723–4 clothbound

Contents

List of Figures

List of Tables

Notes on the Contributors

Carlos Budnevich L. is Manager of Financial Analysis, Banco Central de Chile. He has been Professor of Economics at Universidad Católica de Chile and Universidad de Chile, and has held positions as an Economist at Corporación de Investigaciones Económicas para Latinoamérica (CIEPLAN) and the Superintendencia de Bancos. He holds a PhD in Economics from the University of Pennsylvania.

Rudi Dornbusch is Ford Professor of Economics and International Management at the Massachusetts Institute of Technology

G. K. Helleiner is Professor of Economics at the University of Toronto and Research Coordinator for the Intergovernmental Group of Twenty-Four on International Monetary Affairs (G-24).

Louis Austin Kasekende is Executive Director, Research and Policy Function, at the Bank of Uganda.

Damoni Kitabire is Acting Director of Budget, Ministry of Finance, Republic of Uganda.

Guillermo R. Le Fort-V. is Head of the International Division of the Central Bank of Chile, and a member of the Governor's advisory team in macroeconomic and financial policy matters. Formerly he was a Senior Economist at the International Monetary Fund (IMF) and Assistant Professor of Economics at the University of Chile. He holds a PhD in Economics from the University of California at Los Angeles.

Matthew Martin is Director of External Finance for Africa, (EFA), an economic policy research, advisory and capacity-building organization funded by multilateral and bilateral donors. EFA specializes in national debt reduction strategies, and external and domestic financing of development, and is currently working with over twenty African and non-African governments.

Aziz Ali Mohammed was the head of the G-24 Liaison Office in Washington when this paper was written. Previously he was Chairman of the G-24 Deputies and Special Advisor to the Governor of the State Bank of Pakistan, after a distinguished career in the International Monetary Fund.

Yung Chul Park is Professor of Economics at Korea University, and the President of the Korea Institute of Finance. He previously served as the chief economic adviser to former President Doo Hwan Chun, and as President of the Korea Development Institute.

Chi-Young Song is Assistant Professor in the Division of Economics, Kookmin University, Seoul, Korea. At the time of writing he was a Research Fellow at the Korea Institute of Finance. He received his PhD from Brown University.

John Williamson was Senior Fellow at the Institute for International Economics in Washington, DC, when this paper was written. He is currently on leave from the Institute and serving as Chief Economist for South Asia in the World Bank.

Preface to the 1999 Reprint

The East Asian crisis of 1997–8 and its profound implications for the economic performance of the global economy have lent new importance to the debate on capital account regimes in developing countries and elsewhere. Previously hell-bent on liberalizing all investment flows, the OECD nations and the International Monetary Fund (IMF) now tread far more cautiously in this sphere. Proposals for a new global financial architecture are now discussed in G-7 Summit conferences. The debate over the destabilizing role of short-term private international capital flows has changed from discussion of *whether* to try to control them toward *how* to do so. New sources of financing to forestall or address financial crises in emerging economies have been slapped together in an *ad hoc* fashion. Recognition of the key importance of appropriate regimes for the capital account in emerging and developing economies is now universal.

At the time that the chapters presented in this book were originally commissioned and written there was considerably greater confidence within OECD governments and within the IMF – in the efficacy of free international capital movement. Within many developing countries, however, there was still deep concern over the potential risk in premature 'opening' of the capital account. This volume had its origins in a concentrated research effort to shed light on capital account issues, undertaken as part of the research programme of the Intergovernmental Group of Twenty-Four on International Monetary Affairs (G-24), the developing country caucus within the IMF and World Bank.

The G-24 Research Programme is financed by the International Development Research Centre (IDRC) of Canada and the governments of Denmark and The Netherlands as well as the G-24 countries themselves. In 1994, the IDRC made a special grant to the G-24 Research Programme to enable it to explore issues arising in the capital account of the developing countries, and all of these papers were thereby made possible. The first six chapters in this book were originally prepared under contract with the United Nations Conference on Trade and Development (UNCTAD) which administers the Trust Fund which finances the G-24 Research Programme. These chapters were originally published in the G-24 research series, *International Monetary and Financial Issues for the 1990s*, volumes VII and

VIII (United Nations, New York and Geneva, 1996 and 1997) The seventh chapter was prepared for the G-24 as a 'position paper' in the run-up to the 1997 annual meetings of the IMF. All of these contributions now seem even more relevant to current international policy debate than they were when originally prepared.

The Group of Twenty-Four is most grateful to the IDRC for its support of this project. I should also like to thank Detlef Kotte of UNCTAD for his editorial work in the preparation of these papers for publication and Barbara Tiede at the University of Toronto for her assistance in the preparation of the final manuscript.

G. K. HELLEINER

List of Abbreviations

ADR	American Depository Receipts
ALADI	Association for Latin American Integration
BIBF	Bangkok International Banking Facilities
BIS	Bank for International Settlements
CFA	Communauté Financière d'Afrique
CPI	Consumer price index
EC	exchange certificates
EEF	Exchange Equalization Fund
FDI	Foreign Direct Investment
FEMA	Foreign Exchange Management Act
FFCT	Financial Foreign Currency Title
G-7	Group of Seven
G-10	Group of Ten
G-24	Group of Twenty-Four
GAB	General Arrangements to Borrow (of IMF)
GATS	General Agreement on Trade in Services
GATT	General Agreement on Tariffs and Trade
GDI	gross domestic investment
GDP	gross domestic product
IMF	International Monetary Fund
IOSCO	International Organization of Securities Commissions
LIBOR	London Inter-Bank Offer Rate
MAI	Multilateral Agreement on Investment
MSBs	monetary stabilization bonds
NAFTA	North American Free Trade Agreement
NDA	net domestic assets
NFA	net foreign assets
NIEs	newly industrializing economies
ODA	Official Development Assistance
OECD	Organization for Economic Cooperation and Development
OFI	other foreign investment
RBZ	Reserve Bank of Zimbabwe
SBI	Sertifikat Bank Indonesia
SBPU	Sural Berhaga Pasar Uang
SDR	special drawing right
SET	Stock Exchange of Thailand

SSA	sub-Saharan Africa
TNC	transnational corporation
UNCTAD	United Nations Conference on Trade and Development
VDR	variable deposit requirements
WTO	World Trade Organization

1 Capital Account Regimes and the Developing Countries: Issues and Approaches

G. K. Helleiner[1]

I INTRODUCTION

Debate over the role of volatile private capital flows in international payments and appropriate government policies relating to them has a long history. The League of Nations produced an influential study of exchange-rate experience in the interwar period that addressed some of these issues (Nurkse, 1944); policy debate thereon sharpened in the preparations for (and at) the Bretton Woods conference in 1944; and it resurfaced repeatedly as current and capital account convertibility was restored to an increasing number of developed countries in the post Second World War period (Helleiner, 1994).

In the developing countries, the early discussions tended to centre upon the benefits and costs of foreign direct investment and the problems of 'capital flight' rather than those of the volatility of (then virtually non-existent) portfolio financial flows. With the dramatic expansion of commercial bank lending to the developing countries in the 1970s and the subsequent debt crisis of the 1980s, attention shifted to analysis of sovereign debt, default, emergency lending, and possible 'workout' schemes, with particular reference to the respective roles of government, banks and the international financial institutions. The difficulties encountered with financial liberalization and the 'opening' of external capital accounts in the Southern Cone of Latin America in the late 1970s generated a burst of research and discussion of necessary prerequisites or concomitants of a liberalized capital account and related issues of optimal sequencing (e.g. Diaz-Alejandro, 1985; McKinnon, 1991; Corbo and DeMelo, 1986). With the sharp increase in private international portfolio capital flows to developing countries in the 1990s, particularly to countries in Asia and Latin America, interest in the problems and possibilities they create began to accelerate, as did discussion of the appropriate external capital account regime for these countries.

By the early 1990s several general analytical studies of these questions had already been undertaken (e.g. Williamson, 1991; Akyüz, 1992; Reisen and Fischer, 1993). In the past few years, however, there has been an unprecedented burst of books, papers and conferences on the problems created for developing countries by massive and volatile international flows of private capital, larger for them than ever before, and appropriate policy responses.[2] Both the International Monetary Fund (IMF) and the World Bank have directed a great deal of further attention, during this period, to the problem of volatile private capital flows and the management of capital surges (notably in IMF, 1995b and 1995d; EDI, 1995; Corbo and Hernandez, 1996). Indeed, in some respects, as will be seen, IMF documents have altered their message over this short period, as analysis and experience accumulated. Not only has the IMF directed increased research attention to capital account issues in recent years but, in 1995, its Executive Board also authorized increased attention to them in its surveillance activities. By 1997, the IMF was actively discussing an amendment to its Articles of Agreement, to authorize it to pursue capital account liberalization as well as its traditional liberalization in the current account. Of course, none of this recent experience or the analysis thereof has altered the prime need for macroeconomic policy to create a sound framework for private domestic savings and investment decisions, which remain at the core of successful long-term development.

Among those who first directed developing-country attention to these problems were Calvo (1996) and Mohammed (1996), whose papers at the Group of Twenty-Four (G-24) technical conference (in Cartagena) in early 1994 stimulated lively debate there. A modest research programme was launched by the G-24 shortly thereafter to attempt to shed greater light on the policy issues raised by emerging capital account experience. In the mean time, the Mexican crisis of late 1994 and early 1995 stimulated further public debate and policy discussion. Many other new studies have since been published, as already noted, some of them overlapping those of the G-24 project, the results of which appear in this volume.

This volume includes case studies of a number of developing countries: in Latin America, Chile and Colombia (by Le Fort V. and Budnevich); in Asia, Indonesia, Malaysia, Thailand and the Republic of Korea (by Park and Song); and in Africa, Kenya, South Africa, Uganda, Zambia, Zimbabwe and the United Republic of Tanzania (by Kasekende, Kitabire and Martin). The case studies do not include any countries that adopted currency board arrangements like those of Argentina. Nor do they include Eastern European or other economies in transition. By now there have been numerous other published studies of Asian and Latin American experiences in the IMF and elsewhere. IMF accounts of some of these countries' practices (Chile, Colombia, Indonesia, Malaysia, Thailand and the Republic of Korea) may be found in a recent paper (1995b, pp. 80–94) and summary versions of three of them (Chile, Colombia and Malaysia) in another (1995e, pp. 38–44).

It also includes two more general papers on capital account issues – John Williamson's assessment of the possibility of an IMF financing role in financial crises, and Rudi Dornbusch's analysis of the efficacy of cross-border payments taxes and alternative capital account regimes. Since Williamson's paper was written, the IMF and the Group of Ten have taken some steps in the direction of such an IMF role, but the relevance of his main points is as great as ever. In the last chapter of this volume, Aziz Ali Mohammed assesses the principal issues surrounding the treatment of the capital account in the IMF, as of early September 1997 (some considerable time after the other papers in the volume were completed). Appendices present those paragraphs of the G-24 communiqué of 20 September 1997 that relate to capital account issues and the special statement on these issues agreed by the IMF's Interim Committee on the next day.

The purpose of this first chapter is to introduce the six subsequent ones and, more particularly, to summarize their major results, place them into the context of ongoing debate, consider some of their policy implications at national and international levels, and suggest further research requirements. It first surveys the current state of knowledge as to the new forms, and roles, of private capital flows to developing countries in the 1990s and appropriate national and international policy responses to the problems and possibilities they create. Section II describes the growth of these flows in the 1990s, and some of their effects in recipient countries. Section III addresses the question of alternative capital account policies for developing countries, including the rationale and efficacy of various kinds of direct and indirect controls over international capital flows. In Section IV, the possibility of improved international arrangements is considered, including the provision of increased liquidity, better procedures for orderly debt workouts, and clarified international regimes. Section V presents issues deserving further research. There follows a brief conclusion.

II THE NEW PRIVATE CAPITAL FLOWS TO DEVELOPING COUNTRIES IN THE 1990s

Increased Size and Altered Composition

Private capital flows to developing countries, after slumping in the 1980s, increased dramatically, and to unprecedented levels, in the first half of the 1990s. According to the IMF, net private flows in the 1989–95 period were, on average, about ten times those of the 1983–8 period, whereas net official flows had fallen by more than half (see Table 1.1). According to the World Bank, between 1990 and 1993 private capital flows to developing countries rose nearly fourfold, before stabilizing at about $160–70 billion in 1994–5 as United States' interest rates rose and the Mexican crisis hit (World Bank, 1996, pp. 10–11). These private flows remain, however, highly concentrated. Only about twenty developing countries are today considered creditworthy by international capital markets and banks (World Bank, 1996, p. 11). Foreign direct investment is almost equally concentrated. In recent years, the African continent has received only 4 per cent of total net private flows.

In the 1990s there was a sharp increase in international portfolio investment, both in debt instruments and in equity, in developing countries. The relative importance of bank lending to developing countries fell drastically; that of foreign direct investment also fell, although its absolute size grew very rapidly. Much higher proportions of external capital were also now directed to private-sector borrowers than to governments in developing countries. Tables 1.2 and 1.3 summarize the overall composition of capital flows to the major developing areas and selected countries (studied in this volume) in recent years. Private flows have accounted for very substantial percentages of individual recipient countries' GDP in the 1990s (e.g. 6 to 8 per cent in Colombia and Chile, respectively; 10 to 13 per cent in Thailand and Malaysia, respectively). Foreign direct investment has been relatively more important in Asia than elsewhere, but the relative contribution of portfolio flows has risen nearly everywhere. In some of the sub-Saharan African countries, 'private transfers' have reached remarkable levels (e.g. 9 per cent in the United Republic of

Table 1.1 Developing countries: capital flows, 1973–95[a] (annual average, $ billion)

	1973–7	*1978–82*	*1983–8*	*1989–95*	*1994*	*1995*
All developing countries						
Net private capital flows[b]	10.2	26.0	11.6	114.3	149.0	166.4
Net direct investment	3.6	9.0	12.6	39.8	61.3	71.7
Net portfolio investment	0.2	1.7	4.3	41.5	50.4	37.0
Other net investments	6.4	15.3	−5.2	33.1	37.3	57.8
Net official flows	11.0	25.5	29.5	11.7	2.6	27.3
Change in reserves[c]	−20.2	−21.7	−9.6	−56.8	−57.9	−75.7
Africa						
Net private capital flows[b]	4.5	4.3	0.5	4.9	11.9	9.8
Net direct investment	1.0	0.3	1.1	2.1	2.2	2.1
Net portfolio investment	0.1	−0.3	−0.4	−0.3	1.1	0.1
Other net investments	3.4	4.3	−0.1	3.0	8.6	7.6
Net official flows	2.4	7.2	6.6	2.0	1.5	2.8
Change in reserves[c]	−1.4	0.4	−0.4	−2.1	−5.1	−1.4
Asia						
Net private capital flows[b]	4.3	13.9	11.2	45.7	75.1	98.2
Net direct investment	1.4	3.0	5.6	24.4	41.9	52.4
Net portfolio investment	0.1	0.2	0.9	10.1	16.0	18.5
Other net investments	2.8	10.7	4.7	11.2	17.1	27.3
Net official flows	4.0	7.4	6.4	7.2	6.0	5.9
Change in reserves[c]	−6.9	−7.0	−18.0	−38.9	−61.6	−50.0
Middle East and Europe						
Net private capital flows[b]	−10.3	−21.1	1.9	29.7	11.4	19.0
Net direct investment	−1.3	−0.1	1.2	0.9	−0.5	0.0
Net portfolio investment	0.0	−0.2	5.0	13.6	15.9	8.4
Other net investments	−9.1	−20.8	−4.3	15.2	−4.1	10.5
Net official flows	2.3	6.6	6.6	−2.6	−1.4	−3.8
Change in reserves[c]	−14.2	−17.6	9.5	−1.4	−0.2	−2.6
Latin America and the Caribbean						
Net private capital flows[b]	11.7	28.9	−2.0	34.0	50.7	39.5
Net direct investment	2.5	5.8	4.7	12.4	17.7	17.1
Net portfolio investment	0.0	2.0	−1.2	18.1	17.4	10.0
Other net investments	9.2	21.1	−5.6	3.6	15.6	12.3
Net official flows	2.3	4.4	9.8	5.1	−3.5	22.4
Change in reserves[c]	2.2	2.5	−0.7	−11.4	9.0	−21.7

[a] Net capital flows comprise net direct investment, net portfolio investment and other long-and short-term net investment flows, including official and private borrowing.

[b] Because of data limitations, other net investments may include some official flows.

[c] A minus sign indicates an increase.

Source: IMF, *World Economic Outlook*, May, 1996 p. 35.

Tanzania, 4 per cent in Uganda), although knowledge as to what they really are remains sparse.

Table 1.2 Percentage composition of external long-term capital flows to developing countries, 1994

	Private			*Official*	*Total*	*Total flows*
	Net debt flows	*FDI*	*Portfolio equity flows*			*(in % of GDP)*
All developing countries	21.1	38.6	16.8	23.4	100	3.9
East Asia	25.4	50.5	14.8	9.4	100	5.6
Indonesia	17.9	23.2	40.4	18.5	100	5.2
Republic of Korea	64.4	10.9	33.9	−9.2	100	2.0
Malaysia	14.4	63.2	19.2	3.2	100	9.7
Thailand	87.5	13.9	−11.7	10.3	100	3.2
South Asia	−0.4	9.0	45.1	46.3	100	3.5
Latin America and the Caribbean	30.7	40.7	25.7	2.9	100	3.2
Chile	39.8	43.6	21.1	−4.4	100	7.9
Colombia	38.9	62.6	21.1	−22.5	100	2.2
Europe and Central Asia	19.7	31.2	7.2	41.8	100	2.6
Middle East and North Africa	3.1	35.8	1.0	60.1	100	2.4
Sub-Saharan Africa	4.4	14.8	4.3	76.5	100	5.1
Kenya	−260.4	3.8	0.0	356.6	100	1.5
Zambia	−13.5	12.6	0.0	100.8	100	13.6
Zimbabwe	−45.6	10.3	14.7	120.6	100	6.3

Source: Calculations by the author, based on World Bank, *Global Economic Prospects and the Developing Countries* (Washington, DC: World Bank, 1996), pp. 84–5.

These new flows can be partly explained as a once-for-all (permanent) stock adjustment on the part of the world's investment community (notably insurance companies, mutual funds and pension funds) to newly liberalized international financial markets, both in developing countries and in the industrialized world, and the perception of new profit opportunities in emerging markets, particularly in countries that have achieved sound macroeconomic fundamentals and a receptive environment for foreign capital. (Other capital flows may also be of such a 'one-off' portfolio adjustment nature, e.g. returning

Table 1.3 Major types of private capital inflow to selected developing countries, 1990–4 (per cent of GDP)

		FDI	*Net flow of short-term debt*	*Net flow of long-term debt*[a]	*Private transfers*[b]	*Total private flows*
Latin America						
Chile	(1990–4)	2.4	3.1	1.2	-	7.7
Colombia	(1993–4)	3.0	−0.3	3.8	-	6.3
East Asia	(1990–4)					
Indonesia	(1990–3)	1.3	-	4.1	-	5.5
Republic of Korea	(1991–4)	0.2	0.4	1.8	-	2.4
Malaysia	(1991–3)	7.7	4.7	0.4	-	12.8
Thailand	(1990–4)	1.7	6.1	2.6	-	10.5
Sub-Saharan Africa	(1990–3)					
Kenya		0.3	0.4	0.2	1.9	2.8
South Africa		0.0	0.3	0.0	0.0	0.3
United Republic of Tanzania		0.3	−0.4	0.0	9.1	9.1
Uganda		0.1	−0.2	0.0	4.7	4.7
Zambia		2.9	−0.9	0.0	−0.3	1.7
Zimbabwe		0.2	0.8	0.8	0.3	2.0

[a] Including net portfolio equity flows, except in Malaysia.
[b] Shown only for sub-Saharan African countries.
Source: Kasekende, Kitabire and Martin; Le Fort and Budnevich; and Park and Song; all in this volume.

flight capital or purchases of privatized assets.) Since global investors still allocate small fractions of their portfolios to developing countries and capitalization in emerging markets can still expand, such flows may continue for some time. Once such stock adjustment has been completed, however, the flows resulting from it can be expected to fall to more 'normal' levels (around which they will continue to fluctuate). It would be helpful, in such circumstances, to address the possibilities for smoothing the macroeconomic adjustment in recipient countries to these one-off shifts in global portfolio choices.

The new private capital inflows to developing countries can also be seen, however, in terms of an *ongoing* and perfectly normal response on the part of more globally oriented investors to changing incentive structures – including relative rates of interest, exchange-rate expectations, political volatility, and so on. Private capital inflows may also be procyclical, increasing in 'good' times and falling, even reversing in direction, in 'bad' times; such flows, often found in primary exporting countries and in part essentially speculative, create obvious extra problems for attempts at macroeconomic stabilization. If recent international capital flows (into developing countries) are *not* significantly the product of 'one-off' stock adjustment, but reflect normal response to changing incentives, their surge in one direction is likely to be reversible.

In any case, newly liberalized international and domestic financial markets certainly create new opportunities for international incentive-responsive private capital flows and short-term volatility in such flows. When large institutional investors alter their overall international portfolio composition only marginally (for them) they can have dramatic consequences for individual national asset markets and exchange rates. Some of the surge towards developing countries' financial markets in the early 1990s *is* undoubtedly attributable to the low interest rates in the United States (and other industrialized countries) at that time (Calvo *et al.*, 1993).

External circumstances have always been understood to play an important role in setting the context for national macroeconomic management, particularly in small open economies. Shocks in the external terms of trade have long been recognized as a particular problem for developing countries. Now changes in global interest rates, and their effects upon private international capital flows, are revealed as a further *major* source of exogenous shocks. 'Contagion effects' from financial events elsewhere (e.g. 'tequila effects') are also now an important additional source of exogenous shock; of the countries studied in this volume, the 'tequila effects' of the Mexican crisis were most notable in Thailand, Malaysia and, to some extent, South Africa. Policy changes – particularly in exchange regimes – in geographically contiguous countries are another potentially significant source of exogenous influence upon domestic macroeconomic experience, as shown in some recent African experience (e.g. Kenya and Uganda, and the Communauté Financière d'Afrique (CFA) franc zone and its neighbours). Realignments of major currency exchange rates can also profoundly affect developing countries' real effective exchange rates and hence their prospects for external balance: for example, the nominal appreciation of the yen against the dollar in the 1990s brought depreciation of many East Asian currencies *vis-à-vis* the yen (Park and Song, in this volume).

Impacts and Responses

Capital inflows are generally welcome in developing countries for their role in financing investment, and thereby assisting in long-term development, and/or in shorter-term smoothing of consumption. It has long been recognized, however, that where there are significant domestic microeconomic 'distortions', profit-motivated inflows can be immiserizing. Prior to and during the debt crisis of the 1980s there was a great deal of discussion as to how the proceeds of external bank lending (mainly to governments) had been used, and whether they had contributed to development. Always there has been appropriate concern as to whether the government had its economic policy fundamentals 'right'. There is obviously a continuing need to understand how capital inflows are ultimately used, and whether recipients' national policies may contribute to any 'misdirection'.

Concern with the potentially undesirable *macroeconomic* consequences of private inflows, even when policies in the recipient country are basically sound, is much more recent. Surges of inflowing private capital create macroeconomic problems, above all through their effects on either the exchange rate or the domestic money supply, together with the risk of their abrupt cessation or capital outflow.

If the central bank attempts to maintain stability in the exchange rate, private capital inflows will expand the monetary base (as the central bank increases its foreign exchange reserves). To prevent consequent overheating of the domestic economy, and a real appreciation of the currency, the central bank may seek to sterilize the domestic monetary consequences, through open-market operations – in government securities or in the interbank market (as in Malaysia) or, more usually, through the issue of its own securities; or through increased reserve requirements; or via the redeployment of government deposits from the commercial banks to the central bank.

Tightened domestic monetary policy may, however, involve significant quasi-fiscal losses for the central bank as it pays higher interest rates on its domestic liabilities (including those earned by foreigners) than it earns on its foreign-exchange reserves. To the extent that interest rates increase in consequence of such sterilization policies, they may induce a further fillip to external capital inflows. (Interest rates are presumably lowered through private capital inflows in the first place, however, and inflows will, in any case, cease once a new portfolio equilibrium is reached.)

Increasing bank reserve requirements may also 'redirect capital flows to domestic borrowers through channels other than the domestic banking system – such as through domestic markets for equity and real estate. If this disintermediation is effective, the macroeconomic stabilization problem would remain' (Fernandez-Arias and Montiel, 1996, p. 73). Domestic agents may also resort increasingly to offshore borrowing. Clearly the structure of the domestic financial system and, in particular, the interest of foreign investors in other domestic assets and their access to them are important to overall macroeconomic outcomes.

One obvious additional (or alternative) possible response to surging capital inflows is to tighten the fiscal regime, and this is frequently appropriate, particularly in countries previously running large fiscal deficits. But recent experience indicates that many countries experiencing monetary and exchange-rate pressures from private capital inflows had already achieved fiscal balance or even surpluses (e.g. Chile, the Republic of Korea and others). In any case, as a recent IMF paper argues, 'In most countries ... it is difficult to use fiscal policy as a short-run response, and it may also exacerbate the problem of unsustainable inflows if confidence in economic policy grows strongly' (IMF, 1995d, p. 5). Thus macroeconomic policy instruments other than or additional to fiscal ones must usually be deployed to respond effectively to capital surges.

If the central bank instead allows the value of the domestic currency to appreciate in response to capital inflows, this will have undesirable consequences for the overall incentive structure. The current account of the balance of payments is likely to deteriorate in response to currency appreciation, and the economy will become increasingly vulnerable to a sudden reduction or reversal of the capital inflows. (The same results follow from real currency appreciation stemming from domestic price inflation with a stable nominal exchange rate, such as may follow from unsterilized central bank intervention in the foreign exchange market.) The critical question is whether the capital inflows that are associated with such an increasing current account deficit are likely to be sustainable and, if so, at what level. Countries operating a pure floating exchange-rate system (in some African countries, they seem to have had few options) are consequently faced with amajor set of problems: appreciating and potentially unstable currencies, rising current account deficits and rising external debt.

In the many developing countries where there are relatively weak domestic financial markets, there are likely to be further difficulties created by surges of external private capital, either inward or outward. They can easily spark increased volatility in domestic markets for financial assets and real estate. Capital surges have been associated with stock market and property market booms; and outflows with corresponding busts. Where domestic financial markets are thin and/or weakly supervised, even modest inflows of external private capital can overwhelm both local financial institutions and their regulatory authorities, and create additional macroeconomic management problems. Even in relatively strong financial systems, deposit insurance, whether explicit or implicit, creates moral hazard that may encourage overenthusiastic foreign depositing in domestic banks, and overenthusiastic (and, particularly when there is rapid expansion, inadequately supervised) bank lending to domestic agents.

Although the increased inflow of foreign portfolio capital in the 1990s did not destabilize national financial markets in the four Asian countries studied in this volume, in the sense of increasing average weekly exchange-rate, interest-rate or stock-market volatility, these countries did experience episodes of extreme stock-market volatility which appeared to be associated with foreign capital flows – e.g. a stock market boom in late 1993 and early January 1994 in Malaysia, followed by rapid decline again in the first half of 1994; and sudden stock-market declines in early 1995 in Thailand and Malaysia in response to the Mexican crisis in early 1995, and the Gulf War in the second half of 1990. Similarly, there were at the same times sharp interest-rate changes in response to the same external capital surges, and the pressures on policy that they created.

Many developing countries maintain various forms of control over external capital account transactions. The ease and speed with which private capital can flow internationally depends partly on the nature of the capital asset or liability, but, no less importantly, on the costs of the flows to private transactors, as influenced by such capital controls – in the form of restrictions, regulations and taxes, both direct and indirect. To an analysis of such policies for the capital account we now turn.

III POLICIES FOR THE CAPITAL ACCOUNT IN DEVELOPING COUNTRIES

Benefits and Costs of International Financial Integration, and the Rationale for Controls

Capital flows internationally with or without governmental controls over the capital account. Increasing numbers of countries have opted for full capital account convertibility and integration with global capital markets. This is a clear policy option for all developing countries today.

The principal gains from capital account liberalization at the national level, and from global financial integration more generally, are those deriving from the increased efficiency of both national and global capital markets that they can create. By easing or removing constraints on private decision-making, governments permit private agents to make savings and investment decisions on a freer basis. The result should be less 'distorted' intertemporal decision-making both within individual liberalizing nations and at the global level. Within the (relatively capital-scarce) developing countries, no less than elsewhere, this can be expected, in the best-case scenario, to include greater international portfolio diversification for their own investors; greater diversification of capital sources on the part of their public and private borrowers; greater competition and thereby increased efficiency for their financial services sectors; deeper financial markets and the increased efficiency of intermediation that it brings; and greater domestic savings and investment. These potential advantages are great enough to motivate open capital accounts in the OECD and to inspire most countries (and now the IMF) to declare capital account liberalization to be an ultimate objective, whatever their current practices. But none of these potential gains is assured, and capital account liberalization also involves risks and potential costs.

Capital controls have traditionally been employed to permit domestic monetary authorities to pursue monetary policies more independently of international interest rates than they otherwise could do (frequently, although not so much in recent years, within the context of a fixed-exchange-rate system). Such measures are both easier to make effective and theoretically more defensible on a temporary basis than as a long-run system for maintaining a fundamentally inappropriate exchange rate. Domestic interest rates have typically (although not universally, e.g. not in Indonesia) been deregulated in financial reforms associated with capital account liberalization. Total capital account openness would generate, in equilibrium, domestic nominal interest rates equal to the 'world' rates plus a premium reflecting the market's exchange-rate expectations and its assessment of other country risks associated with the imperfect enforceability of international contracts.[3] Since the resulting domestic interest rates could be inappropriate to domestic needs, there has been interest in policies that could drive a (variable) wedge between domestic rates and these fully market-determined rates. Stated differently, the unwanted private capital flows engendered by official efforts to set domestic rates that are 'appropriate' for domestic needs create an obvious interest in policies that could reduce such flows. In some instances, where governments were using the inflation tax and/or reducing domestic debt service costs via *lowered* domestic interest rates, controls over outflows carried primarily a fiscal purpose. In Chile and the Republic of Korea, on the other hand, domestic interest rates have been maintained at rates *above* those in the major financial markets in industrial countries by means of controls over capital inflows.

Controls over outflows, notoriously difficult to enforce, have also traditionally been motivated by a desire to utilize domestic savings for the purpose of domestic investment. An older literature has long argued that the potential vulnerability of developing countries' external payments positions or exchange rates to volatile private expectations legitimates controls over capital outflows, and should make capital account outflows the very *last* to be liberalized (e.g. Williamson, 1991).

In the 1990s, however, capital controls have frequently been motivated by the desire to stabilize the domestic economy in a world of volatile private capital surges, either inward or outward. There is by now plenty of evidence that developing countries can encounter severe macroeconomic management problems, even financial crises, in consequence of surges of private capital flow. Such surges are presumably easier and therefore both more likely and more frequent when capital flows are 'freer'.

According to much current wisdom, it is critically important for development that countries maintain a stable and appropriate real exchange rate, and thus a stable and sustainable current account, and a reasonably stable macroeconomy. Such stability is seen by many as more important for the achievement of an adequate level and efficiency of investment than the details of incentive structures which purport to have microeconomic efficiency benefits. For this purpose, it may be desirable to moderate overall capital flows that are not driven by long-term economic fundamentals. From this motivation it is but a small further leap to the objective of attempting to influence the *composition*, as well as the overall size, of capital flows so as to achieve more stable and more productive inflows.

In the face of the limits to the efficacy, in terms of macroeconomic management objectives, of the available fiscal, monetary and exchange-rate policy instruments, the monetary authorities of many developing countries have sought to deploy direct and indirect controls over private international capital flows as additional macroeconomic policy instruments. Such capital controls typically seek to reduce the level, slow the pace or alter the composition of private capital flows.

Further measures to restrain expansion of consumer expenditures which might otherwise be associated with capital inflows (and, in many cases, with import liberalization) may also be considered appropriate, for example, limits upon domestic consumer and mortgage credit, or compulsory private savings programmes (McKinnon and Pill, 1995). These may be able to reduce the prospect of credit-driven booms in private consumption of the recent Mexican type.[4]

There are also prudential grounds for controls over international capital flows in the developing-country context. Increased openness in the capital account may involve domestic banks and other financial institutions in increased risks, both because of increased deposit volatility and because of increased foreign exchange risk. Capital account liberalization therefore is likely to require strengthened prudential supervision and information disclosure. According to some, prudential requirements or market 'standards' relating to a country's international financial transactions are separate issues, not strictly part of the issue of capital account convertibility (IMF, 1995d, p. 11); others, however, prefer to consider these issues more holistically, evidently finding it difficult to distinguish control measures purely on the basis of their purported or presumed motivation (IMF, 1995b, pp. 13–16).

Capital account convertibility is obviously not a matter of all or nothing. Some types of transactions may be free while others are not; and the tightness of restrictions may vary in the same country over time. In this respect, as in trade policy and the analysis of the current account, 'openness' can have a variety of interpretations. There is as yet no agreed way of measuring the degree of openness in the capital account (Montiel, 1994).[5] For the present, there seems little alternative but to rely on descriptive accounts, such as the IMF offers in its *Annual Reports on Exchange Restrictions*, for data on the extent of capital account convertibility and changes therein.

Direct regulation of international capital flows, both inward and outward, has evidently been common in developing countries. A summary of existing capital controls in 155 developing countries,

Table 1.4 Capital controls in developing countries, 1994

Category	*Number of countries maintaining controls*
Any form of capital control	119
Comprehensive controls	67
on outflows	67
on inflows	17
Foreign direct investments	107
of non-residents	84
of residents	35
Profit repatriation and capital liquidation	34
Taxes on capital transactions	9
Non-resident-controlled enterprises	6
Portfolio investments	61
of non-residents	30
of residents	33
Security issuance by non-residents	15
Security issuance abroad by residents	6
Debt-to-equity conversion	2
Financial transactions	78
of non-residents	41
of residents	66
Trade-related financial transactions	7
Deposit requirements for borrowing from abroad by residents	2
Deposit accounts	83
of non-residents in foreign exchange	37
of non-residents in local currency	52
of residents abroad	29
of residents in foreign currency with domestic banks	23
Other capital transfers	70
Personal capital transfers	34
Blocked accounts	24
Real-estate transactions	
of non-residents	23
of residents	30

Source: IMF, *Annual Report on Exchange Restrictions* (Washington, DC: IMF, 1995), p. 35.

based on IMF data, is given in Table 1.4. Of the 155 developing countries surveyed by the IMF, 119 employ some form of control over international capital flows, although 75 have accepted Article VIII obligations in respect of the current account. (For further discussion of the IMF Articles, see Section IV under 'The IMF and Capital Controls'.) The forms of these controls are numerous and the degree of their use varies greatly both across countries and over time. Some may be motivated more by the need to monitor than the desire to restrict. Table 1.4 shows that regulation of outward flows has been considerably more frequent than that of inward flows. Regulation of outward flows also has a longer history and remains fairly pervasive. Restrictions on residents' external investments and holdings of foreign currencies are frequent, at least in the form of upper limits, often based purely on prudential objectives, on the proportion of total assets that financial institutions may place abroad. Of inward flows, foreign direct investment is much more frequently regulated than purely financial flows. But there is evidently increasing interest in and resort to controls over the latter. In general, positive lists (in which only those transactions listed are 'free') are more restrictive than negative lists (in which only those activities listed are restricted, regulated or prohibited).

Influencing the Composition of Inflows

There seems to be general agreement that some forms of external private capital inflow are more attractive to the recipient country than others. From the standpoint of future macroeconomic stability, the longer-term and the more stable are inflows of capital, the better. This would suggest a preference for longer-term investments – in long-term loans, equity and/or in the form of foreign direct investment,[6] particularly that which takes the form of physical flows of capital goods. Such flows are more likely to be based on long-term economic fundamentals and should be less susceptible to short-term volatility. (Some 'reliable' development assistance may also carry these desirable attributes.)

If it is possible to distinguish between long-term and short-term investments, long-term ones are clearly preferable. Categorization of portfolio capital flows, however, is often difficult. In some sub-Saharan African countries, for instance, the authorities have little idea about the detailed composition of such capital flows. Informed analysts conjecture that much of what is at present recorded as private 'transfer' in some African countries is actually more appropriately categorized as private capital flow, quite probably quickly reflected in real investment (Kasekende *et al.*, in this volume). If the authorities do not know which flows are which, they will obviously face great difficulties in developing appropriate controls or macroeconomic stabilization policies. Indeed, in some developing-country circumstances, authorities are said to be inhibited in their attempts to collect more accurate information on private capital flows by their fear of frightening market participants, discouraging real investors and stimulating undesired outflows (ibid.).

Short-Term versus Long-Term Flows

Short-term capital inflows (and outflows) have been an important element in the recent experience of many developing countries (including Thailand, Malaysia and several sub-Saharan African countries, where such flows have dominated). These include:

- short-term external borrowing (lending) by domestic commercial banks or other local firms;
- increased (decreased) non-resident holdings of domestic currency deposits in local banks;
- sales (purchases) of short-term money-market instruments to (by) non-residents;
- reduced (increased) resident holdings of foreign-currency deposits (where these are allowed); and
- swap transactions – sales (purchases) of foreign currency simultaneously unwound by forward market contracts.

Some of these flows may be directly related to real international trade in goods and services. A high proportion, however, may be unrelated to any real transactions, whether international or domestic. If so, they may be highly volatile. In Zambia in the late 1980s, for instance, there were sharp reversals in the direction of such flows involving year-on-year changes amounting to 6–8 per cent of GNP (Kasekende *et al.*, in this volume).

Unfortunately, it is often difficult to distinguish flows that are related to real transactions from purely financial ones, or short-term from long-term flows. The Republic of Korea *has* consciously tried to treat capital account transactions related to real investments differently from (more liberally than) purely financial transactions but this is inherently very difficult. Over many years, it has proved difficult even to distinguish current from capital transactions.

Long-maturity external obligations may seem, in principle, less vulnerable to volatility than short-maturity ones; but if there are active secondary markets, long maturities may be highly liquid. Longer-maturity instruments are thus not necessarily less volatile in their short-term behaviour than nominally short-term ones (Claessens *et al.*, 1995). According to the IMF, 'financial asset flows have become increasingly fungible ... [making it] more difficult for ... countries ... to maintain the effectiveness of their controls' (IMF, 1995d, p. 18). Indeed, OECD (Organization for Economic Cooperation and Development) and European Union codes on capital flows have abandoned efforts to distinguish short-term capital flows from others, and this indicates that others may eventually be forced along the same route (IMF, 1995d, p. 9). Monetary authorities in Chile, among other countries, have nonetheless found it possible to encourage longer-term bank deposits and longer-term credits via carefully structured bank reserve requirements and 'minimum stay' regulations respectively (Le Fort and Budnevich, in this volume).

Foreign Direct Investment versus Portfolio Capital

Foreign direct investment (FDI) is generally believed to be motivated differently, to behave differently, and to create different macroeconomic (and developmental) effects from portfolio capital flows. Foreign direct investors are presumed to base their decisions on longer-term economic and political fundamentals and thus to be less volatile in their short-term behaviour. FDI also often takes the form of real flows of capital equipment and brings technology and/or managerial and marketing skills along with its capital.

As far as stability and macroeconomic consequences are concerned, however, these presumed differences can be overdone. Foreign direct investment flows can also be volatile. Transnational corporations (TNCs) manage liquid funds as well as flows of real goods and services, and they usually do so very effectively. Foreign direct investors can also, when appropriate, borrow from foreign or domestic financial institutions in pursuit of their international financial flow objectives. FDI can therefore be associated with higher, rather than lower, variability in capital flow, reflecting TNCs' capacities for managing international intrafirm financial transactions to respond quickly to changing national circumstances. Some of these

FDI-related flows may be recorded as portfolio flows in traditional statistical systems.

The regimes for foreign direct investment in developing countries are usually quite different from those for portfolio capital, and they are not typically primarily motivated by short-term macroeconomic management considerations. In many ways, FDI inflows are treated more liberally than foreign portfolio capital because of the presumed advantages brought by its longer-term motivation, and the potential managerial, technological and export market-opening attributes associated with it. On the other hand, there are often selective prohibitions, controls and approval procedures – designed to protect strategic sectors or to ensure national benefits of various kinds – that are more stringent for FDI than for 'arm's-length' portfolio capital (IMF, 1995d). Although controls over inward foreign direct investment are not usually primarily directed at reducing the volatility of capital flows, they can be. Chile has instituted 'minimum stay' regulations for direct investors to complement its reserve requirements for portfolio investors, in pursuit of its macroeconomic stabilization objectives.

Debt versus Equity

External portfolio investment in domestic equities clearly involves fewer risks to the borrowing country than debt. External debt requires servicing regardless of domestic economic circumstances and the roll-over of its principal can never be assured. Foreign owners of equity can, of course, choose to exit at any time, but when they do so as a group they must first find domestic buyers and, when they do so, they may be forced to take capital losses that ease the blow to the capital-losing country. There is therefore a risk management rationale for developing countries to favour portfolio equity inflows over debt-creating ones (although they may, on average, be more expensive). It can be argued that the shift towards equity borrowing in the 1990s has already imparted an important stabilizing influence on developing-country borrowers, relative to their variable-interest bank borrowing in the 1970s (Williamson, 1996).

Efficacy of Controls

According to some analysts, direct controls (and, for that matter, sterilization) can only be effective in the short run: 'given the worldwide integration of financial markets and the sophistication of financial intermediaries, *such policies do not seem to work in the long run*' (Corbo and Hernandez, 1996, p. 84).

It is well known that controls over capital outflows are difficult to enforce and that considerable capital flight will occur when market participants deem it warranted, even in the tightest of control regimes – via misinvoicing of trade transactions, leads and lags in external payments, alterations in the terms of trade credit, changes in overseas workers' remittances, and so on. Expectations effects, as always, can also generate unexpected results. The tightening of controls may constitute a signal to investors, generating greater net outflows than before; similarly, liberalization of outflows may trigger more inflows.

But it would be a considerable logical leap to the conclusion that controls are *always totally* ineffective. Particularly in the large-scale formal financial sector, they are likely to have *some* effect. The issue is usually, rather, whether the actual social benefits of such controls warrant their administrative and other (including efficiency) costs; and, more fundamentally, whether domestic macroeconomic management is, or is about to become, sound.

Controls over capital outflows are *not* universally associated, as some seem to imply, with payments crises or preludes to currency devaluation and payments liberalization. Many developing countries have maintained such controls over outflows over *very long* periods of time, and varied them in response to their external payments positions (e.g. IMF, 1995d, p. 21).

Controls over capital inflows are inherently easier to make effective than controls over outflows. Foreign owners of capital are likely to be concerned to hold legal title to their financial assets in the country, providing them with motivation to abide by domestic regulations where they exist. At the same time, the domestic monetary authorities, not usually facing crises in the circumstances of surging inflows, are in a much stronger bargaining position in seeking compliance with the rules. Needless to say, it will still be impossible to prevent the usual range of evasions through leads and lags, misinvoicing in the current account, and the like. (Similar argument is now made by the IMF in 1995b, p. 108.) Needless to say, it would be easier to make controls work if the monetary authorities at both ends of the flows cooperated – as they rarely do at present except with reference to the 'laundering' of illegal funds.

Dooley's recent survey (1995) of the academic literature on capital controls (which has mainly been addressed to attempts at control of unwanted *out*flows) concludes that they *have* often successfully driven wedges between domestic and international interest rates, thereby generating government revenue and reducing the costs of public domestic debt servicing (pp. 29–32); but in developing countries, contrary to the evidence for developed countries, they have not succeeded in influencing the volume or composition of capital flows, or exchange-rate levels (pp. 34–5). This study is also sceptical, in view of the distortions they create, of their overall benefit: cost ratio (see also Mathieson and Rojas-Suarez, 1993).

Analyses of recent developing-country experience in this volume, by those closer to policymaking, however, suggest more optimistic conclusions regarding the efficacy of capital controls, particularly those relating to *in*flows (Le Fort and Budnevich, and Park and Song, in this volume). Many developing-country macroeconomic managers evidently believe it *is* possible to influence not only the pace but also the composition of external private capital inflows.

Recent Policy Response to Capital Surges

As has been seen, many developing countries have encountered large surges of capital inflow in the 1990s, surges which have significantly complicated the tasks of macroeconomic policymakers in recipient countries. Analysts have noted the contrast between the Latin American and Asian experiences with private capital inflows in the early 1990s: in Asia, foreign direct investment played a greater role, investment rates typically rose more, and the real appreciation of currencies was more limited than in Latin America (e.g. Calvo *et al.*, 1996; Corbo and Hernandez, 1996). The studies that follow confirm these results (Le Fort and Budnevich, and Park and Song, in this volume). They also find that in some sub-Saharan African countries, private capital inflows began to increase noticeably in the 1990s, to the point where their size relative to GDP (gross domestic product) was as large as in Asia and Latin America (Kasekende in this volume).

How can the policy responses of the countries studied in this volume be briefly summarized? In the sub-Saharan African countries studied, such as Uganda, Zambia and the United Republic of Tanzania, macroeconomic policy response has consisted primarily in letting the exchange rate reflect the increased capital flows; and this has not yielded results with which policymakers can be fully content. In the East Asian countries studied (Indonesia, the Republic of Korea, Malaysia and Thailand), on the other hand, strenuous efforts were made by macroeconomic policymakers to preserve incentives for their tradable goods sectors by preventing too much real currency appreciation. Inevitably this involved the use of activist policies in currency and financial markets, and pragmatic resort to direct and indirect capital controls that varied in their intensity in response to changing external circumstances. In Chile and Colombia, too, policymakers sought to moderate the exchange-rate effects of the new capital inflows by 'managing' exchange rates, monetary sterilization and judicious resort to capital controls, principally in the form of indirect taxes (via reserve requirements).

The experience reviewed and the analysis conducted in these studies suggests that the vigorous use of market-friendly policy instruments – particularly official participation in financial markets, and direct and indirect taxes (rather than direct controls) on certain international capital flows – has helped many developing countries in their pursuit of traditional macroeconomic objectives in the context of volatile international flows of private capital, and could help more. The most important such instruments are:

- flexible central bank intervention in the foreign-exchange market, with varying limits and 'bands', and without overly rigid adherence to nominal exchange-rate targets;
- flexible intervention by the monetary authorities in domestic financial markets and/or provision to them of new financial instruments for purposes of monetary sterilization;
- maintenance of fiscal discipline;
- use of reserve requirements (deposits in foreign currency in the central bank) on domestic bank deposits of non-residents, domestic foreign currency deposits, and all external borrowing, bond issues or lines of credit. (These deposits have sometimes included a minimum time period, sometimes varied with the maturity, and have typically been designed to discourage shorter-term flows.)

The 'successful' managers of capital surges in East Asia and Latin America also often buttressed their more 'market-friendly' instruments with more direct regulations.

Regulation of *inward* flows of portfolio capital has involved:

- overall quantitative restrictions or even prohibitions on some types of flows (e.g. some short-term flows in Malaysia in early 1994);

- regulation or restrictions on borrowing or issuance of securities abroad by residents;
- restrictions on access by foreigners to domestic stock and financial markets, or limits on foreign ownership of shares of domestic corporations (which often vary with the sector of activity);
- restrictions and conditions on (and sometimes incentives for) foreign direct investment, varying with different kinds and sectors, including minimum length of stay (e.g. in Chile, one year).

Obviously, such controls on capital flows can be liberalized or tightened over a wide range of restrictive possibilities. Governments have often varied their capital account regulations so as to pursue their macroeconomic objectives as external circumstances changed. The Republic of Korea systematically tightened or eased restrictions on both capital inflows and outflows in response to developments in the current account of its international payments. To counter excessive inflows, some governments have at times eased regulations only on outflows (e.g. Thailand). They have also varied their reserve requirements on foreign borrowing.[7]

The East Asian and Latin American countries studied in this volume thus appeared remarkably successful in responding to surges of private capital inflows in the 1990s through a judicious combination of exchange-market intervention (to moderate real currency appreciation), monetary sterilization, fiscal discipline, and the careful and changing use of direct controls on both inward and outward flows to dampen volatile short-term movements.

It is always difficult to assess the effects of policy in the absence of clarity as to the relevant counterfactual. Those with faith in the perfectibility of markets may argue that the provision of greater information is always more socially efficient than governmental interventions. Still, government interventions, including direct controls, *did* frequently seem to be effective in terms of their own declared (and limited) macroeconomic objectives. It is important to recognize that the purpose of controls in the more 'successful' cases was generally *not* to maintain a fundamentally unsustainable exchange rate, but to assist in *real exchange-rate stabilization*. In some cases, there may also have been a longer-run concern to prevent undue real currency appreciation and its detrimental effects for the tradables sector. The policy objective was always a stable and appropriate overall incentive structure, and thus effective macroeconomic management for development.

Capital controls or taxes, whether direct or indirect, are not a panacea. If used to support weak macroeconomic policy they can even be harmful. Nor are they without difficulties or costs. In Dornbusch's words, however, 'while a near-perfect system of managing capital flows would be desirable, something that falls even far short may still do the job much better than doing nothing' (See Chapter 6). There are many recent examples of reasonable success with their use in developing countries and many more examples of recent developing-country difficulties with capital surges that might have been eased through greater use of such controls.

Policymakers should draw pragmatic conclusions from these recent experiences, like those of a recent literature survey of the same subject: 'In view of the multiplicity of factors that should in principle influence the response of macroeconomic policies, no single combination of policies is likely to be optimal in all cases' (Fernandez-Arias and Montiel, 1996, p. 76).

New Policy Instrument: A Cross-Border Transactions Tax?

There are strong theoretical and practical grounds for relying on *taxes on* international transactions rather than direct controls. Such taxes (often known as a 'Tobin tax') are likely to interfere less with the allocative efficiency of the relevant capital markets, and to be administratively no more (and maybe even less) demanding. They overcome the difficult administrative task of distinguishing long-term from short-term flows by leaving market agents to decide what types of flows will be altered. They also have the important side-benefit of raising fiscal revenues (some of which can be used to fund their own administrative costs). Some developing countries have levied taxes on international financial transactions, most notably Brazil from 1994 onwards; and their experience deserves more study. Obstfeld is among those who have argued that: 'A coherent case can be made for a Tobin tax in the context of stabilizing developing countries, which need to manage exchange rates and have relatively shallow financial markets, and where the cost of failed stabilization is extremely high' (Obstfeld, 1995, p. 188). Such taxes have also been advocated for OECD countries (Eichengreen *et al.*, 1995) and active professional debate continues over the merits and feasibility of a worldwide Tobin tax (e.g. Felix, 1995; Kenen, 1995; Frankel, 1995; Spahn, 1995; ul Haq *et al.*, 1996).

In Chapter 6 of this volume, Dornbusch argues for a (small) tax, levied by individual countries, which could be varied over time, on all international (cross-border) transactions so as to discourage short-term capital flows and lengthen investor horizons. Such a tax, he argues, is superior to administrative controls in that 'a maximum of market choice and discipline is maintained and a minimum of bureaucratic control intrudes'.

He suggests that most of the relevant problems of tax evasion could readily be overcome by imposing the tax on *all* transactions in foreign exchange, whether for trade in goods or services, or for international capital movements. Since the tax applies to all cross-border flows rather than only to financial transactions, and since its object is to moderate instability in cross-border flows not financial asset markets, the arguments concerning the ineffectiveness of financial transactions taxes, he argues, are irrelevant. There could be some negative effects on international trade but, at the tax rates contemplated, they would be minimal. Rather, he argues, the tax would smooth the process of national integration into the world economy.

IV IMPROVING INTERNATIONAL ARRANGEMENTS

The Provision of Liquidity in Response to Capital Surges

To the extent that private international capital flows are subject to volatile and herd-like ('disequilibrating') behaviour that does not accurately reflect 'fundamentals' there is a case for official intervention. As has been seen, this may involve efforts to slow the pace or change the composition of these flows. But official intervention more frequently is a matter of *responding* to capital flows which have not been, and probably could not be, controlled.

Recent analysis has not said much about the possibility of increased direct cooperation, for the purpose of more effective macroeconomic management, between the monetary authorities of the capital-losing and capital-gaining countries. This is somewhat surprising since there are evidently considerable under-exploited opportunities for such mutual assistance (see, for instance, Felix, 1993). Some such cooperation takes place bilaterally on an *ad hoc* basis and, among the central banks of the major industrial countries, in the activities of the Bank for International Settlements (BIS). Except in emergencies, such as those of Mexico in 1982 and 1994–5, however, little direct cooperation is normally found between Northern and Southern monetary and financial authorities.

For some years there has been discussion of means for the provision of emergency credits to developing countries facing large and sudden capital outflows that are not associated with changes in domestic economic fundamentals. It is easy to envisage circumstances in which the changes in interest rates and/or exchange rates that would be required in the capital-losing developing country to restore capital market stability are impossible or undesirable; or in which there is a prospect of major defaults on external debt; or in which there is a risk of inappropriate and internationally damaging intervention via controls or taxes on international transactions. In such circumstances, there is a strong case for official intervention in the form of the provision from abroad of official credit to offset the disequilibrating flows.

In order to be effective and, in particular, to serve as credible 'signals' to markets and as catalysts for other official sources, such credits would have to be provided in very large amounts and at very short notice. The 1994–5 Mexican crisis, described by the IMF's Managing Director as 'the first financial crisis of the twenty-first century', and generating the largest IMF loan to a member in its history (both absolutely and in relation to its quota), demonstrated the urgent need for significantly improving upon current arrangements. Progress has now been made towards improving 'early warning systems' via sharpened data systems, and towards the significant expansion, principally for this purpose, of the IMF's General Arrangements to Borrow (GAB).

The key issues for the construction of an effective mechanism for the provision of official finance in response to the problems created by disequilibrating private capital flows are identified by Williamson in Chapter 6 of this volume as follows: (*i*) the criteria for judging the eligibility of countries for such assistance, including, for instance, upper bounds on prior current-account deficits (expressed as percentages of GDP) adjusted to reflect different means of financing, previous debt loads, and so on; (*ii*) the need for speed in response, and therefore prior authorization of later 'automatic' access; (*iii*) the necessary size of the resources to be supplied, where they might come from, and through which channels; (*iv*) the appropriate maturity on the credits, the upper limits upon individual country access to them, and the need, evident in the Mexican case, to provide them on a longer-term basis in some instances.

Such credits are best provided, Williamson also argues, through the IMF, rather than through the BIS or the G-7 (Group of Seven), so as to preserve a fully multilateral approach to such crises, which could quickly generate systemic consequences, and so as to buttress the role of the Fund in international monetary and financial affairs. They should also rely on 'special financing' for such credits, including the possibility of creation of special drawing rights (SDRs), in order not to risk 'crowding out' other IMF lending.

The new arrangements in this sphere build upon the GAB. As long as they do not reduce the prospect for an IMF quota increase (and they might), these financing arrangements are likely to be additional. Developing countries have reasons for concern, however, as to many elements of the new scheme for the provision by the Group of Ten (G-10) and other countries of increased IMF finance for crisis lending. In particular, there are grounds for doubt as to whether its resources will be sufficient, whether its procedures for determining eligibility and activation are appropriate, or whether the new arrangements are likely to succeed in achieving their stated objectives. In particular, they fail to provide finance for the majority of developing countries whose payments crises are unlikely to generate 'systemic' consequences. Developing countries have also expressed their concern over the unrepresentative decision-making processes, outside the IMF, employed in setting up the new arrangements (G-24 Communiqué, 21 April 1996, para. 11). It is not surprising, therefore, that further regional financing mechanisms are being actively discussed, most notably in the Asian context with the active participation of the Bank of Japan.

What is clear is that in the new world of volatile private capital flows, traditional measures of the adequacy of international liquidity, based primarily upon the relationship between owned foreign-exchange reserves and imports of goods and services, are obsolete. Appropriate guidelines for reserve management in a world of large and volatile capital flows are unfortunately still nowhere to be found. Presumably new guidelines would have to take account of stocks (of external debt, domestic money supply, etc.) as well as flows. The capacity of the IMF, with current resources, to address the likely liquidity requirements of emerging markets in coming years remains very much in doubt. IMF quota increases and further SDR issues are minimum necessary steps in the rebuilding of a credible multilateral liquidity system.

Orderly Debt Workouts

The experience of the 1980s has demonstrated that financial crises in developing countries may also reflect more fundamental problems, problems of 'solvency' that cannot be addressed solely by the provision of increased liquidity. In the absence of an agreed international framework for dealing with these more fundamental solvency problems, the 'workouts' have been slow, *ad hoc*, and consequently socially costly and often inequitable.

Whereas, within national jurisdictions, bankruptcy procedures provide the legal means for reducing the inefficiencies and inequities that can be associated with such workouts, there are no such agreed arrangements for sovereign debtors in international financial markets. There has been increasing governmental realization that improvements in current international arrangements are both desirable and possible (e.g. Sachs, 1995a and 1995b; Eichengreen and Portes, 1995; Group of Ten, 1996). Many private financial institutions continue to oppose such reforms, no doubt believing that eventual governmental bailouts are a brighter prospect for them than officially sanctioned write-down of sovereign debt.

Where financial crises have 'fundamental' origins, there can be no substitute for reform, restructuring and improved (and usually changed) management. External financial support can be essential for the success of efforts to reform and restructure fiscal, financial and macroeconomic management systems. Its objective must be to assist governments and countries to restructure themselves with minimum social cost and to do so in such a way as to minimize moral hazard. Sachs has stressed the need for financial assistance at three critical points in a debt workout: a standstill on debt servicing obligations at the outset; 'fresh working capital during restructuring, so that critical governmental functions don't collapse' (1995a, p. 20); and eventual debt reduction to assist in the restoration of solvency (1995a and 1995b). At each of these points there are severe collective action problems in that individual creditors have little incentive, by themselves, to assist. Hence many see the need for a significantly enhanced role for a multilateral financial institution like the IMF to establish appropriate principles, set the conditions, and organize the financing for more orderly and efficient sovereign debt workouts.

The recent report of the Group of Ten sides with those (like Eichengreen and Portes, 1995) who have argued for the incorporation of new provisions in international loan contracts and bond covenants that clarify the means for collective representation and decision-making on the part of lenders and bondholders in the (what they hope is unlikely) event of future difficulties with debt servicing. How such provisions are to be pushed upon unwilling market participants remains a question.

The G-10 report also suggests that the IMF could both signal its approval of a (unilateral) cessation of external debt servicing and assist in the provision of working capital by conditional lending to governments that have entered into external arrears. There is already a precedent for such IMF practice in the case of arrears on bank loans. The new IMF financing arrangements discussed in the previous section can clearly be deployed in support of orderly workouts of sovereign debt problems as well as to provide emergency liquidity, at least for some of its members. Adding the support of orderly debt workouts to the financial responsibilities of the IMF, however, can only raise further doubts as to the adequacy of IMF resources for the effective performance of its twenty-first century role.

The longer-term nature of the reform and restructuring processes involved in orderly debt workouts and the potential need for more sizeable external resources than the IMF, by itself, is able to provide both suggest an important complementary role for the World Bank. In low-income countries, the development of joint IMF–Bank programmes based upon ostensibly locally developed policy framework papers already has a considerable history. Analogous approaches would seem to be appropriate for future debt workouts in middle-income countries.

The IMF and Capital Controls

Under the IMF Articles of Agreement (Article VIII),[8] members are required to seek current account convertibility, though by no means all have done so. Of the 125 low-and middle-income countries with populations of over one million, 51 had by 1995 accepted the obligations of the IMF's Article VIII (see Table 1.5). Under Article VI, however, members are permitted to retain capital controls[9] and, as noted above, about three-quarters of them (119 of 155) do so.

An obvious difficulty in making the current Articles function is distinguishing between international flows in the capital account and international flows in the current account. Where there is convertibility in the current account it is likely to be extremely difficult to exercise fully effective control over international capital flows. The

Table 1.5 Developing countries[a] that have accepted IMF Article VIII obligations, 1994

Argentina	Jamaica	Papua New Guinea
Bangladesh	Jordan	Paraguay
Bolivia	Kenya	Peru
Chile	Kyrgyz Republic	Poland
Costa Rica	Latvia	Republic of Korea
Croatia	Lebanon	Saudi Arabia
Dominican Republic	Lithuania	Singapore
Ecuador	Malaysia	South Africa
El Salvador	Mauritius	Sri Lanka
Estonia	Mexico	Thailand
The Gambia	Moldova	Trinidad and Tobago
Ghana	Morocco	Tunisia
Guatemala	Nepal	Turkey
Haiti	Nicaragua	Uganda
Honduras	Oman	Uruguay
India	Pakistan	Venezuela
Indonesia	Panama	Zimbabwe

[a] Low and middle-income countries with population of one million or more.
Source: IMF, *Annual Report on Exchange Restrictions* (Washington, DC: IMF, 1995).

desire for effective capital account controls may therefore generate pressure for the maintenance or reintroduction of controls in particular types of current-account transactions, notably in financial and other services. Where the domestic administrative and managerial capacity is particularly weak, as in some sub-Saharan African experience, the decision to 'free' international payments on current account is likely to imply freedom for both current and capital transactions; it is simply impractical to attempt to make fine distinctions in the context of weak administrative and statistical systems (Kasekende *et al.*).

In recent years, the IMF has actively promoted capital account convertibility as well as current-account convertibility for all of its members, and it now reports upon capital controls in its surveillance of members' exchange-rate policies and exchange restrictions. In a series of speeches in 1994 and 1995, the Managing Director of the IMF vigorously advocated capital account convertibility and floated the idea of revising the Articles of Agreement to promote that end, an idea considered in more detailed fashion in a recent Fund paper (IMF, 1995d) and now being discussed in the Executive Board.

In Article IV consultations with industrial countries the IMF has generally been strongly supportive of capital account liberalization.

In those with developing countries, according to a recent IMF survey of this subject (1995d), it has approached the issue of capital controls on a case-by-case basis; however, 'the tightening of controls over capital movements ... was generally discouraged'. The IMF survey speaks of 'a general distaste for such controls as a way of addressing balance of payments difficulties', although 'prudential limits on foreign exchange risk exposure have been endorsed' (1995d, p. 6).

In its technical assistance, the IMF appears frequently to have been more forceful:

> Traditionally, the IMF's technical assistance in the area of foreign-exchange systems focused on efforts to facilitate current-account convertibility in its member countries; however, from the mid-1980s the focus shifted toward encouraging the adoption of full capital account convertibility. Common themes in technical assistance supporting a move to capital convertibility have included the ineffectiveness of existing controls, improved transparency associated with a free exchange system, the benefits of recognizing an informal market through which a significant proportion of transactions was already taking place, and the need to develop a competitive and efficient exchange system. (ibid.)

In 1995–6, the IMF appeared to modify its approach. A series of research papers and conferences have portrayed a more nuanced IMF position – to the effect that controls may serve some useful purposes, in particular circumstances, and when employed on a temporary basis (IMF, 1995d, pp. 4, 6, and 22–3; IMF, 1995c). In late 1995, an IMF report argues:

> *during times of surges in inflows a country might consider measures to influence the level and characteristics of capital inflows, such as taxes on short-term bank deposits and other financial assets, reserve requirements against foreign borrowing, and limits on consumption credit.* In this regard, the experiences of Chile, Colombia, and Malaysia have been revealing .... In countries facing large and potentially unsustainable capital flows, a mix of intervention, sterilization, fiscal consolidation, *and some direct measures to discourage short-term portfolio flows or to influence their composition may be appropriate.* The mix of policies will, naturally, vary from country to country.
> (IMF, 1995b, p. 27, my italics)

In its background paper (in the same document) it concludes, 'In light of the recent experiences of countries that adopted measures designed to curb short-term capital inflows, it appears that, at least in the short run, the policies were effective in either reducing the volume of capital inflows or affecting their composition, or both' (ibid., p. 108). Even in the longer term, there seems to be IMF acceptance that liberalization of the capital account serves no purpose if it must subsequently be reversed. Thus, the proposition that the IMF stands for an open capital account, plain and simple, is no longer correct (see also Dornbusch, Chapter 6).

In places, these same IMF documents nevertheless state strong caveats that reflect the basic IMF position, for example: 'It should be noted, however, that comprehensive restrictions on capital flows can be highly distorting and their effectiveness tends to erode over time. Capital controls on outflows are generally viewed as confiscatory taxes and, if applied during periods of exchange market stress, may aggravate a crisis of confidence' (IMF, 1995b, p. 27).

Whatever the eventual advantages of an open capital account, it is generally agreed that there may be difficulties in the transition and that some sequences of policy reform make more sense than others. Generally, there seems to be agreement that *domestic* stabilization and financial reforms (particularly the strengthening of prudential regulation and the creation of solvent and sound banking and financial institutions) are a prerequisite, or at least a corequisite, for successful external capital account liberalization (IMF, 1995d). If domestic banks or other financial institutions are fragile and weakly supervised, a large inflow of funds can be very inefficiently intermediated with the prospect of bubbles and future crises. It is also generally agreed that trade liberalization should precede or, at least, accompany liberalization of the external capital account. In some cases, reforms may move concurrently and with speed; but experience in the Southern Cone and elsewhere in the late 1970s and early 1980s illustrates the danger that underlying weaknesses in the financial sector can be aggravated and further problems created by premature and overly rapid capital account opening.[10]

On the basis of the experience to date, reviewed in this volume and elsewhere, one must conclude that capital controls – both indirect and direct – have played an important positive role in the macroeconomic management of a great many developing countries. Some see such controls as purely temporary or transitional, pending the liberalization and strengthening of domestic financial markets and/or the achievement of domestic macroeconomic stability. But such temporary or transitional conditions are likely to continue for a considerable period in most developing countries. Moreover, private capital surges have continued to create severe macroeconomic problems in countries that have ostensibly already come through such reforms; and controls, albeit usually temporary, have been an important part of the policy armoury for responding to them. It would certainly seem premature at this time, and, quite possibly, inappropriate for a much longer time, to consider an amendment to the IMF Articles of Agreement that required all members to commit themselves to the achievement of an open capital account.

If an amendment relating to capital account issues is required, it is most urgent in the anomalous provisions describing the IMF's authority, under Article VI, to lend in Mexican-type circumstances. Section 1 of Article VI prohibits the use of the Fund's general resources 'to meet a large or sustained outflow of capital' and authorizes the IMF to require members 'to exercise controls to prevent such use'. The capital outflows to which future IMF loans are likely to have to respond may be 'large', 'sustained' or both. It would be wise to attempt to clarify the IMF's role and responsibilities in future 'twenty-first century' financial crises. This may also involve, as argued by some in the IMF, expansion of its jurisdiction over 'payments and transfers and multiple currency practices related to international capital movements. No other international agency exercises jurisdiction over such transactions' (IMF, 1995a, p. 32). In light of the declining share of current transactions in total exchange transactions and the difficulty in distinguishing current from capital transactions, some argue, the IMF may be unable to pursue its broader responsibilities without such a modification of its formal jurisdiction (ibid., pp. 31–2). For these reasons, some amendments to the IMF's Articles, such as are now under discussion, are appropriate. A commitment on the part of all IMF members to total capital account convertibility does not belong, however, on the current agenda.

In his analysis of recent discussions of capital account issues in the IMF, in Chapter 7 of this volume, Aziz Ali Mohammed questions the need for an amendment to the IMF's Articles of Agreement and argues that if there is one it should leave maximum discretion for liberalization with member governments. The G-24 communiqué of 20 September 1997 (see Appendix 1 at the end of the book) makes clear the developing countries' continuing caution with regard to capital account liberalization and any proposed amendments to the

IMF's Articles. The IMF Interim Committee's statement on the next day (see Appendix 3 at the end of the book) speaks of the need for a new IMF mandate: 'bold in its vision, but cautious in implementation', to promote 'an orderly liberalization of capital movements'. Developing countries will evidently now focus upon the means for ensuring an appropriate degree of caution as the IMF moves more vigorously to promote overall liberalization.

Other International Regimes

International regimes relating to capital account transactions can have a variety of purposes, for example, facilitation of cross-border transactions (including harmonization of accounting, disclosure or other regulatory standards), encouragement of competition in financial services, achieving and maintaining financial stability, and so on (White, 1996). Controls and regulations relating to international capital flows are not the same thing as controls relating to foreign financial institutions or the services they provide. The IMF has rules relating only to the former. The World Trade Organization (WTO) is among the multilateral bodies striving to develop a regime for the latter (Zutshi, 1995), but also active in these issues are the BIS, International Organization of Securities Commissions (IOSCO), OECD, the European Union, North American Free Trade Association (NAFTA), and other regional bodies. There are evidently considerable clutter, confusion and overlapping jurisdictions in the international regimes for capital flows and financial transactions. Are these various regimes mutually consistent? Are the needs of the developing countries different and are they taken into account? Is the march towards liberalization of financial services in developing countries any more defensible than the arguments for the total liberalization of their external capital accounts? Many emerging market policymakers will identify readily with the Dornbusch assessment that 'Liberalization of world trade in financial services is the most fiercely lobbied issue of the day' (Chapter 6). These issues urgently require more detailed and comparative analysis.

A further (sub)question relates to the potential role of regional agreements and institutions. Freedom of portfolio capital flows and (most) FDI is central, for instance, in the NAFTA. It is also obviously a key feature of the CFA franc zone. If the world economy evolves on a regionalized basis, as some predict it will, one could easily envisage large regions within which capital, as well as trade in goods and services, would flow relatively freely but between which some controls remained. Negotiations concerning future capital account regimes and supportive financial arrangements among central banks may thus be at their most vigorous on a bilateral or plurilateral (regional) basis, for example in the Free Trade Area for the Americas, or the Asia-Pacific Economic Cooperation Conference (APEC), or the successors to the Lomé Convention.

In some cases, as has been suggested for sub-Saharan Africa, such arrangements might increase the credibility of governmental policy commitments by providing an 'agency of restraint' on governments with deficient 'track records' (Collier, 1991). But such 'opening', as has been seen, may be inappropriate or premature. It is also quite possible that the United States (or other reserve-currency countries) might attempt to 'link' future trade policies to capital account regimes in much the same manner as they now link them to intellectual property ones. As always in these matters, and other things being equal, the interests of smaller and less developed countries are more likely to be protected in fully multilateral arrangements than in discriminatory ones.

Global Macroeconomic Management

Implicit in the increased sensitivity to international interest rates of private international capital flows to (and from) developing countries is the need for greater consideration of the fairly immediate consequences for these flows of the macroeconomic policies of the major industrialized countries. Many analysts argue, with the wisdom of hindsight, that the Volcker anti-inflationary 'shock' of 1979 was a major contributor to the international debt crisis of the 1980s. Yet the links between interest rates in the United States (and, to a lesser extent, Germany, Japan and other industrial countries) and macroeconomic developments in developing countries are much tighter today, by virtue of the increased integration of their capital markets, than they were then. Those who model the functioning of today's global economy must take account of these new linkages through the capital account and the increasingly important potential feedback effects from the economic performance of the developing countries to that of the high-income countries. Macroeconomic policymakers in the major industrial countries, and those who assess or advise them (including the IMF), must recognize, as never before, the potential *global* economic consequences of their policy choices.

V ISSUES REQUIRING FURTHER RESEARCH

Efficacy of Alternative Policy Instruments

Evidently the countries of Asia and Latin America studied in this volume considered that a degree of exchange-rate management, within the context of a generally flexible regime, was critically important to the provision of adequate incentives to their tradables sectors. To this end, they found a variety of policy instruments to reduce the incentives for unwanted capital flows and to sterilize the domestic monetary consequences of such flows as nevertheless took place. Rather than continuing the quasi-theological debate over the efficacy of capital account convertibility, the most useful research and policy debate would therefore now seem to concern the relative efficacy of these various instruments. The issues surrounding the choice of policies of exchange-rate management and sterilization are, by now, fairly well understood. The experience with various policies relating directly to the capital account, many of recent origin, however, has not as yet been as widely shared. In particular, there would seem to be a need for more comparative research and discussion on the most cost-effective instruments for influencing the volume, composition and productive usage of capital flows in countries with thin and vulnerable foreign exchange and financial markets.

Behaviour of Agents in Financial Markets

Much of the policy debate seems to hinge on the assumed behaviour of different agents in financial markets. Imperfect substitutability between domestic financial assets (including those denominated in foreign currencies) and otherwise identical foreign assets implies that either foreigners or nationals (or both) see differences between them. But do foreigners and nationals behave similarly in their substitution of one for the other? It is often implied that OECD investors are sluggish in their response to new opportunities where they require entry into unaccustomed areas like developing-country markets; and they are skittish and prone to early departure at the first hint of potential trouble. On the other hand, it is also often said, for instance in discussions of the 1994–5 Mexican crisis, that because domestic residents of developing countries are so much better informed about national affairs than foreigners, they will be the first to move their funds in or out in response to changing domestic circumstances; some domestic holdings of government debt may therefore be inherently more unstable than foreigners' holdings. Can these alternative hypotheses be tested? Do such ownership traits offer any presumptions as to the likelihood that capital flows may be volatile? Do they offer guidance as to the efficacy of alternative kinds of taxes or controls on international capital flows?

In the same vein, do large institutional investors like pension funds, mutual funds or insurance companies – the new external investors in developing countries' bonds and equities – typically take a longer view than commercial banks as they construct their international investment portfolios? Might they be persuaded, or encouraged through incentives, to do so?

Interaction between Domestic Financial Markets and External Convertibility

Where domestic financial liberalization and macroeconomic stabilization create, for a time, high real and nominal interest rates, there are strong incentives for short-term capital (not least in the form of trade credit) to move in. Where capital controls are inoperative or where they have been abandoned, as in some of the African cases analysed in this volume, very large capital flows (relative to GDP) can result. More generally, external capital flows (inward or outward) of even quite modest size can easily 'swamp' the relatively thin and fragile financial markets and financial institutions of individual developing countries. Where such flows are relatively 'free' and where, as in the majority of developing countries, business 'confidence' is subject to some uncertainty, the domestic financial environment is inherently volatile. Statistical reporting systems have often failed to keep up with the new monitoring requirements: foreign purchases and sales of domestically issued financial instruments require new reporting arrangements beyond those already in place for internationally issued ones. The interactions between domestic reforms and external capital account regimes demand more careful study than they have so far received.

The Impact of 'Dollarization'

The implications of liberalizing the financial system to the extent of authorizing domestic residents to hold foreign currency deposits and domestic financial institutions to do local business (offering deposit facilities and loans) in foreign currencies are not fully explored in this volume. Changes of this kind have been prominent in recent developing-country reforms, and they have profound implications for macroeconomic management.

Where foreign-currency denominated financial transactions (notably bank deposits and loans) are permissible, further problems of macroeconomic management may arise. As long as there are no reasons for doubt about the value of the domestic currency, particularly if there is a peg to the currency of a major trading partner, there need be no such problem. Speculation against the national currency, however, may work extremely rapidly in the context of a partly 'dollarized' system. Pressure on the exchange rate via 'capital flight' does not then require that financial assets, whether owned by foreigners or nationals, actually leave the country; they need only leave the national currency. Even if the domestic currency is fully backed by foreign-exchange reserves, in a currency-board system, difficulties may arise as the values of longer-term domestic currency financial assets fall. (Where there is a loss of confidence in the soundness of domestic banks and/or the domestic financial system, of course, investors *will* seek to leave the country, or more properly, the country's financial institutions, wherever located. These issues are elaborated in Rojas-Suarez and Weisbrod, 1995.)

Even if banks' dollar assets and liabilities are balanced (as often required), their dollar liabilities are likely to be shorter-term than their dollar assets, such transformation being the essence of successful commercial banking. The central bank cannot act as a (dollar) lender of last resort, beyond early limits set by its own foreign-exchange reserves, if there should be a 'run' on the banks' dollar deposits. The Mexican example showed a similar problem with over-reliance by the government on short-term dollar-denominated (or dollar-indexed) debt. Although *tesobono* debt was not large, in terms of the usual indicators, it exceeded dollar foreign-exchange reserves, preventing the central bank from rescuing the government once panic set in. The need for an *external* lender of last resort in domestically dollarized systems has frequently been noted (e.g. by Calvo, 1996).

The impact of 'dollarization' and related policy issues clearly merit further analysis.

The Potential of Tobin–Dornbusch Taxes

This volume does not seriously explore the benefits and costs of a globalized version of the taxes on cross-border transactions advocated by Dornbusch for individual nations, or other related schemes such as the Tobin tax. Others have recently explored the issues surrounding the Tobin tax (e.g. Felix, 1995; Frankel, 1995; Kenen, 1995; Spahn, 1995; ul Haq *et al.*, 1996) and more work in this sphere, particularly on the Dornbusch variant, would be appropriate.

VI CONCLUSIONS AND RECOMMENDATIONS

Private international capital flows have become a much more important and potentially volatile element in many developing countries' economies. Their macroeconomic policymakers must acquire accurate and timely information as to their size and composition. The IMF should do all in its power to assist member countries with weak data on these flows to improve them. Monetary authorities in the developed countries should also actively assist and cooperate with those in developing countries in the collection of data, monitoring of developments, and, in some cases, implementation of controls on international private capital flows. Global macroeconomic modellers and macroeconomic policymakers in the major industrial countries must take account of the increased sensitivity to interest rates of private capital flows to (or from) developing countries, and the potential for significantly increased feedback effects from the developing countries' performance to the global economy, in their models and policy decisions.

The IMF should be encouraged to recognize capital account controls, direct and indirect, as important macroeconomic policy instruments in most developing countries for the foreseeable future. A revision in the IMF Articles of Agreement to require capital as well as current-account convertibility of all its members would be inappropriate at this time. The IMF should be encouraged, however, to expand its role, in conjunction with other relevant bodies, in the surveillance of international capital markets; this would be facilitated by an amendment to its Articles of Agreement. Early efforts should be made to clarify rules and jurisdictions relating to international capital account transactions and international financial institutions in the many areas in which there are potential overlaps, e.g. those of the

IMF, the WTO and other international and regional institutions or agreements.

The IMF should be formally mandated to lend into financial crises in developing countries, both to provide emergency liquidity and, in conjunction with the World Bank and others, to support orderly workouts of sovereign debt problems. (This may also require amendments to its Articles of Agreement.) Decisions as to the appropriate procedures for activating such lending and the decisions actually to lend should be taken via the fully multilateral decision-making mechanisms of the IMF. To permit it to perform its role, the IMF will have to be provided with significantly expanded resources, particularly through quota increases and SDR issues.

More understanding is required of the behaviour of agents in financial markets, and the efficacy of alternative policy instruments in the capital account and in financial markets more generally. Strengthened research could be helpful in such other areas as: the implications of dollarization, interactions between domestic financial markets and external convertibility, the potential of Tobin–Dornbusch taxes, and appropriate measures of reserve adequacy.

Notes

1. For comments on an earlier draft, and without implicating them in the contents of the current version, I would like to thank Andrew Cornford, Roy Culpeper, Dinesh Dodhia, Rumman Faruqi, Eric Helleiner, Louis Kasekende, Guillermo Le Fort. V., Aziz Ali Mohammed, Chi-Young Song and John Williamson.
2. These include Calvo, Leiderman and Reinhart, 1993, 1994, 1996; Claessens, Dooley and Warner, 1995; Corbo and Hernandez, 1996; Dooley, Fernandez-Arias and Kletzer, 1996; Dornbusch and Park, 1995; Edwards, 1995; Fernandez-Arias and Montiel, 1996; Ffrench-Davis, Titelman and Uthoff, 1994; Ffrench-Davis and Griffith-Jones, 1995; Grilli and Milesi-Ferretti, 1995; Hausmann and Rojas-Suarez, 1996; IMF, 1995a, 1995b, 1995c, 1995d; Quirk, 1994; Rojas-Suarez and Weisbrod, 1995; Schadler *et al.*, 1993; UNCTAD, 1994; EDI, 1995).
3. In a recent study of nine Latin American and Asian countries with liberalized capital accounts in the 1987–94 period, exchange risk was far more important than country risk (or remaining capital controls) in 'explaining' such premia (Frankel and Okongwu, 1996).
4. Mexican private savings fell from 15.5 per cent to 7.7 per cent of GDP in the 1989–93 period (Schadler *et al.*, 1993).

5. There is no agreed method in the current or trade accounts either, but there is a much more extensive empirical literature on the subject, including an important (and remarkably under-cited) one that finds little correlation among alternative such measures (Pritchett, 1991). There seems to be some consensus on the use of the percentage premium on the black market as against the principal official exchange rate as a measure (at least in an ordinal sense) of the strength of *overall* foreign-exchange controls or official currency misalignment.
6. There may be significant differences, however, within items which are categorized similarly. Under the heading of long-term loans, for instance, East Asian borrowers averaged bond maturities of nearly twelve years in 1995 whereas Latin American borrowers averaged only three years; and Latin American spreads over comparable government benchmark bonds were nearly three times as high as East Asia's (World Bank, 1996, p. 11).
7. Where they exist, they could also vary their taxes on foreign exchange transactions, as advocated by Park and Song in this volume.
8. Under Article VIII: 'no member shall, without the approval of the Fund, impose restrictions on the making of payments and transfers for current international transactions' (section 2) or 'engage in any discriminatory currency arrangements or multiple currency practices' (section 3). These Articles have never been amended.
9. Section 3 of Article VI of the IMF's Articles of Agreement states that 'members may exercise such controls as necessary to regulate international capital movements, but no member may exercise these controls in a manner which will restrict payments for current transactions or which will unduly delay transfers of funds in settlement of commitments.'
10. The World Bank has adopted quite similar approaches (see, for instance, World Bank, 1996, p. 11).

References

Akyüz, Y. (1992) 'On Financial Openness in Developing Countries' in UNCTAD, *International Monetary and Financial Issues for the 1990s,* vol. II (New York and Geneva: United Nations).

Calvo, G. A. (1996) 'The Management of Capital Flows: Domestic Policy and International Cooperation' in G. K. Helleiner (ed.) *The International Monetary and Financial System: Developing Country Perspectives* (London: Macmillan).

Calvo, G. A., L. Leiderman and C. M. Reinhart (1993) 'Capital Flows and Real Exchange Rate Appreciation in Latin America: The Role of External Factors', *IMF Staff Papers*, vol. 40, no. 1, March.

Calvo, G. A., L. Leiderman and C. M. Reinhart (1994) *The Capital Inflows Problem: Concepts and Issues* (San Francisco: International Center for Economic Growth).

Calvo, G. A., L. Leiderman and C. M. Reinhart (1996) 'Inflows of Capital to Developing Countries in the 1990s', vol. 10, no. 2, *Journal of Economic Perspectives* (Spring).

Claessens, S., M. P. Dooley and A. Warner (1995) 'Portfolio Capital Flows: Hot or Cold?', *World Bank Economic Review*, vol. 9, no. 1, (January).

Collier, P. (1991) 'Africa's External Relations: 1960–1990', *African Affairs* (July).

Corbo, V. and J. DeMelo (eds) (1986) 'Liberalization with Stabilization in the Southern Cone of Latin America', *World Development,* vol. 13, no. 8 (August).

Corbo, V. and L. Hernandez (1996) 'Macroeconomic Adjustment to Capital Inflows: Lessons from Recent Latin American and East Asian Experience', *World Bank Research Observer,* vol. 11, no. 1 (February).

Diaz-Alejandro, C. F. (1985) 'Goodbye Financial Repression, Hello Financial Crash', *Journal of Development Economics* vol. 19. no. 1/2 (September/October).

Dooley, M. (1995) 'A Survey of Academic Literature on Controls Over International Capital Transactions', *NBER National Burea of Economic Research Working Paper Series* 5352 (November).

Dooley, M., E. Fernandez-Arias and K. Kletzer (1996) 'Is the Debt Crisis History? Recent Private Capital Inflows to Developing Countries', *World Bank Economic Review,* vol. 10, no. 1 (January).

Dornbusch, R. and Y. C. Park (eds) (1995) *Financial Opening: Policy Lessons for Korea* (Seoul: Korea Institute of Finance and International Centre for Economic Growth).

EDI (Economic Development Institute, World Bank) (1995) 'Managing Economic Reform under Capital Flow Volatility', selected readings for First Annual Seminar on Managing Economic Reform in an Uncertain World.

Edwards, S. (ed.) (1995) *Capital Controls, Exchange Rates and Monetary Policy in the World Economy* (Cambridge and New York: Cambridge University Press).

Eichengreen, B. and R. Portes (1995) *Crisis? What Crisis? Orderly Workouts for Sovereign Debtors* (London: Centre for Economic Policy Research).

Eichengreen, B., J. Tobin and C. Wyplosz (1995) 'Two Cases for Sand in the Wheels of International Finance', *Economic Journal*, vol. 105 (January).

Felix, D. (1993) 'Suggestions for International Collaboration to Reduce Destabilizing Effects of International Capital Mobility on the Developing Countries' in UNCTAD, *International Monetary and Financial Issues for the 1990s,* vol. III (New York and Geneva: United Nations).

Felix, D. (1995) 'Financial Globalization versus Free Trade: The Case for the Tobin Tax', *UNCTAD Discussion Papers*, no. 108 (November).

Fernandez-Arias, E. and P. J. Montiel (1996) 'The Surge in Capital Inflows to Developing Countries: An Analytical Overview', *World Bank Economic Review,* vol. 10, no. 1 (January).

Ffrench-Davis, R. and S. Griffith-Jones (eds) (1995) *Coping with Capital Surges: The Return of Finance to Latin America* (Boulder, CO, and Ottawa: Lynne Rienner and International Development Research Centre).

Ffrench-Davis, R., D. Titelman and A. Uthoff (1994) 'International Competitiveness and the Macroeconomics of Capital Account Opening', *UNCTAD Review*.

Frankel, J. (1995) 'How Well Do Foreign Exchange Markets Function: Might a Tobin Tax Help?', *Working Paper C95-058*, Center for International and Development Economics Research, University of California at Berkeley.

Frankel, J. and C. Okongwu (1996) 'Liberalized Portfolio Capital Inflows in Emerging Markets: Sterilization, Expectations, and the Incompleteness of Interest Rate Convergence', *International Journal of Finance and Economics,* vol. 1, no. 1 (January).

Grilli, V. and G. M. Milesi-Ferretti (1995) 'Economic Effects and Structural Determinants of Capital Controls', *IMF Staff Papers*, vol. 42, no.3, September.

Group of Ten (1996) *The Resolution of Sovereign Liquidity Crises*. Official Document.

Hausmann, R. and L. Rojas-Suarez (eds) (1996) *Volatile Capital Flows: Taming their Impact on Latin America* (Inter-American Development Bank, Washington, distributed by Johns Hopkins University Press Baltimore).

Helleiner, E. (1994) *States and the Reemergence of Global Finance: From Bretton Woods to the 1990s* (Ithaca and London: Cornell University Press).

IMF (1995a) *Issues in International Exchange and Payments Systems,* April (Washington, DC: International Monetary Fund).

IMF (1995b) *International Capital Markets,* August (Washington, DC: International Monetary Fund).

IMF (1995c) 'Roundtable on Responses to Sudden Capital Inflows', reported in *IMF Survey,* 22 May.

IMF (1995d) Capital Account Convertibility: Review of Experience and Implications for IMF Policies, *Occasional Paper 131*.

IMF (1995e) *Annual Report on Exchange Restrictions* (Washington, DC: International Monetary Fund).

IMF, 1996, *World Economic Outlook*, May (Washington, DC: International Monetary Fund)

Kenen, P. B. (1995) 'The Feasibility of Taxing Foreign Exchange Transactions', *Working Paper*, no. 29, Center for Economic Policy Studies, Princeton University.

Mathieson, D. J. and L. Rojas-Suarez (1993) 'Liberalization of the Capital Account: Experiences and Issues', *IMF Occasional Paper*, no. 103.

McKinnon, R. (1991) *The Order of Economic Liberalization: Financial Control in the Transition to a Market Economy* (Baltimore: Johns Hopkins Press)

McKinnon, R. and H. Pill (1995) 'Credible Liberalizations and International Capital Flows: The "Over-Borrowing" Syndrome', Department of Economics, Stanford University.

Mohammed, A. (1996) 'Implications for IMF Policies Arising from Effects on Developing Countries of Industrial-Country Macroeconomic Policies' in G. K. Helleiner (ed.) *The International Monetary and Financial System: Developing Country Perspectives* (London: Macmillan).

Montiel, P. (1994) 'Capital Mobility in Developing Countries: Some Measurement Issues and Empirical Estimates', *World Bank Economic Review*, vol. 8, no.3 (September).

Nurkse, R. (1944) *International Currency Experience* (League of Nations).
Obstfeld, M. (1995) 'International Currency Experience: New Lessons and Lessons Relearned', *Brookings Papers on Economic Activity*, no. 1.
Pritchett, L. (1991) 'Measuring Outward Orientation in Developing Countries: Can It Be Done?', *Policy Research Working Paper*, no. 566 (Washington, DC: World Bank).
Quirk, P. J. (1994) 'Capital Account Convertibility: A New Model for Developing Countries' in T. Balino and C. Cottardli (eds) *Frameworks for Monetary Stability* (Washington, DC: International Monetary Fund).
Reisen, H. and B. Fischer (eds) (1993) *Financial Opening: Policy Issues and Experiences in Developing Countries* (Paris: OECD).
Rojas-Suarez, L. and S. R. Weisbrod (1995) Financial Fragilities in Latin America: The 1980s and 1990s, *IMF Occasional Paper,* no. 132.
Sachs, J. (1995a) 'Do We Need an International Lender of Last Resort?', Frank D. Graham Lecture, Princeton University, 20 April, mimeo.
Sachs, J. (1995b) 'Alternative Approaches to Financial Crises in Emerging Markets', November, mimeo.
Schadler, S., M. Carkovic, A. Bennett and R. Kahn (1993) 'Recent Experiences with Surges in Capital Inflows', *IMF Occasional Paper,* no. 108.
Spahn, P. B. (1995) 'International Financial Flows and Transactions Taxes, Survey and Options', *IMF Working Paper 95/60.*
Ul Haq, M., I. Kaul and I. Grunberg (eds) (1996) *The Tobin Tax: Coping with Financial Volatility* (New York and Oxford: Oxford University Press).
UNCTAD (United Nations Conference on Trade and Development) (1994) 'Controls on International Capital Movements' in *Trade and Development Report, 1994* (New York and Geneva: United Nations), pp. 95–115.
White, W. R. (1966) 'International Agreements in the Area of Banking and Finance: Accomplishments and Outstanding Issues', Bank for International Settlements, mimeo.
Williamson, J. (1991) 'On Liberalizing the Capital Account' in R. O'Brien (ed.) *Finance and the International Economy,* vol. V (Oxford, for the *Amex Bank Review*).
Williamson, J. (1996) 'Prospects for Avoiding Crises with Liberalized Capital Flows', Institute for International Economics, Washington, DC, mimeo.
World Bank (1996) *Global Economic Prospects and the Developing Countries* (Washington, DC: World Bank).
Zutshi, U. (1995) 'Aspects of the Final Outcome of the Negotiations on Financial Services of the Uruguay Round', *UNCTAD Discussion Papers*, no. 109 (December).

2 Capital Account Regulations and Macroeconomic Policy: Two Latin American Experiences

Guillermo Le Fort-V. and
Carlos Budnevich L.[1]

I INTRODUCTION

A new policy debate has arisen in Latin American countries after international investors' recent reawakening to opportunities in emerging markets. Two polar positions have been defined in this policy debate. On the one hand, the 'integrationists' defend financial integration on the grounds that free market operation will always produce the best result for the developing economy. On the other, the 'isolationists' consider financial integration dangerous for macroeconomic stability, and prefer a developing world without market-determined international capital movements. The regulations that limit international financial integration have been at the centre of this policy debate, as they define the degree of financial integration and the distance between reality and these two polar positions.

The debate is in itself surprising. An international macroeconomist from only five or ten years ago would be extremely puzzled to see that the external financing problems that some Latin American countries are struggling with today relate no longer to the lack, but rather to the excess, of external financing. Colombia and Chile were denied access to external financial markets operating on a voluntary basis during the second half of the 1980s. Many analysts back then considered that market-based external financing was not to be resumed in the immediate future. But everything changes, and so did the lenders' perceptions of the risk involved in holding emerging market assets. In the mid-1990s, market-based external financing, including medium- and long-term lending, direct investment and portfolio investment, has been abundant for both countries.

In our opinion the polar positions are both to be rejected. Any developing economy has the need for international financial integration, not only because of the external financing needs of a rapidly growing economy, but also because of the long-term advantages that can be derived from financial development, including risk diversification and the efficient provision of financial services. Despite these advantages, the immediate and complete opening-up of the capital account implies very significant potential costs for macroeconomic stability in a developing economy. Several experiences with negative effects of excessive spending and external indebtedness prompted by private capital flows have already been recorded. Thus, the discussion that has been focused on the question of the convenience or inconvenience of opening the capital account should instead be focused on the particular strategy for international financial integration.

The approach that has been favoured in both Chile and Colombia is one of gradual and limited financial integration. Foreign-exchange market regulations and capital account intervention (including regulations) have been used to limit the secondary effects of international financial integration and to deter interest-rate arbitrage, destabilizing speculation, bubbles and overshooting behaviour of asset prices (including the real exchange rate). The strategies differ in the instruments used and in the emphasis of policies and objectives, but both place particular emphasis on neutralizing the disturbances to the current account and domestic prices caused by net capital inflows. The regulations are not exclusively based on macroeconomic policy considerations. They also relate to the potential problems derived from public insurance of the liabilities of financial institutions, and the need for monitoring and limiting their risk-taking. Both deposit insurance and exchange-rate guarantees may encourage over-intermediation of international funds by banks and an increase in systemic risk, expanding therefore the vulnerability of the banking system (see Le Fort, 1994).

This chapter describes and analyses the policies followed in Chile and Colombia regarding their external capital accounts during the 1990s. The policies are analysed and assessed in the context of the macroeconomic and financial results obtained in the period. The first section of the chapter deals with the main analytical issues relating to international financial integration, its costs and benefits, its implications for monetary and exchange-rate policy, and the main limitations to financial integration. The second section describes the experience of regulated financial integration in Chile during the 1990s, including a brief historical review, a review of foreign-exchange market regulations and the regulations on capital movements, and the results in the capital account and at the macroeconomic level. The third section of the chapter is devoted to an analysis of the Colombian case, including a review of the main regulations and intervention schemes in the foreign-exchange markets and the regulations for different types of capital movements, with special emphasis on the reserve requirement system, and the results obtained. The last section presents our concluding remarks.

II MAJOR ISSUES IN INTERNATIONAL FINANCIAL INTEGRATION

This section analyses some important issues relating to the integration of the so-called emerging markets with the world's financial markets without making reference to specific countries. To some extent, this integration is the result of the change of views of investors regarding the risks represented by emerging markets, and to some extent it is the result of an explicit financial integration strategy pursued by developing countries during the 1990s. The issues discussed include the benefits and costs of financial integration, the implications of integration for monetary and exchange-rate policy, and the policy instruments used to limit international financial integration.

The limits imposed by policy upon the international integration of financial markets should be seen as instrumental to more effective monetary and exchange-rate policies. Given that these instruments have some shortcomings, they should be used only to a certain extent; the need for their use arises mainly from the concern about the effects of abundant external financing on the current account and debt positions. This concern in general relates to the fact that large current account deficits and increasing external indebtedness erode a country's creditworthiness, rendering domestic macroeconomic stability vulnerable to external financial turbulence.

Benefits and Costs of Financial Integration

Benefits

An open capital account has important benefits for an economy with an outward-oriented development strategy, characterized by the growth of the sectors in which the country has comparative advantage. In principle, and perhaps oversimplifying, it can be said that the opening-up of the capital account can be associated with two types of benefits:

(1) *Development of the financial services sector*. A developing economy may have comparative advantage in the production of financial services; if that is the case, an export sector would develop after the elimination of restrictions to international financial integration. However, it is also possible that foreign competition may take control of this sector, and the country may become a net importer of financial services. In any case, international integration would imply lower costs and better quality for users of financial services. Financial integration then permits reduced cost of capital and more efficiently provided financial services to help in the intertemporal stabilization of consumption. In some cases, comparative advantage in financial development partly stems from experience derived from earlier liberalization attempts, which resulted in the development of regulatory frameworks that have operated successfully, and now offer these countries the possibility of benefiting from the existence of scale economies. It must be stressed that in developing economies, capital account openness implies larger net capital inflows on a sustained basis, due to the higher productivity of capital typical of these countries because of the abundance of labour and the availability of natural resources. This capital inflow allows for higher growth and a reduction in the cost of capital.

(2) *Greater diversification of the asset portfolio of domestic economic agents*. This can result from financial integration, by permitting the composition of domestic portfolios to be independent of the composition of domestic production. In a financially closed economy, the composition of domestic asset portfolios tends to be closely related to that of domestic output. After all, domestic financial assets represent rights to domestic income streams

which are basically determined by production. In a financially integrated economy, foreign securities that derive returns from external productive activities which are independent from those of domestic activities allow for greater domestic income stability through greater diversification. Incomes of domestic residents become more stable to the extent that their portfolios include assets that derive their returns from activities more or less independent from domestic exports. Such diversification may be used to compensate for the (often great) volatility of national income that affects open economies due to the variability of individual export prices.

Costs

Financial openness can also impose several costs, some of which are only incurred during the transition to a fully integrated economy. Among these costs can be distinguished:

(1) *Transitional costs*. One way of looking at the process of financial integration is that it constitutes a way to overcome a stock imbalance. Financial liberalization allows stock adjustments, directing capital towards regions where the expected profitability of capital is greatest, or to where opportunities exist for risk diversification at a reasonable cost in terms of profitability. It is clear that in countries like Chile and Colombia, the returns to capital are typically higher than in the developed world, a condition for foreigners to invest and finance investments in these countries. Full integration implies a jump in asset prices within a relatively short period of time, and a massive inflow of foreign capital that lasts until the stock adjustment is completed and risk-adjusted domestic rates of return converge to the levels of foreign rates. If this process takes place in a short period of time, then, macroeconomic imbalances can be developed in the form of overly rapid growth in investment, wealth and consumption, real currency appreciation, inflationary pressures and a widening current-account deficit. It can create destabilizing wealth and expenditure effects, resulting in confusing signals to domestic consumers with detrimental effects on domestic savings, exchange-rate stability and the stability of the growth process (see Budnevich, 1994, for a model of this kind of transition).

(2) *Policy costs*. In a financially open economy monetary policy loses its ability to affect domestic macroeconomic conditions without affecting the external balance. In general, an increase in the real interest rate directed at controlling inflationary pressures will also result in currency appreciation, both in nominal and real terms. The appreciation helps in reducing inflation, but may generate a larger current account deficit. In fact, under some conditions, in a financially open economy, monetary authorities may be forced to choose between the inflationary target and the external balance objective. It is true that a tighter fiscal policy may be used in place of monetary restraint under these circumstances; however, real world fiscal policies lack the flexibility needed for short- or medium-term stabilization, particularly when the fiscal accounts are already in balance or in surplus.
(3) *Real costs*. Financial integration leaves the economy exposed to the turbulence of international capital markets, adding a risk factor and volatility to the exchange market which may affect macroeconomic balances. International capital markets can move very rapidly and almost without warning signals, from an optimistic lending phase in which funds are abundant and relatively cheap, to a pessimistic phase in which funds are not available and a sharp adjustment is forced. The recent case of Mexico and that of most Latin American countries in the 1980s come to mind in this respect.
(4) *Systemic risk costs*. Economic agents tend to perceive the existence of publicly provided insurance to liabilities of financial institutions and institutional investors, whether or not it has been explicitly offered. This implicit or explicit insurance requires regulations that limit risk-taking by those institutions. Full and unrestricted international financial integration allows portfolio selection from a wider set of assets, making it more difficult for public authorities to control and monitor their risk-taking.

Financial Integration, and Monetary and Exchange-Rate Policy

The perceptions of foreign investors of the risk and returns from investment in the Chilean and Colombian economies have changed significantly following institutional changes and the successes of macroeconomic policy. This change has resulted in a very significant reduction in the risk premium demanded by investors in these countries, which in turn has resulted in sizeable capital inflows that have modified the degree of integration of the domestic financial markets into the corresponding international markets. It can be said that in economies like Chile and Colombia, the risk-adjusted marginal efficiency of capital has increased to levels above those prevailing in the developed world. As a result, capital tends to move into these economies, reducing the domestic cost of capital and increasing the prices of domestic assets.

Financial integration implies that the integrating economy is fully open to financial arbitrage. Consequently, domestic real interest rates are forced to reflect the external real interest rate and a country-risk premium. Any deviation from this requirement of risk-adjusted international interest-rate equalization implies changes in the opposite direction in the real exchange rate.[2] However, the domestic interest rates required to generate domestic macroeconomic equilibrium may be higher than the rates forced by international arbitrage. In these conditions, when domestic interest rates are increased, in addition to the standard closed economy response in terms of a lower expansion of domestic expenditure, in the financially open economy, a real appreciation of the domestic currency takes place. The real exchange-rate adjustment shifts demand towards the rest of the world, alleviating pressure on domestic output but also increasing the current account deficit.

The size and duration of the arbitrage effect of the domestic interest-rate change on the real exchange rate depend on, among other factors, the time-horizon of arbitrageurs and the expected duration of the new interest-rate differential. The shorter their time-horizon, the lower the impact on the real exchange rate. It also depends upon the effect on the country-risk premium of the currency appreciation. If the increase in the country-risk premium brought about by the real appreciation of the currency is significant, then the impact on the exchange rate is minimized.

International arbitrage may imply that the real exchange rate becomes and remains, for significant periods of time, out of line with respect to the authorities' external equilibrium objective. Consequently, the current account deficit may exceed, in the medium term, the level that is sustainable over a longer term, rendering the economy vulnerable to a forced external adjustment.[3] Such an adjustment is triggered if external creditors no longer consider it safe to continue lending to an addictive borrower. The market's automatic correction mechanism is the effect of the larger current account deficit on the country-risk premium and on expectations of currency depreciation. If larger deficits make market participants uneasy, then this by itself should stop or even reverse the capital inflows and thus correct the real exchange rate. However, it seems that market participants are not always very sensitive to this risk, and that they typically only react when it is too late, after the external conditions have worsened so much that a very large and painful domestic expenditure adjustment is needed.[4]

A first policy response to the real appreciation of the currency is to try to compensate for the effect of capital inflows on the exchange rate. This has been done through the intervention of the monetary authority in the foreign-exchange market. However, the purchase of foreign exchange by the central bank has thereby become the main source of domestic liquidity creation. To limit the effects of exchange market intervention on monetary conditions, the central banks have used different forms of sterilization, including the sale of bills or forcing the temporary holding of foreign-currency certificates. However, this sterilization is costly for the central bank and losses arise from the international interest-rate differential and the real currency appreciation: the central bank acquires assets that yield the international interest rate and that depreciate in real terms, while having to issue liabilities that pay the higher domestic interest rate and keep their real value. As a transitory mechanism, sterilized intervention works; however, over the longer term, its effectiveness is impaired by the resulting financial losses.

A second alternative is to reduce the domestic interest rate. However, this reduction would create an increase in domestic expenditure that would put pressure on the price level, force a real currency appreciation and increase the current account deficit. An obvious solution is to reduce the interest rate and at the same time compensate for the effect on expenditure via tighter fiscal policy. An austere fiscal policy directed at controlling the expansion of aggregate expenditure, limiting both public and private expenditure expansion, is a must for the final success of any stabilization effort. However, there are political limits to what fiscal policy can deliver, and thus restrictions or limitations to international financial integration may be required to preserve macroeconomic stability.

It is generally suggested that another way to compensate for capital inflows is by opening the economy to capital outflows, allowing domestic residents, firms and financial institutions to hold assets abroad. Although a valid tool to favour the diversification of domestic portfolios, this is not effective as a tool to reduce net capital inflows.

As domestic residents increase their holdings of foreign assets, they reduce their demand for domestic assets. A lower demand for domestic assets, *ceteris paribus*, is reflected in lower asset prices and higher asset returns, which serve as an additional attraction for foreign capital inflows.[5] Furthermore, by making exit easier, facilitating capital outflows reduces the risks faced by foreign investors (see Labán and Larraín, 1993).

Limitations on international financial integration give additional degrees of freedom to monetary and exchange-rate policies, allowing adjustments in domestic interest rates that cannot be arbitraged to the exchange rate. In practice, these restrictions give room for the use of monetary policy to reduce domestic inflation gradually, while keeping the current-account deficit at reasonable levels.

The problem created by capital inflows for the effectiveness of monetary policy is better dealt with by a flexible exchange rate. In this connection, exchange-rate stability is costly because it facilitates the international arbitrage of interest rates. If the central bank actively tries to achieve exchange-rate stability, it faces additional costs in terms of higher reserve purchases, and in the end is forced to accept a more appreciated currency. In this sense, avoiding rules for official intervention, increasing the width of the exchange-rate band, and using a basket of currencies rather than a single currency to peg the reference rate are measures that increase the effectiveness of monetary policy, by helping to insulate against excessive capital inflows. The *ex ante* volatility of the exchange rate also tends to deter short-run capital inflows as it removes exchange-rate 'guarantees' and thus helps to support a higher real exchange rate (see Sanhueza, 1995).

Limitations to Financial Integration

In order to reduce the need for sterilized intervention, several restrictions to international financial integration have been used. These restrictions, by limiting the possibilities of financial arbitrage, have given some room for the operation of monetary policy as it seeks to achieve domestic macroeconomic equilibrium. In most cases the restrictions to capital transactions introduce registration procedures for international capital transactions. These procedures can be important sources of information for measuring the external accounts, and also for the tax authorities; but they also involve obvious administrative costs.

The first type of restriction is the use of dual foreign-exchange markets. One market, the formal one, is used for current account transactions and authorized capital flows, and the other, the informal one, is used for other financial flows. In this scheme, financial arbitrage takes place in the informal market, permitting this secondary exchange rate to deviate from the authorities' target rate. Since the formal market is not subject to arbitrage, the current account is isolated from exchange-rate volatility. During the days of scarce foreign financing, the informal rate reflected a more depreciated domestic currency than the rate in the formal market. The opposite should be the case under abundant external flows.

The dual exchange-rate scheme has one serious shortcoming – the existence of leaks that allow for arbitraging the differential between the exchange rates in the two markets. These leaks not only render the exchange restrictions ineffective, creating pressure towards the equalization of the exchange rates, but also imply significant costs. The leaks include the over-and under-invoicing of current-account flows, and they tend to increase in importance as the absolute value of the premium becomes larger. The leaks, in general, result in quasi-fiscal losses and transfer of resources from the central bank to those agents that discover ways to buy foreign exchange in one market and sell it in the other at a premium. Additional costs of the leaks are the regulations and administrative costs incurred in the effort of preventing them.

A second type of restriction is the imposition of reserve requirements or other more direct measures that increase the marginal cost of external financing. The reserve requirements increase the cost of foreign financing since they demand the use of additional resources to finance the required deposit in the central bank. The reserve requirements may relate to all forms of foreign financial flows; however, in practice, they have not generally affected direct investment and other forms of equity financing, suppliers' credits on imports, or advanced export returns.[6]

In general, the financial cost effects of the reserve requirements tend to be greater for short-term financing and therefore work particularly against short-term arbitrage. In Chile, the required reserves must be kept in the central bank for a period of one year, diminishing the relative financial burden for longer-term operations. In the case of Colombia, however, the requirement is variable depending on the maturity of the loan; for longer maturities the reserve requirement ratio is lower, implying discrimination against short-term inflows.

Mechanisms like these reserve requirements have certain limitations. First, they can be avoided by using vehicles that are not affected by the requirement; for example, accelerated export returns, supplier credits, or equity investments. There is a limitation, however, on what can be brought in through these alternative vehicles. The requirements can also be evaded by not registering capital flows, although penalties may be imposed on those who evade the regulations.

Reserve requirements are effective only under expectations of a stable real exchange rate, and thus are unable to stop a speculative attack created by expectations of exchange-rate adjustments. The capital gains that can be made with a discrete exchange-rate jump cannot be sufficiently reduced by the financial cost of the reserve requirement. This implies that, despite the reserve requirement, only exchange rates that are consistent with market expectations can be successfully defended. The equilibrium trend of the exchange rate, even if it represents a significant real appreciation of the currency, cannot be influenced by such policies. An exchange-rate adjustment can be spread more over time, but only to a certain extent. Reserve requirements as well as other restrictions to financial integration increase financing costs for individuals and firms, limit business opportunities for the financial sector, and reduce portfolio diversification for domestic agents. They also affect the equity–debt mix, and create financial segmentation that tends to favour big over small enterprises, and to encourage informal means of financing. They are thus not free of private and social costs. There are also costs derived from weaknesses of the regulations that make reserve requirements not completely effective. In a country like Chile, with a long and deep-seated law-abiding tradition, these effects are more important than direct evasion.

Other types of restriction affect the ability of domestic firms and financial institutions to issue debt or stock in international capital markets. These restrictions can take the form of discretionary authorization or conditions like a minimum credit rating, minimum amount issued, or others. In this respect, the purpose of the restrictions is not only related to limiting the external capital inflows but also to screening the companies that are authorized to participate in international capital markets. Since the actions of each firm generate externalities to others, in the sense that all of them are seen as firms belonging to a particular country, some type of screening process is required. Finally, restrictions may be applied to portfolio investors from abroad in the form of quantitative restrictions on entry into domestic markets, or minimum stay (or permanence) requirements.

Restrictions on international financial integration are effective to a certain extent but could not be considered a cure-all or a way to completely isolate the domestic economy from the realities of the international financial markets. There are always ways to circumvent the restrictions, ways that tend to be reinforced the larger the risk-adjusted interest-rate differential. Consequently, only to a certain extent is it possible to use these restrictions to give some room for manoeuvre to domestic monetary policy.

III REGULATED FINANCIAL INTEGRATION IN CHILE

During the 1990s, important policy measures have been taken to regulate the financial integration of the Chilean economy with international markets. These measures, together with the recognition of the Chilean economy in financial centres, have allowed for increasing financial integration and for important changes in the composition of Chilean capital flows during the 1990s. The foreign-exchange market and capital flow regulations existing in the Chilean economy are briefly reviewed in this section. In addition the results derived from this strategy are presented.[7]

The regulations are directed to reducing potential effects on macroeconomic stability, increasing the effectiveness of monetary policy, and imposing prudential regulations on banks and institutional investors. They have taken the form of exchange-market regulations, capital flows regulations and other related policies.

A Brief History of Regulations

Financial activity, which had been repressed for years by negative real rates of interest and administrative allocation of credit, and with the majority of financial institutions under government control, entered an accelerated liberalization process in the 1970s. After decades of financial repression, the supervisory institutions lacked the experience necessary to impose prudential regulations effectively. The result was a financial system with insufficient capitalization, that went into bankruptcy in the early 1980s. A deep recession, beginning at the end of 1981, further eroded the solvency of financial institutions which were already in a very vulnerable position. The trigger for the crisis was a sharp reduction in external capital inflows and a deterioration in the terms of trade, causing a sharp adjustment in domestic expenditure. The financial crisis spread throughout the financial system by the beginning of 1983.

The volatility of international capital flows played a very important role in setting off the crisis. A significant proportion of capital flows entering the country in the period prior to the 1982 crisis had been intermediated by the financial system. The removal of restrictions to capital inflows, when domestic interest rates, duly adjusted for exchange risk, greatly exceeded international rates, generated a massive capital inflow which financed a strong expansion of domestic spending. Subsequent external debt problems provoked a drastic change in the direction of capital flows, forcing an adjustment and contributing to the deepening of the crisis of the financial system.

The financial institutions recovered from the crisis in the second half of the 1980s. A macroeconomic policy characterized by caution and a concern to control the expansion of expenditure has resulted, during the 1990s, in moderate current-account deficits. Macroeconomic policy has defined a target range for the medium-term current-account deficit of between 3 and 4 per cent of gross domestic product (GDP). External financing has more than exceeded financing requirements, resulting in significant increases in international reserves. International reserves increased by almost $10 billion in the period 1990–5, reaching a level of around $14 billion by the end of that period despite the prepayment of public external debt of about $1.5 billion.

The policy of external financial opening pursued by the Chilean authorities in the 1990s is characterized by the maintenance of a series of regulations which affect the foreign-exchange market and the capital account, and limit the degree of integration of external and domestic markets.

Foreign-Exchange Market Regulations and Intervention

During the 1990s the Chilean foreign-exchange market has evolved from a dual market to an increasingly unified market. The formal foreign-exchange market is affected by regulations and access restrictions, while the informal foreign-exchange market is fully liberalized. Total unification has not been achieved yet, but the exchange-rate differential in both markets is almost non-existent – less than a 0.5 per cent difference on average in 1995. The dual exchange market was conceived as a way to isolate the formal-market exchange rate – the one at which trade flows were carried out – from the volatility of capital flows, particularly portfolio outflows, that must be carried out through the informal exchange market. Over time, however, the duality has lost relevance.

Some transactions must be effected through the formal market: in particular, all foreign portfolio capital inflows. Investors and borrowers obtain, in exchange, the right to access the same market at the time of servicing the debt or remitting profits or capital. Other capital outflows, including foreign direct investment and portfolio investment by residents, cannot be carried out through the formal market. Finally, there are transactions that can be carried out in either of the two exchange markets. These include exports and imports of goods and non-factor services.

The dual-exchange-market approach has been gradually revised. Increasing confidence has allowed the reduction of exchange restrictions, particularly those affecting export proceeds. In several steps, the export surrender requirements were first reduced and then completely eliminated (on 16 June 1995). The exchange-market regulations that remain in place are mostly related to capital flows.

The formal foreign-exchange market operates under a managed float within an exchange-rate band. Intervention by the central bank is directed at maintaining the nominal and, through it, the real exchange rate within a range consistent with a sustainable current-account position. In an indexed economy like that of Chile, changes in the nominal rate only affect the level of the real exchange rate for a limited period. It is understood that the real exchange rate cannot be permanently affected through the nominal rate, and that it is necessary to create adequate conditions in terms of real variables to attain that result.

The authorities understand 'external equilibrium' to mean the maintenance of a deficit in the current account of the balance of payments, which, while allowing the use of a reasonable amount of external saving for financing domestic investment, still ensures that the increase in external debt is compatible with the long-term growth of the Chilean economy without introducing a significant source of further external vulnerability for the country. In practice, this means a deficit on current account of the order of 3 to 4 per cent of GDP. Obviously this target is interpreted as an average since in any given year the current account deficit must be permitted some divergence from the average.

Since the market has been at, or close to, the more currency-appreciated end of the exchange-rate band, the central bank, as noted above, has accumulated a significant amount of net international reserves, while a significant portion of the external public debt has been prepaid. The monetary impact of official intervention in foreign-exchange markets has been sterilized through the issuance of central bank debt.

Regulations on Capital Movements

The regulation of capital movements differentiates between direct investment and debt flows. Direct investment is favoured due to the presumed positive externalities associated with it, including access to international markets and the transfer of management techniques and technology. As a consequence, the direct-investment regime is fairly liberal, while the regulations are designed to limit foreign indebtedness, particularly that of a short-term nature. The only important restriction for direct investment is the one-year minimum stay. Portfolio investment through American Depository Receipts (ADRs) placed in New York is limited by credit-rating and minimum-amount conditions.

Direct Investment Inflows[8]

Direct investment is subject to a minimum stay of one year for the principal. Profits, with the single exception of investment performed through debt conversions, are not subject to time limitations. The rules that allowed for foreign investment through debt conversions were eliminated in mid-1995.

Portfolio Investment Inflows and ADRs[9]

Procedures relating to bonds and ADRs – which represent the acquisition of shares of domestic companies by foreigners – set limits on the right to issue these types of instrument in terms of minimum amount and risk classification. Initially the minimum amount demanded for the issuing of non-financial firms' ADRs was 50 million United States dollars ($). As of September 1994 this was reduced to $25 million. At the same time it was decided to reduce the issuers' required long-term debt risk rating to BBB or better for non-financial companies, and to BBB+ or better for banking institutions. This rating has to be granted by three internationally recognized risk-rating agencies.

Since July 1995, the secondary ADR inflows have been subject to the 30 per cent reserve requirement that relates to most forms of foreign indebtedness. In addition, in November 1995, for those companies that have at least one previous issue, the minimum amount for primary issues of ADRs (not subject to the reserve requirement) was reduced to $10 million. A condition imposed on the new primary issues is that all previous issues of the same company become subject to the same regulations as the last issue.

Other Portfolio Capital Inflows

Regulations on debt-related capital flows and on deposits of non-residents are tighter. Instead of minimum-stay or credit-rating requirements, these types of flows are influenced by a reserve requirement. The purpose of the reserve requirement is to increase the cost of external financing, and consequently increase the level of the domestic interest rate at which international arbitrage results in external inflows. At present, the reserve requirement ratio is 30 per cent of the value of the loan, bond or deposit, and the reserve deposit must be placed at the central bank in US dollars.

Loans and Bonds[10]

External loans and bonds issued abroad are subject to a 30 per cent reserve requirement, to be kept in the central bank for a period of one year, irrespective of the maturity of the loan or bond. In all cases, the reserve deposit must be constituted in US dollars; however, an alternative to the deposit is the payment, in advance, of the financial cost implied by the reserve requirement. In addition, bonds are subject to regulations similar to those that affect ADRs. There is a minimum amount of bonds to be issued ($25 million for corporate bonds), and a minimum risk rating of BBB for non-financial issuers and BBB+ for banks.

Deposits and Credit Lines[11]

External credit lines, used mainly to finance trade operations, are also subject to the 30 per cent reserve requirement which is applied on the average balance of the month. Foreign-currency deposits are treated similarly: like placements in foreign currency, they are also subject to the reserve deposit of 30 per cent, applied on the average balance of the month.

Capital Outflows

With respect to the acquisition of foreign assets by Chilean residents, regulations are rather liberal with the sole exception of prudential restrictions imposed on banks and institutional investors.

Foreign Investments by the Chilean Non-Financial Private Sector[12]

Foreign investments carried out by individuals and by non-financial companies are not in practice subject to any restrictions. The only limitation is related to access to the formal foreign-exchange market, which is not always granted. In any case, the informal market is readily available at a rate roughly the same as in the formal market. This measure has greatly facilitated Chilean investment abroad, which has boomed since 1990. Chilean investment abroad is concentrated mainly in the financial services, electrical, and transportation and telecommunications sectors.

Foreign Investments by Chilean Institutional Investors[13]

Foreign investments by pension funds, mutual funds and life- insurance companies are subject to certain limits as to the amounts and types of foreign assets that they can hold. These restrictions were recently upgraded by the central bank after the approval by Congress of a new capital market law. Pension funds are authorized to hold up to 9 per cent of their total funds in foreign assets, which may include a variety of fixed-income assets and company shares; the latter are limited to 4.5 per cent of the fund. Life-insurance companies are limited to investments of up to 10 per cent of their funds in foreign assets. The limit on general-insurance companies is 15 per cent of their reserves, and for mutual funds the limit is 30 per cent of the fund.

Foreign Investments by Chilean Banks

Regulations on foreign asset holdings by commercial banks are associated with the problem of systemic risk and deposit insurance affecting the banking system. Foreign financial investments by commercial banks are limited to 25 per cent of the bank capital and reserves, and restricted to bills and bonds issued or guaranteed by foreign governments or central banks. Banks are also authorized to use foreign-currency deposits and credit lines to finance trade within the Association for Latin American Integration (ALADI). In addition, commercial banks can acquire stock of foreign banks or establish branches abroad provided that the domestic banks have a capital-adequacy index of 10 per cent or more. (This index, based on the Basle Convention, measures capital as a proportion of the value of total assets adjusted by credit risk.) Only to the extent that bank supervision can be effective in monitoring the risk of foreign assets is further liberalization possible in this area.

Capital Account and Macroeconomic Results

The international perception of the reduction of the risk of Chilean investment is reflected in several indicators. The investment-grade rating for Chilean public debt, equivalent to Standard & Poor's A– which is given by the most prestigious international agencies, is the highest in Latin America and comparable to that of some countries in Southern Europe and South-East Asia.

The reduction in the international perception of risk in the Chilean economy has resulted in a substantial increase in the supply of external funds available for the country. Net capital inflows have been significant over the last five years, averaging 6.6 per cent of GDP over the period 1990–4, with a maximum of 9.4 per cent of GDP in 1990. With a current-account deficit averaging only 1.5 per cent of GDP, the available external financing has been more than necessary or desired and, as a result, net international reserves increased markedly, by about $10 billion, to a level equivalent to 26 per cent of GDP which represented more than one year of imports by the end of 1995 (see Table 2.1).

Table 2.1 Chile and Colombia: balance of payments, 1990–4 (per cent of GDP in dollars)

	Chile			*Colombia*		
	Balance of payments	*Capital account*	*Current account*	*Balance of payments*	*Capital account*	*Current account*
1990	7.7	9.4	−1.7	1.2	−0.3	1.5
1991	3.5	3.2	0.3	4.2	−2.1	6.3
1992	5.8	7.4	−1.6	2.2	0.0	2.2
1993	1.2	5.7	−4.5	−2.1	2.4	−4.5
1994	6.1	7.5	−1.4	0.3	4.6	−4.3

Note: A minus sign indicates a deficit.
Source: Calculations by the authors, based on data of the Banco Central de Chile, Banco de la República de Colombia, IMF and Departamento Administrativo Nacional de Estadistica (DANE), Colombia.

An important question is whether under these circumstances the existing capital account regulations have been effective. In particular the reserve requirement has been under scrutiny. If the effectiveness of this measure is judged against its success in checking overall capital flows, the regulations have not been effective since inflows have continued at a significant pace. However the effectiveness of regulations should be measured only in terms of their objectives, which do *not* include drying up the capital account. The first objective is to favour equity over debt financing and long-term financing over short-term financing. The second is to give more freedom for monetary policy which can be tightened without resulting in large current-account imbalances.

As a consequence of the capital account regulations, a significant change in the composition of the capital account occurred in the 1990s. Foreign direct investment and longer-term portfolio investment (associated mainly with the placement of ADRs) grew in importance relative to external indebtedness (see Table 2.2). Indeed, net foreign investment plus portfolio investment grew from about 3 per cent of GDP in 1990 and 1.2 per cent of GDP in 1991, to 2.5 per cent in 1993 and 4 per cent in 1994.[14] In recent years there has also been a change in the composition of external borrowing, with a trend towards a larger share of medium-and long-term debt and a consequent reduction in external short-term financing. In fact, in 1990 external short-term debt financing amounted to 4.6 per cent of GDP, while in 1994 short-term financing was equivalent to 2.4 per cent of GDP (see Table 2.3).

Table 2.2 Chile and Colombia: capital account balance and foreign direct investment, 1990–4 (per cent of GDP in dollars)

	Chile		*Colombia*	
	Capital account balance, excluding net FDI	*Net FDI*	*Capital account balance, excluding net FDI*	*Net FDI*
1990	6.4	3.0	−1.6	1.3
1991	2.0	1.2	−3.2	1.1
1992	5.9	1.5	−1.8	1.8
1993	3.2	2.5	0.8	1.6
1994	3.9	3.6	2.4	2.2

Note: A minus sign indicates a deficit.
Source: Calculations by the authors, based on data of the Banco Central de Chile, Banco de la República de Colombia, IMF and Departamento Administrativo Nacional de Estadistica (DANE), Colombia.

Table 2.3 Chile and Colombia: time structure of non-investment capital flows, 1990–4 (per cent of GDP in dollars)

	Chile		*Colombia*	
	Medium- and long-term capital	*Short-term capital*	*Medium- and long-term capital*	*Short-term capital*
1990	2.2	4.6	0.5	−0.5
1991	−0.2	1.4	0.3	−2.5
1992	0.6	4.5	0.4	0.4
1993	1.1	2.4	1.9	2.1
1994	2.5	2.4	5.7	−1.1

Source: Calculations by the authors, based on data of the Banco Central de Chile, Banco de la República de Colombia, IMF and Departamento Administrativo Nacional de Estadistica (DANE), Colombia.

Monetary policy has been tight, with short-term real interest rates averaging 6 per cent per annum while inflation came down from almost 30 per cent in 1990 to 9 per cent in 1994. This reduction has been based on the control of expenditure expansion. Expenditure control has paid off not only in terms of lower inflation but also in that the current account deficit has averaged less than 2 per cent of GDP in the 1990s. Expenditure control has been achieved through interest rates that were higher than the standards in the developed world. Despite strict monetary policy, the economy has been able to grow at an average of close to 7 per cent per year in 1990–5. Exports have led the expansion; for example, during 1995 real GDP grew by 8.5 per cent, and exports by 11 per cent in real terms.

Expenditure control would not have been possible if capital account regulations had not been effective, because otherwise capital inflows would have made it impossible to keep interest rates above international levels (see Table 2.4). It is possible to conclude that reserve requirements have been effective in limiting the international integration of fixed-income financial markets. The international interest-rate differential would not have been possible without this type of restriction. Longer-term markets show, *ex ante*, a similar spread to short-term markets. The explanation seems to be that for longer terms the insurance premium against country risk is higher, thus offsetting the lower financial effect of the reserve requirement.

At the same time an important segment of the Chilean equity market has been effectively integrated with international stock markets through the ADRs. However, the risks associated with the price of each particular stock, or even with a composite index, make it very difficult to perform international financial arbitrage through this mechanism.

It is important to note that the reserve requirement cannot be used to avoid a trend of real appreciation of the domestic currency. Indeed in Chile the real effective value of the currency has shown an appreciating trend averaging 4 per cent per year during the last five years. The currency appreciation trend has been an equilibrium trend, in the sense that it has been consistent with a sustainable deficit in the current account of the balance of payments of less than 2 per cent of GDP. In the face of expectations of currency appreciation, the reserve requirement is ineffective in stopping capital inflows. The financial cost implied by the requirement, that is, 2 or 3 percentage points per annum, can be easily offset by an expected appreciation of 1 per cent or 2 per cent in the following few weeks.

Domestic financial indicators show that the capital account regulations have not impaired the financial system. In fact, despite the regulations, the financial system and the capital markets have achieved very significant development in Chile over the last few years. An indication of the rapid development of the banking system is the expansion of total liabilities of the financial system to the private sector, which have increased from 47 per cent of GDP in 1990 to 67 per cent of GDP in 1995. At the same time, the real rate of return on capital of domestic banks has been kept at a high and stable level. On average, between 1990 and 1994 commercial banks earned 20 per cent, in real terms, on their capital and reserves.

The results in the stock market are even more remarkable. On average, the stock-market index in terms of United States dollars rose 40 per cent per year in the period from December 1989 to December 1995. As a consequence, total stock-market capitalization towards the end of 1995 reached 125 per cent of GDP, compared to 50 per cent of GDP in 1990.

Moreover, the country shows a strong international financial position. Total external debt net of international reserves is just equivalent to 10 per cent of annual GDP or 35 per cent of annual exports.

IV CAPITAL ACCOUNT AND EXCHANGE-RATE POLICY IN COLOMBIA

During the first half of the 1990s, the Colombian economy was engaged in a wide-reaching programme of structural reform. The programme included the opening of the economy to international trade through the elimination of administrative restrictions on imports and a generalized reduction of tariffs; bilateral international trade agreements with Venezuela, Mexico and Chile; the creation of a Ministry of Foreign Exchange and a Foreign Commerce Bank; the introduction of measures increasing the flexibility of the exchange-rate regime; the enhancement of possibilities to acquire external financing for national agents; the removal of restrictions on external investment and the establishment of national treatment for foreign investors; the reduction of the overall taxation rate; labour-market liberalization and partial privatization of the social security system; privatization of some public enterprises; and the reform of the Central Bank Charter to grant its legal independence.

Exchange-Rate Regime and Sterilization

Since the end of the 1970s, Colombia had used a crawling-peg exchange-rate regime. The Banco de la República, Colombia's central bank, made a daily announcement of the rate at which the bank was willing to engage in foreign-exchange transactions. Towards the mid-1980s, the rate of currency devaluation consistently lagged behind inflation differentials, resulting in a sustained real appreciation. The response of the Banco de la República was an acceleration of the devaluation programme, even above the inflation differential, improving competitiveness at the cost of higher inflation.[15]

In 1991, the Banco de la República was granted political independence through a constitutional reform. The new Central Bank Charter formally established a commitment to the reduction of inflation. In a context of stubborn inflationary pressures and a tendency to currency appreciation, the Banco de la República reformed the exchange-rate regime, introducing exchange certificates (ECs), aiming at a more flexible and market-oriented exchange rate. In this way, the first formal exchange market in many years was established.

The need and scope for using monetary sterilization policy depend on the cross-border mobility of capital. As its benefits, one can mention the recovery of monetary control and the avoidance of excessive intermediation through the banking system without increasing intermediation costs associated with a reserve requirement. Among the associated costs, it is worth mentioning that monetary sterilization has implied an increase in interest rates and an increase in the quasi-fiscal deficit.

The intervention mechanism in Colombia combined, in the same transaction, exchange-market intervention and sterilization. The central bank purchased foreign exchange with ECs, a dollar-denominated financial instrument issued by the Banco de la República that initially was redeemable in pesos at full value and on demand. The redemption price, in pesos, of these instruments was determined daily by the central bank, and corresponded to its liquidation price at the maturity date. This price was similar to the exchange rate and was called 'the representative rate'.

The maturity of ECs was extended to three months in June 1991, and to one year in October 1991. These financial instruments could be sold at a discount in the secondary market, and the central bank opened a discount window to redeem ECs at 87.5 per cent of their value, that is, at a discount of 12.5 per cent. Foreign exchange was sold to the Banco de la República in exchange for the ECs at the exchange-certificate redemption rate, the official exchange rate fixed by the central bank. This rate was adjusted in a crawling-peg fashion, creating a gap with respect to the market rate. This gap was fundamentally determined by domestic interest rates (since the ECs were substitutes for other peso-denominated financial assets) and the expected rate of change of the official exchange rate. When interest rates rose, the gap widened and the market rate for the peso appreciated, converging to the exchange-rate floor which was 87.5 per cent of the official exchange rate, the value at which the Banco de la República bought back new ECs.

The nominal value at time T of an 'EC-dollar' was equal to the official exchange rate (ER) at time T. The market value of an 'EC-dollar' with maturity date of $T+1$, which claims the right to one dollar, and is bounded by the discount price at which it can be sold to the Banco de la República (the floor), must be determined as a function of the expected official exchange rate (ER) at time $T+1$, and the opportunity cost given by the interest rate of peso-denominated debt issued by the Banco de la República. The price in pesos could be written as:

$$P_{ecdollar} = \frac{E(ER_{T+1}/ER_T)}{(1+r)} \times ER_T$$

The floor price is determined by the Banco de la República, which buys an 'EC-dollar' at a discount of 12.5 per cent of the official exchange rate:

$$P_{ecdollar} = 0.875ER_T$$

If the foreign-exchange market works efficiently, the EC price should correspond to the market exchange rate which depends positively on the level of the official exchange rate and its expected rate of devaluation, and negatively on the interest rate.

The ECs tied the hands of the Banco de la República in the conduct of its monetary policy. If the central bank raised interest rates through open-market operations, the market exchange rate (the price in pesos of the EC dollar) would be pushed to the floor, and intermediaries would liquidate their EC stocks. As the stock of ECs in the market fell, the monetary stock would increase, eliminating the initial interest-rate rise, unless it was sterilized with peso-denominated debt. The system operated practically as a pseudo flotation-band, given that by arbitrage the market price could never fall below what we have called the floor. If the market rate rose above the official rate, agents would lower their stock of ECs, which is equivalent to buying dollars from the Banco de la República to sell them to the market.

Back in the crawling-peg years, monetary sterilization had been carried out through open-market operations. ECs were introduced with the objective of eliminating the need for such sterilization, or performing it directly in the exchange market. The system was of very limited effectiveness. As long as market operators accumulated EC stocks, the flow of dollars going into the market and, hence, central bank intervention were reduced. At the point when the flow of EC liquidations was equal to the issuance of new certificates, however, the sterilization effect of EC was nullified. The attempts at forcing an increase in the EC stock through longer maturity for the ECs were bound to fail.[16]

In January of 1994, the EC system was discontinued, and an exchange-rate band of ± 15 per cent around a central parity entered into operation. The central bank intervened, within the band, in both the spot and future exchange markets. The Banco de la República announced daily the central parity for the next ten days, and the rate of devaluation of the central parity was initially set at 11 per cent. Parallel to the band, a 'monetary corridor' was established, that is a band for M1 which the central bank is committed to maintain through operations in its peso-denominated debt. In December 1994, and as the market rate put pressure on the band, the band's central rate was appreciated by 7 per cent. As a compensation, the rate of subsequent devaluation of the central parity was increased to 13.5 per cent.

Foreign-Exchange Restrictions and Public Debt Policy

In 1991 a formal foreign-exchange market was created, substituting for the previous exchange controls through licences, a mechanism that had existed since 1967. Resolutions 55 and 57 authorized banks, financial corporations, and to some extent savings funds and commercial financing corporations, to operate as authorized dealers in the exchange market. Resolution 57 stipulated that the more important trade and investment operations, including imports, exports, and foreign investment and loans, must be channelled through the formal exchange market.

The authorized dealers in the market could negotiate foreign-exchange proceeds coming from the activities required to be in the formal market, but also currency coming from other activities. Dealers were also authorized to trade among themselves and with the Banco de la República. The transactions and the exchange rates were to be reported daily to the Banking Superintendent and central bank. Resolution 55 authorized the Banco de la República to intervene in the exchange market through transactions in ECs, certificates that were denominated in dollars but payable in pesos. They were freely negotiable and could be liquidated at the Banco de la República before their maturity at a discount. The Banco de la República could not negotiate dollars with the public, but only with authorized intermediaries, by means of ECs, or with the government.

Two measures forced dealers to align their rates with the official exchange rate. In order to sell dollars to the Banco de la República, a domestic agent had to buy ECs through a market dealer. In order to acquire dollars from the central bank, the agent had to liquidate ECs, obtaining them in the secondary market. As mentioned above, the principal objective of the new regime was to give more flexibility to the exchange rate, avoiding the cost of sterilized intervention. This was the first step towards a flexible exchange rate, which allows more flexibility in monetary policy to stop inflationary pressure.

Before the establishment of the EC regime, the Banco de la República had centred its monetary policy on the sterilization of the effects of significant capital flows coming from abroad. This implied a financial burden for the central bank as the cost of its domestic debt grew continuously.[17] Inflation continued unabated as the Banco de la República tried to compensate for the observed real appreciation through a more aggressive devaluation calendar that reduced additional capital inflows. By 1991, there was a widespread perception that the devaluation programme was not sustainable. The devaluation–intervention–sterilization cycle was too costly for the Banco de la República, and the expectations of real appreciation that ensued generated a more vigorous capital inflow. Exchange-rate flexibility was the only way out of this pervasive cycle.

The EC system produced, in the short run, an effective sterilized intervention. As domestic agents accumulated their EC stocks, the pressure concentrated on the exchange market until the floor was reached and pressure on money creation started. In 1993 though, the ECs started to mature, causing a new impulse for monetary creation that needed to be sterilized through debt issues. The ECs gave some degree of freedom in the short term, but by no means monetary policy independence, as it was not a stable sterilization tool. What appears obvious is that the exchange market was forced to evolve gradually towards a system of managed floating. The EC's term was an adaptation period, thought to create the necessary institutional background for the development of the market. Domestic open-market operations were the principal source of sterilization before, during and after the EC system.

More recently, the exchange reforms included Resolution 21 which had the objective of advancing more quickly than Resolution 57 in facilitating transactions with international markets. The reforms were oriented towards speeding up long-term investment flows and holding out speculative capital. The reforms applied to the capital market were mainly:

- simplification of authorized exchange-market operations;
- extension of the types of operations not required to be made through the formal foreign-exchange market;
- authorization to make payments for exports and imports in Colombian pesos;
- an increase in the possibilities of obtaining loans abroad;
- liberalization of capital outflows to foreign markets.

The public debt policy, on the other hand, had the following objectives: to diversify internal financial alternatives, to develop the national financial market, to improve the external debt time profile, and to expand the possibilities for public corporations to engage directly in foreign financing. Consequently, during 1993 and 1994, long-term bonds were issued and placed in international markets at interest rates that were more favourable than those of previous issues of external debt. Part of the resources generated were used to prepay outstanding debt.

Bonds were issued not only by the central government. About 60 per cent were issued by public enterprises, including Ecopetrol, the Financiera Electrica Nacional and the Bank of Colombia. These issues, along with the low international interest rates, helped to improve the liquidity and solvency of Colombia as an international debtor.

Reserve Requirements and Capital Account Regulations

During the second half of the 1980s, the Colombian current account registered a sustained surplus. At the beginning of the 1990s, the authorities reacted to this surplus with measures to liberalize external trade, consisting mainly of a reduction of import tariffs, a mix of sterilized interventions to neutralize the monetary effects of capital inflows, and reserve requirements to limit the attractiveness of those inflows. Moreover, capital account liberalization in conjunction with tax forgiveness led to capital repatriation. As a result, the current account went into deficit and a surplus in the capital account was created, which increased further in 1992 and 1993, due to relatively low international interest rates. Net international reserves grew rapidly in 1991 and 1992, but the increase slowed down in 1993 as a result of a reduction in sterilized intervention in the foreign-exchange market.

In 1993, the Banco de la República reformed the exchange ordinance, aiming at making foreign-exchange transactions more flexible but at the same time maintaining some control over speculative capital movements. Article 30 of Resolution 21 of the Banco de la República introduced a reserve requirement ratio of 47 per cent on any credit in foreign exchange obtained by a resident that had a total repayment period of up to 18 months. The deposits associated with the reserve requirement were considered as exchange operations and were to be made through exchange-market intermediaries. Upon deposit of the required reserve, the Banco de la República issued a certificate corresponding to the reserve requirement ratio multiplied by the amount of the loan. The remaining part of the loan could enter freely. The certificate was denominated in US dollars, was non-negotiable, had a maturity of one year, and was redeemable at its nominal value in pesos at the official exchange rate. It was called 'Financial Foreign Currency Title' (FFCT). The Banco de la República could, if it considered it necessary, acquire the titles before their maturity, applying a discount of 13 per cent on their nominal value at the official exchange rate on the day of issue if the buyback was performed immediately. If redemption was made at a later date, the corresponding official exchange rate had to be applied.

In 1994, the reserve requirements were modified, allowing for differentiation according to the maturity of the loan. Resolution 7 of 1994 introduced reserve requirements for operations of less than 36 months, the Banco de la República issuing FFCTs in exchange. For certificates with a maturity of 12 months the reserve requirement ratio was 93 per cent, for a maturity of 18 months, 64 per cent, and for a maturity of 24 months it was 50 per cent.

Certificates could be partitioned to the agents' preference, and the central bank could buy back only those with a maturity of 12 months, at a 55 per cent discount on the official exchange rate at the day of issue. Finally, Resolution 22 of 1994 established a new schedule of reserve requirements, extended to maturities of up to five years (see Appendix 2.1). This shows that in Colombia there is discrimination against short-run capital inflows: the shorter the maturity, the higher the reserve requirement. The reserve requirement is applied for the duration of the operation. The Colombian authorities have tried to eliminate possibilities for arbitrage, as the reserve requirement ratios were set so as to close the arbitrage gap. The objective was clearly to increase the cost of short-term capital inflows, in parallel with the liberalization of the capital account.

It is important to mention that this system differs from that used in Chile, where the reserve requirement has been oriented towards closing the gap of interest-rate arbitrage only for operations of up to one year. For longer maturities, greater uncertainty and risk may act as deterrent to longer-term arbitrage. Appendix 2.2, however, shows that under the assumption of risk neutrality and flat term structures of interest rates and expectations of devaluation, the reserve requirement which eliminates arbitrage for different durations increases with the length of the maturity.

The Capital Account and Macroeconomics

During the first half of the 1990s, Colombia experienced a significant accumulation of international reserves, especially at the beginning of the decade. Recently this accumulation has slowed down as a consequence of the movement of the current account from a significant surplus to deficit. We interpret this evolution as the result of the liberalization of external trade which led to an import boom and to a sudden adjustment of the stock of durable consumption goods. We reject the hypothesis that this behaviour was driven by capital inflows. The surplus in the capital account, which at the beginning of the 1990s was moderate, started to increase significantly in the last two years. Our interpretation is that the current account deficit caused the capital account surplus to increase. This is because trade liberalization, while generating an expansion in imports which needs to be financed, usually also increases the availability of voluntary external financing. Thus, the current account deficit contributed to balance-of-payments equilibrium through a capital account surplus, partly generated by better expectations of the future income stream.

With respect to the composition of the capital account, there is a stable trend towards an increase in foreign direct investment (FDI). Annual FDI flows have accounted for between 1 and 2 per cent of GDP. Capital flows not related to FDI evidenced greater volatility and a steeper trend growth. Debt flows have increased from 1 to 5 per cent of GDP. Short-term financing has oscillated around zero; in some years there was an increase in short-run indebtedness and in others there was a net repayment of external debt. In controlling short-term capital inflows Colombia has been more successful than Chile where such inflows represented, on average, 3 per cent of GDP.

In any event, it is important to recall that the reserve requirement theoretically need not affect the path of the real exchange rate. Without a reserve requirement, it is quite possible to obtain the same path, but with higher public debt and higher losses for the central bank. Some authors have therefore argued that the reserve requirement is ineffective. But how can an authority maintain higher interest rates than the rest of the world without increasing public debt to infinity and without a deep misalignment in the real exchange rate? If the reserve requirement were ineffective, market interest rates would be lower than they are, or public debt would be very high. That capital controls have been effective is indicated by the fact that even under high domestic interest rates and low private disposable income, due to the fiscal surplus and to inflation, there are no heavy capital inflows into Colombia. Both Chile and Colombia have managed to keep high interest rates without an explosive path of public debt. Moreover, real exchange rates have been aligned with fundamentals. This shows the effectiveness of capital controls. It is important to say that both countries had already attained fiscal equilibrium before the turn of the decade, generating conditions for a sustainable fiscal balance.

During the first half of the 1990s, Colombian public finances were in balance, and in some years there was a surplus. Nevertheless, inflation has remained at a level of 20 to 25 per cent per annum – another case of chronic inflation. Despite steady inflation and a crawling-peg system without intervention, there has not been undue pressure in the foreign-exchange market. This also indicates the effectiveness of capital controls. The Colombian economy maintained a moderate growth rate during the first half of the 1990s, with a tendency to acceleration in 1993 and 1994.

V CONCLUDING REMARKS

In this chapter, two successful macroeconomic experiences of Latin American countries during the 1990s have been reviewed. Both Chile and Colombia have registered impressive performances compared to their historical record and to the contemporary results of other countries in the region (see Tables 2.4 and 2.5). They have been able to

Table 2.4 Chile and Colombia: macroeconomic indicators, 1990–4

		Real exchange rate (Dec. 1989=100)[a]	*GDP growth (per cent)*	*Rate of inflation (per cent)*	*Fiscal balance (per cent of GDP)*	*Real interest rate (per cent)*
Chile	1990	112.8	3.3	27.3	0.8	9.4
	1991	106.4	7.3	18.7	1.5	5.4
	1992	97.6	11.0	12.7	2.2	5.2
	1993	96.9	6.3	12.2	1.9	6.4
	1994	94.3	4.2	8.9	1.7	6.3
Colombia	1990	101.0	4.2	29.9	−0.3	4.4
	1991	98.0	2.0	26.8	0.2	4.8
	1992	92.0	3.8	25.1	−0.3	0.0
	1993	91.0	5.2	22.6	0.3	2.4
	1994	90.0	5.6	22.6	2.6	4.7

[a] An increase denotes a depreciation of the domestic currency.
Source: Calculations by the authors, based on data of the Banco Central de Chile, Banco de la República de Colombia, IMF and Departamento Administrativo Nacional de Estadistica (DANE), Colombia.

Table 2.5 Chile and Colombia: savings and investment, 1990–4 (per cent of GDP in dollars)

	Chile		
	Investment[a]	*National savings*	*External savings*[b]
1990	26.3	24.2	2.0
1991	24.5	24.0	0.4
1992	26.8	24.7	2.0
1993	28.8	23.9	4.8
1994	26.8	25.3	1.4

	Colombia			
	Investment[a]	*National savings*	*External savings*[b]	*External savings*[c]
1990	18.5	18.9	−1.5	−0.4
1991	15.9	18.6	−6.3	−2.7
1992	17.2	17.0	−2.2	0.2
1993	20.4	...	4.5	...
1994	...	...	4.3	...

[a] Gross capital formation and inventory accumulation.
[b] Current-account deficit.
[c] Non-domestic savings, defined as investment minus domestic savings over GDP.
Source: Calculations by the authors, based on data of the Banco Central de Chile, Banco de la República de Colombia, IMF and Departamento Administrativo Nacional Estadistica (DANE), Colombia.

achieve sustained growth: Chile at an average rate close to 7 per cent per year, and Colombia at around 5 per cent. The current-account deficit has been kept at reasonable levels in both countries: in Chile at below 2 per cent of GDP, and in Colombia at around 3 per cent. The main difference in terms of macroeconomic performance is that, while Chile has succeeded in gradually reducing inflation to single digits, Colombia has maintained the trends of the past, with moderate inflation of between 20 and 25 per cent per annum.

The capital account regulations applied in the two countries can take part of the credit for the successful macroeconomic performance. Of course, consistent macroeconomic policies and the right microeconomic incentives are the main factors behind this success; however, the macro policies would not have been possible without effective capital account regulations.

Advocates of the two polar views in the policy debate on international financial integration coincide in their assumption that reserve requirements and other qualified capital account regulations, like those used in Chile and Colombia, are ineffective. Some critics (for example Valdés and Soto, 1995) argue that the reserve requirements have been unable to modify appreciating trends of the currencies, and have thus been ineffective in favouring gradual sectoral adjustment processes. Others argue that the regulations have been unable to stop excessive capital inflows and reserve accumulation, thus defending the imposition of quantitative limits on capital flows. We find both types of criticism unfounded.

The fact that the appreciating trend of the Chilean currency has continued at about the same rate after the introduction of a reserve requirement is not an indication of the ineffectiveness of this tool. The reserve requirement allows for maintaining an interest-rate differential in favour of the emerging economy, without having to generate an expectation of currency depreciation to fulfil the arbitrage condition. That is to say, the reserve requirement is successful if a once-and-for-all currency appreciation followed by a depreciating trend is avoided. An appreciating trend could be the result of financial pressures rather than a trend in the equilibrium exchange rate; and rather than indicating weaknesses of the reserve requirement itself, such a sustained trend shows the strength of the existing capital account regulations, including the reserve requirement.

The effectiveness of the reserve requirement can also be seen from the change of the composition of net capital inflows. Increasingly, external financing has been moving from debt to direct investment and equity-based portfolio investment. This implies a more flexible structure of financing, favouring risk-sharing between domestic and external partners. It also allows the attainment of externalities associated with direct investment, in the form of international market access for exports and an inward transfer of technology and management. At the same time, medium- and long-term forms of debt have gained ground and represent increasing proportions of total debt financing.

While there could be leaks in the reserve requirements and other regulations, they do not seem to be of macroeconomic significance. If the leaks were severe, short-term external financing would be of great importance, but that has been the case neither in Colombia nor in Chile. There are periods, however, when short-term financing is more abundant. These are periods in which the expectations of currency appreciation are high. Confronting even a small expected appreciation in a short period of time is an impossible task for the reserve requirement. The gains implied by the change in the value of the currency in a few months cannot be compensated by the financial cost implied by the reserve requirement.

This opens the possibility of using stronger restrictions on capital flows, such as quantitative limits. In our opinion, quantitative limits not only create very significant microeconomic costs and slow down economic and financial development, but also would probably be ineffective. Quantitative controls would create a dual exchange market. Officially authorized transactions would take place at the official rate, and unauthorized capital flows would be carried out at the parallel-market rate, which in this case would be higher than the official rate. When the exchange-rate differential becomes significant, the incentives for arbitraging between the two exchange markets would increase, allowing some private operators to profit by buying foreign currency cheap in the informal market and selling it at a higher price in the formal market. Consider, for instance, an exporter who would sell and even over-invoice his proceeds in the official market, but would try to finance all his imports in the parallel market. The central bank would then be forced to accumulate reserves purchased at a transitory high exchange rate, and big losses would eventually accrue when the rate had to be adjusted.

Overall, the reserve requirement and other capital account regulations, with all their limitations, have played a very important role in these two successful experiences. Perhaps the problem of the critics is that they expect too much from such regulations. One should expect from such measures no more than a contribution to efforts aimed at keeping the current account deficit within reasonable bounds and at sustainable levels, while domestic macroeconomic targets of growth and price stability are attained.

Appendix 2.1

Table 2.A1 Colombia: maturity of FFCT[a] and reserve requirement ratio, according to Central Bank Resolution 22 of 1994

Maturity of FFCT (days)	*Reserve requirement ratio (per cent)*	*Maturity of FFCT (days)*	*Reserve requirement ratio (per cent)*
1–30	140.0	901–930	76.6
31–60	137.2	931–960	75.1
61–90	134.5	961–990	73.6
91–120	131.8	991–1020	72.1
121–150	129.2	1021–1050	70.7
151–180	126.6	1051–1080	69.3
191–210	124.1	1081–1110	67.9
211–240	121.6	1111–1140	66.5
241–270	119.2	1141–1170	65.2
271–300	116.8	1171–1200	63.9
301–330	114.5	1201–1230	62.7
331–360	112.2	1231–1260	61.4
361–390	110.0	1261–1290	60.2
391–420	107.8	1291–1320	59.0
421–450	105.7	1321–1350	57.8
451–480	103.6	1351–1380	56.7
481–510	101.5	1381–1410	55.5
511–540	99.5	1411–1440	54.4
541–570	97.5	1441–1470	53.3
571–600	95.6	1471–1500	52.3
601–630	93.7	1501–1530	51.2
631–660	91.8	1531–1560	50.2
661–690	90.0	1561–1590	49.2
691–720	88.2	1591–1620	48.2
721–750	86.4	1621–1650	47.3
751–780	84.7	1651–1680	46.3
781–810	83.0	1681–1710	45.4
811–840	81.4	1711–1741	44.5
841–870	79.7	1741–1770	43.6
871–900	78.2	1771–1800	42.8

Note: The required reserve is to be kept for the duration of the investment.
[a] Financial Foreign Currency Title (Título en Divisas par Financiaciones).

Appendix 2.2 International Arbitrage and the Reserve Requirement

1. Investment and required reserves for an equivalent period of one year

Consider the arbitrage condition that equates the rate of return of domestic and international financial investment, in this case for an investment with one-year maturity and where the reserve requirement should be kept at the central bank for the same period. In equation (1), i^* is the external interest rate, i the domestic interest rate, ϵ is the reserve requirement ratio (RRR), and ê is the expected depreciation of the domestic currency.

$$(1+i^*) = \frac{(1+i)(1-\epsilon)}{(1+\hat{e})} + \epsilon \tag{1}$$

The solution for the RRR that fulfils this arbitrage condition depends on the international interest rate differential, on the expected rate of currency depreciation, and on the level of domestic and external interest rate according to the following expression:

$$\epsilon = \frac{(i^* - i) + \hat{e}(1+i^*)}{\hat{e} - i} \tag{2}$$

2. Investment and RRR for an equivalent period of X months

For an investment of X months, with the required reserve to be kept for the maturity of the operation, it is possible to obtain an expression similar to (1). The only difference is that the relevant rate is the compound rate for the period in question.

$$(1+i^*)^{X/12} = \frac{(1+i)^{X/12}(1-\epsilon)}{(1+\hat{e})^{X/12}} + \epsilon \tag{1'}$$

and, equivalent to (2):

$$\epsilon = \frac{(1+i^*)^{X/12}(1+\hat{e})^{X/12} - (1+i)^{X/12}}{(1+\hat{e})^{X/12} - (1+i)^{X/12}} \tag{2'}$$

It can be shown that the necessary condition for the RRR to increase with the maturity of the operation, i.e. the partial derivative of ϵ with respect to X to be positive, is fulfilled whenever the domestic interest rate exceeds the external rate adjusted by exchange-rate expectations.

Notes

1. The views presented in this paper represent the opinions of the authors and not necessarily those of the Central Bank of Chile. A first version of this paper was presented at an UNCTAD Conference on Globalization of Financial Markets, held at the Jerome Levy Economics Institute of Bard College, New York, in March 1996. We have benefited from the comments of Y. Akyüz and G. Helleiner and acknowledge the able assistance of O. Landerretche M.
2. Throughout this chapter we use the Latin American definition of the real exchange rate (RER); that is, the RER increases when the domestic currency depreciates in real terms.
3. It is also possible to explain the dynamics of capital inflows, with booms and busts, in terms of bandwagon effects; but this model seems inappropriate for the Chilean reality of the 1990s. There is no evidence of a bubble in asset prices. Asset prices and the real exchange rate appear to be in line with fundamentals.
4. Experiences of the lack of immediate response of market participants in the face of large external indebtedness include the run-ups to the Mexican crisis of the 1990s and the Chilean financial crisis of the 1980s. In both cases, financing was abundant up to a point at which a large adjustment was needed (see Arellano, 1983; Budnevich and Cifuentes, 1993).
5. Institutional investors and banks are subject to regulations and supervision of their investments abroad because of the systemic risk and public insurance problem. These restrictions are not related to the regulation of capital flows to preserve macroeconomic stability. It is important to mention that there are regulatory restrictions that limit bank exposure to foreign currency.
6. An exception to this rule is the reserve requirement imposed on secondary inflows of American Depository Receipts (ADRs) in Chile.
7. For a complete description of the regulations and capital account results in Chile in the 1990s, see Le Fort and Varela (1995).
8. Decree Law 600 (DL-600), and chapters XIX and XIV of the Central Bank Foreign Exchange Regulations (CBFER).
9. Chapter XXVI of the CBFER.
10. Chapter XIV of the CBFER.
11. Chapters III and XIII of the CBFER.
12. Chapter XII of the CBFER.
13. Chapter XXVIII of the CBFER.
14. If we exclude from total foreign investments those performed through external debt instruments, the change in the composition is still more significant. Net foreign investment as a percentage of net capital inflows rose from 20 per cent in 1990 to 44 per cent in 1994. The remainder is

external borrowing which fell from 80 per cent to 56 per cent in the same period.

15. According to Carrasquilla (1995), macroeconomic policy never sought explicitly the reduction of inflation since it constituted an important source of resources for the public sector; he characterized exchange-rate policy as accommodative.
16. At the end of 1992 and the beginning of 1993, the liquidation of ECs forced the monetary authorities to tighten their market operations. The open-market operations were made through the sale of notes issued by the Banco de la República.
17. Carrasquilla (1995) illustrates this with the alarming statistic that the domestic debt of the central bank grew from 1.5 per cent of GDP in 1989 to 7 per cent in 1991.

References

Arellano, J. P. (1983) 'De la Liberalización a la Intervención: El Mercado de Capitales en Chile 1974–1983', *Colección de Estudios CIEPLAN*, no. 11 (December).

Budnevich, C. (1994) 'The Intergenerational and Dynamic Effects of Opening the Capital Account', *Revista de Análisis Económico*, vol. 9, no. 2 (November).

Budnevich, C. and R. Cifuentes (1993) 'Manejo Macroeconómico de los Flujos de Capitales de Corto Plazo: La Experiencia de Chile', *Colección Estudios CIEPLAN*, no. 38 (December).

Carrasquilla B., A. (1995) 'Bandas Cambiarias y Modificaciones a la Política de Estabilización: Lecciones de la Experiencia Colombiana', *Revista del Banco de la República de Colombia* (January).

Labán, R. and F. Larraín (1993) 'Twenty Years of Experience with Capital Mobility in Chile', April, mimeo.

Le Fort, G. (1994) 'The Financial System and Macroeconomic Stability: The Chilean Experience' in S. Faruki (ed.) *Financial Liberalization: Comparative Experience in Asia and Latin America* (Washington, DC: Economic Development Institute of the World Bank).

Le Fort, G. and C. Varela (1995) 'The Chilean Capital Account in the 1990s and Regional Origins of Capital Flows', paper presented at the Pacific Economic Outlook Structural Meeting, Osaka, March.

Sanhueza, G. (1995) 'Volatilidad vs. Nivel del Tipo de Cambio Real', Banco Central de Chile, mimeo.

Valdés, S. and M. Soto (1995) 'New Selective Capital Controls in Chile: Are they Effective?', Universidad Católica de Chile, Santiago, September, mimeo.

3 Managing Foreign Capital Flows: The Experiences of the Republic of Korea, Thailand, Malaysia and Indonesia

Yung Chul Park and Chi-Young Song[1]

I INTRODUCTION

During 1990–4 there was a surge of foreign capital inflows to developing countries in Asia. The net inflow during the period was \$261 billion, more than twice that for the entire 1980s (IMF, 1995a). It represented approximately 50 per cent of total capital inflows to all developing countries.[2]

In contrast with the 1980s, much of the inflow in the 1990s was in the form of portfolio investment. While the share of portfolio investment in total net inflows was 8 per cent on average during 1983–9, it rose to 24 per cent during 1990–4. Net foreign portfolio investment increased from \$10 billion during 1983–9 to \$63 billion during 1990–4. Still, even in the 1990s, foreign direct investment (FDI) has been the most important source of external financing in these countries. The net inflow of FDI increased markedly, from \$36 billion during 1983–9 to \$117 billion during 1990–4, accounting for 45 per cent of the total net inflow. For comparison: in Latin America portfolio investment represented 66 per cent of the total net capital inflow during 1990–4, while FDI represented 30 per cent during that period.

A number of developments in the Asian economies and in the industrial economies have been suggested as causes of the inflow. East Asia, including China, has been the most rapidly growing and dynamic region in the world. The higher demand for capital, arising from the need to sustain a high rate of investment, and favourable growth prospects have attracted a large amount of foreign investment to the region. Such investment has become easier as

East Asian economies deregulated their domestic markets and liberalized capital account transactions. Domestic financial reform and financial-market opening have greatly facilitated foreign investment in domestic securities. Finally, the decline in interest rates and the international diversification of the portfolios of institutional investors in the industrial countries also contributed to increased capital flows to Asia.

Capital inflows in the form of foreign direct and portfolio investment have been crucial in supporting a high rate of investment and gross domestic product (GDP) growth in South-East Asian countries such as Indonesia, Malaysia and Thailand. At the same time, however, inflows of speculative short-term capital have undermined macroeconomic stability because they have resulted in large swings in key financial variables, including the exchange rate. Some countries have therefore resorted to direct control measures to dampen short-term capital movements.

This chapter analyses the experiences with the management of capital flows in four East Asian countries with different economic and institutional structures: Indonesia, Malaysia, the Republic of Korea, and Thailand. These countries have been the major recipients of foreign capital in Asia. Compared to the entire 1980s, the amount of net capital flows to the four countries doubled during 1990–4, totalling $143 billion and accounting for about 55 per cent of total net capital flows to Asian developing countries.

Section II will examine the nature of capital flows in these countries. This is followed by an analysis of the process of and the driving forces behind capital account liberalization. Macroeconomic effects of and policy responses to capital inflows are also analysed. We then consider some of the policy measures that have been implemented and other measures that have been under consideration for dealing with capital inflows.

II TREND AND COMPOSITION OF FOREIGN CAPITAL FLOWS IN THE 1990s

Republic of Korea

The Republic of Korea began to witness a surge in the inflow of foreign capital in 1991. The large interest-rate differential between domestic and foreign financial markets, coupled with the favourable prospects for the economy, made the Republic of Korea one of the most attractive emerging markets, and the liberalization of the capital account triggered a massive inflow, totalling $32.1 billion during 1990–4, more than ten times the total for the 1980s.

However, relative to the size of the economy, the magnitude of the flow to the Republic of Korea has been relatively small compared to other East Asian countries. The capital account surplus between 1990 and 1994 averaged only 2.0 per cent of GDP, compared to 10.1 per cent for Thailand, 10.2 per cent for Malaysia, and 4.0 per cent for Indonesia. The difference is partly attributable to Korea's tighter control of capital movements, but mainly to a relatively smaller current account deficit. In other words, the investment–savings gap of the Republic of Korea has been narrower than in the three other countries (Figure 3.1).

In the 1990s, the capital flows to the Republic of Korea consisted mainly of portfolio investment (Figure 3.2a). Net foreign portfolio investment increased from just $29 million in 1989 to $3.2 billion in 1991, and peaked at $11.0 billion in 1993. The cumulative amount during 1991–4 was $27.2 billion, accounting for 88 per cent of the total foreign capital inflow during the period.

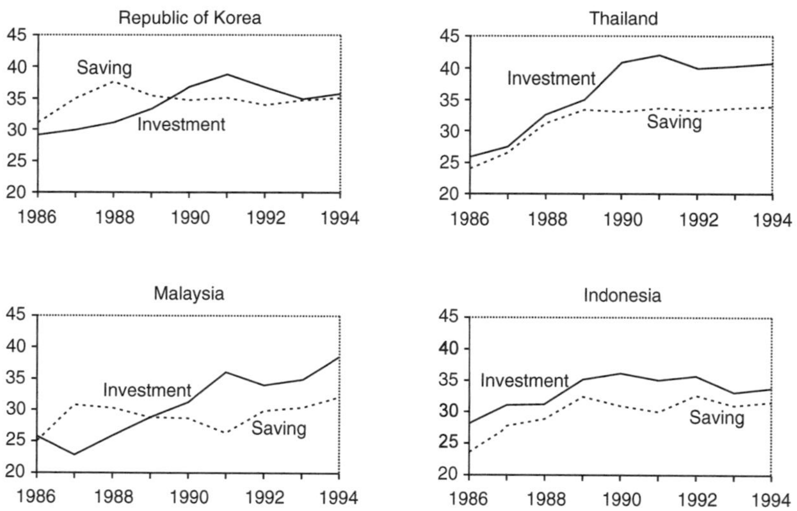

Figure 3.1 Trends of investment and savings, selected Asian countries, 1986–94 (per cent of GDP)
Source: IMF, *International Financial Statistics*, various issues.

FDI was the main source of inflow in the second half of the 1980s, and it peaked in 1991. In the first half of the 1990s, the Republic of Korea became relatively less attractive to foreign corporate investment because of large increases in production costs. There was a net outflow in long-term foreign lending as loan repayments continued (see Park, 1995).

The increase in portfolio investment in the 1990s was due primarily to the softening of rules on overseas issues of securities by domestic firms and the opening of the Korean stock market. A decline in world market interest rates resulting from the recession in the developed countries motivated Korean firms and banks to mobilize cheaper foreign funds available in the international capital markets. At the same time, low interest rates in the industrial economies provided strong incentives for international investors to increase their holdings of securities in the emerging markets, including the Republic of Korea.

The opening of the Korean stock market in January 1992 accelerated the inflow, but issues of securities in international financial markets continued to be a significant portion. From the first quarter of 1992 through to the third quarter of 1995, the cumulative inflow of foreign capital related to overseas issues of securities by domestic firms and banks amounted to $19 billion, accounting for approximately 62 per cent of the total inflow of portfolio investment. The dominance was particularly pronounced during 1994–5, when the Korean stock market performed poorly. Between October 1994 and June 1995, there was a net outflow of non-resident investment in the Korean stock market of $634 million.

Thailand

Thailand has seen a large increase in foreign capital inflows from the late 1980s onwards. Net inflows increased from $1 billion in 1987 to $3 billion in 1988, and skyrocketed to $14 billion in 1993. Between 1988 and 1994 the cumulative net inflow was $70 billion, more than eight times the cumulative amount between 1980 and 1987.

Figure 3.2b depicts the trend of foreign capital inflows in each group; long-term loans, FDI, portfolio investment and other foreign investment (OFI). It shows that OFI, which is the total of short-term borrowing by commercial banks and increase in non-resident *baht* (Thai currency) account deposits, has been a major source of foreign capital inflows. The volume has increased significantly since 1988 mainly due to the large increase in short-term borrowing by financial

a. Republic of Korea

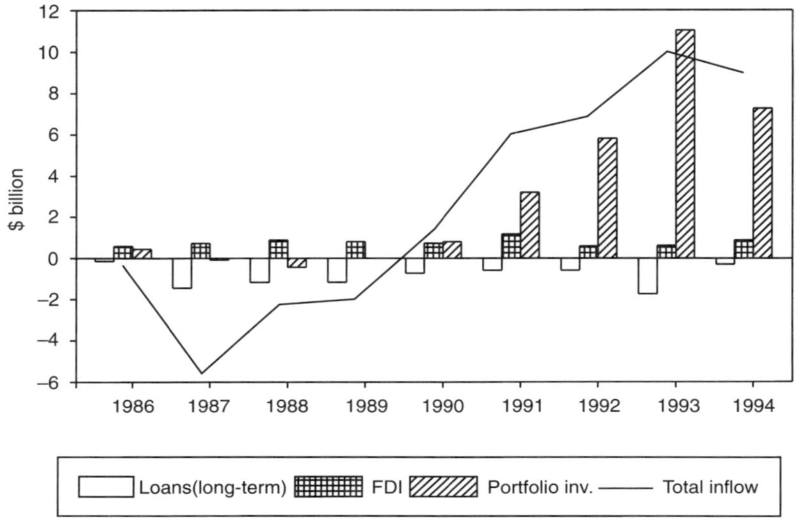

b. Thailand

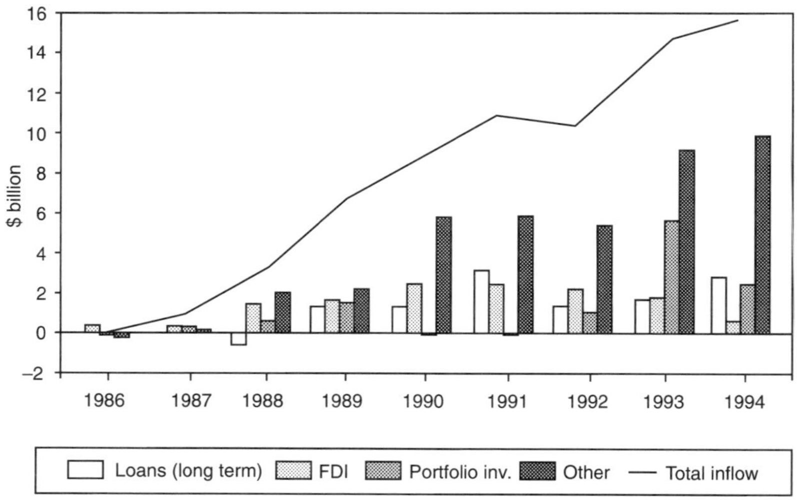

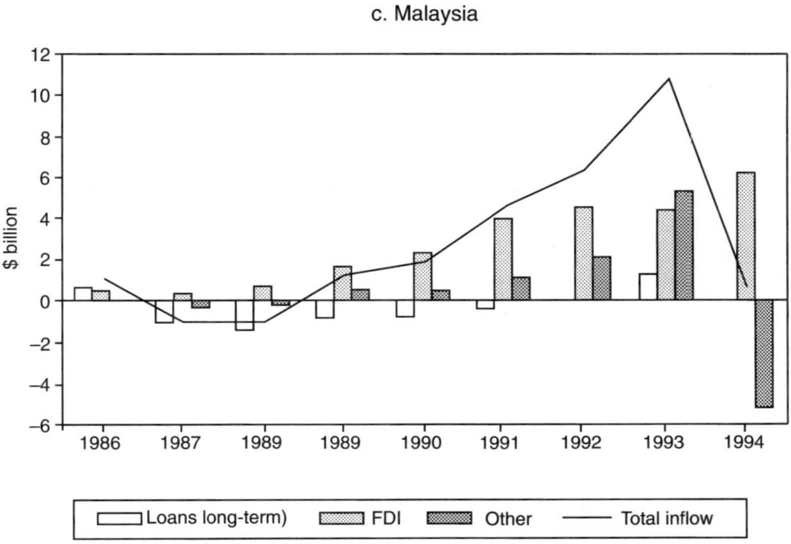

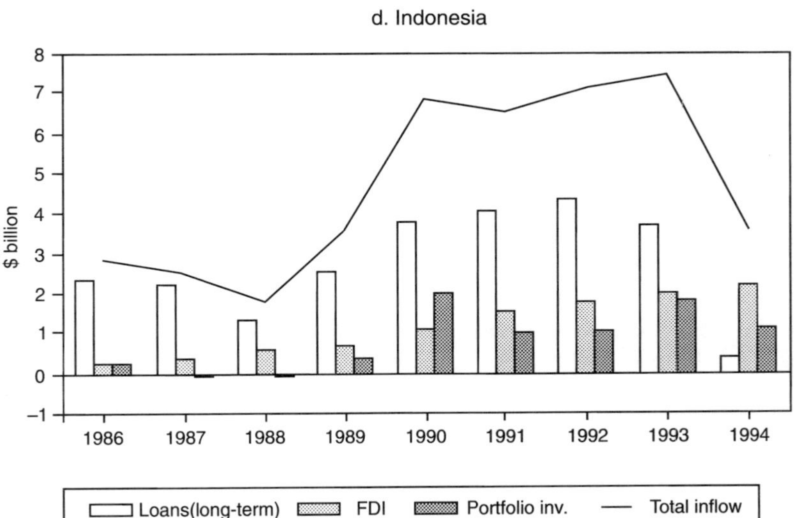

Figure 3.2 Trend and composition of foreign capital inflows, selected Asian countries, 1986–94 ($ billion)
Source: IMF, *Balance of Payments Statistics*, various issues.

institutions. Until 1992, non- bank financial institutions accounted for the largest part of short-term loans, but afterwards short-term borrowing by commercial banks greatly increased, as prompted by the establishment of the Bangkok International Banking Facilities (discussed in Section III, below) in 1993.

It should also be noted that the volume of non-resident baht account deposits has considerably increased since 1991, greatly contributing to the large increase in OFI during the following years. They represent about 41 per cent of the cumulative inflow of OFI during 1991–4. Reasons for this increase include the fact that Thailand offered higher interest rates than industrial economies and that the government has allowed exporters to receive payments from non-resident baht accounts. Foreign companies exporting to Thailand were often inclined to receive payments through non-resident baht accounts in order to minimize their foreign-exchange risk. In addition, foreign investors have used these accounts as a parking place for funds before making other investments, especially portfolio investment, as the Thai stock market showed improvement. In 1994, an increase in commercial banks' short-term borrowing prompted by the establishment of the Bangkok International Banking Facilities in 1993 accounts for most of the inflow of OFI.

Having reached a peak of $2.4 billion in 1990, FDI fell subsequently. An important reason is the country's poor infrastructure, which has lowered potential returns on investment. A general decline in global FDI during 1990–1 and intense competition from developing countries such as China, Vietnam and India are additional causes. It should be noted that Malaysia, which has a relatively good infrastructure and a somewhat more skilled labour force, has maintained substantial FDI inflows. A high interest-rate differential boosted long-term borrowing from abroad, especially during 1989–91.

Foreign portfolio investment rose dramatically in 1993, from $927 million in 1992 to $5.5 billion in 1993, and accounted for more than one-third of the total net inflow of foreign capital. The sharp increase was due to renewed confidence among foreign investors in the Thai stock market after the general election in September 1992, the higher interest-rate differential between Thailand and the industrial economies, and increased stability of the baht. The strong global trend of investing in emerging markets by international institutional investors was also an important cause. In 1994, however, portfolio investment fell substantially as rising interest rates in industrial economies narrowed the interest-rate differential.

Malaysia

In Malaysia, the surge in foreign capital inflows started in 1989, following an outflow of $0.9 billion in 1988. In 1989 the inflow amounted to $1.3 billion and it jumped to $4.7 billion in 1991 and to $10.9 billion in 1993. Between 1989 and 1993, the cumulative inflow was $26 billion compared to $17 billion during the 1980s.

Figure 3.2c also shows that FDI was the principal source of inflow during the second half of the 1980s and until 1992, accounting for about 86 per cent of total net inflows between 1989 and 1992. Sustained fast economic growth with sound economic fundamentals was the main factor driving FDI during this period; deregulation of inward FDI and the introduction of incentives also contributed. Malaysia lifted or relaxed restrictions on foreign ownership and types of FDI, as well as simplifying approval procedures. Generous tax incentives, including total exemption from corporate and income taxes in certain cases, were also introduced. External factors included the continued appreciation of the Japanese yen and rapidly rising labour costs in the Asian newly industrializing economies (NIEs).

Figure 3.2c shows that other foreign investment, negligible until 1990, began to increase significantly in 1991, and in 1993 it exceeded FDI. For Malaysia, OFI includes portfolio investment and commercial banks' short-term external liabilities which are largely associated with their short-term borrowing and increases in non-resident *ringgit* (Malaysian currency) accounts. It amounted to $5.3 billion in 1993, more than two and a half times the 1992 level. It should also be noted that in 1993 there was an unusually high entry in the capital account of $4.0 billion under errors and omissions, something that may be closely related to the inflow of foreign portfolio investment (Aziz, 1994).

The increased inflow of portfolio investment and commercial banks' borrowing was due to a large gap between domestic and foreign interest rates, the promising prospects of the Malaysian economy, and the improved performance of the domestic stock market, partly related to the privatization of several state enterprises.

In early 1994, the Malaysian government implemented several administrative measures in order to curb the inflow of short-term speculative capital. As a result, a large net outflow was recorded under 'other foreign investment'.

Indonesia

Indonesia has experienced massive inflows of foreign capital since 1990. The inflow increased from $3.6 billion in 1989 to $6.8 billion in 1990 and to $7.1 billion in 1992. In cumulative terms, it amounted to $36 billion between 1990 and 1994, compared to $25 billion in the period 1982 to 1989.

Long-term borrowing was the principal form of inflow throughout the 1980s and until 1993 (Figure 3.2d). During 1990–3, it amounted to $16 billion, representing about half of the total net capital inflows. While most borrowing during the 1980s was by the public sector, the level of borrowing by private firms and banks has also increased substantially since 1990. During 1990–3, the net inflow of long-term borrowing by the private and the public sector was $10.6 billion and $3.2 billion, respectively. The corresponding figures for the period 1982 to 1989 had been $0.5 billion and $20.2 billion. The removal of the ceiling on foreign commercial borrowing by banks in 1989 and high domestic interest rates in the early 1990s were the principal factors in the increase in private borrowing. The introduction of a swap facility with Bank Indonesia, the central bank, also helped.

Indonesia's dependence on long-term borrowing has been greater than that of the Republic of Korea, Malaysia and Thailand. Deregulation of inward FDI and an improved economic outlook have helped increase the flow of FDI. Still, Indonesia has not been able to secure enough FDI to fill as much of the investment–savings gap as the other East Asian countries such as Malaysia. This is attributable to poor infrastructure and low-quality labour. The country's access to international capital markets has been limited due to the low credit rating of its domestic firms. Accordingly, Indonesia had to rely on loans with government guarantees.

However, the loan portion of the total capital inflow fell in the 1990s, while that of FDI and portfolio investment rose compared to the 1980s. While FDI and portfolio investment made up only 12 per cent and 7 per cent, respectively, of total inflow during 1982–9, their shares increased to 20 per cent and 18 per cent during 1990–3. Finally, the amount of inward FDI exceeded that of long-term borrowing in 1994.

Most foreign portfolio investment in Indonesia has been made through the stock market in which foreign investors have been allowed to participate since 1987. Increased portfolio investment in the early 1990s was closely related to the deregulation of domestic capital markets such as the simplification of requirements for listing on the stock exchange and the establishment of an over-the-counter market. The bullish stock market and the large interest-rate differential between Indonesia and industrial countries resulted in a large inflow of portfolio investment in 1993. Since 1993, with improved credit rating of Indonesian firms, issues of Indonesian securities in international capital markets have increased.

III LIBERALIZATION OF THE CAPITAL ACCOUNT

Republic of Korea

Since the early 1960s, developments in the current account dictated the way capital controls were implemented. For example, when the current account deteriorated, restrictions on capital outflows were tightened while those on inflows were loosened.

In the first half of the 1980s, the current account continued to be in deficit although the size of the deficit was steadily decreasing. The Korean economy had difficulties in attracting foreign capital because of the high country-risk relating to political instability and the continued depreciation of the Korean *won*. In an effort to ease the difficulties, the government tightened regulations on capital outflows mainly by restricting overseas investment by residents, and took several measures to ease inward capital movements. In 1981, for example, foreign investors were allowed to participate in the Korean stock market through investment trust funds set up exclusively for this purpose[3] and, in 1985, Korean firms were allowed to raise capital overseas by issuing convertible bonds, bonds with warrants, and depository receipts.

The easing led to a sharp increase in borrowing from abroad by domestic firms and banks. In 1986 the current account recorded a surplus which continued to expand until 1989. This surplus resulted from the recovery of the world economy and the rapid appreciation of the Japanese yen which improved the competitiveness of Korean exports. Foreign-exchange reserves, only \$2.8 billion at the end of 1985, reached \$12.6 billion a year later and \$15 billion at the end of 1989. With a view to reducing what it considered excessive foreign-exchange holdings, the government abolished all restrictions on outward foreign direct investment below \$1 million and permitted residents to purchase foreign real estate for business purposes. However, commercial loans to domestic firms were not allowed, except in the case of public enterprises. Issues of bonds and depository receipts by residents were also restricted.

In 1990, the current account balance moved into deficit because of rising domestic wages, real appreciation of the won, and the deterioration of the world economy. The current account worsened in 1991, generating a deficit of $8.7 billion, more than four times the level of the preceding year. The amount of foreign-exchange reserves held by the Bank of Korea fell markedly. Facing difficulties in financing the mounting current account deficit, the government once again liberalized the capital account by amending the Foreign-Exchange Management Act (FEMA).

Under the FEMA, amended in 1991, transactions classified as capital inflows were liberalized first, although the positive list system of control – only those transactions specifically listed are allowed – remained intact. A negative list system – only those transactions specifically listed are not allowed – was adopted for current account transactions. Residents could raise funds by issuing securities abroad under certain conditions. Restrictions on direct investment by non-residents were almost completely lifted. Most importantly, effective from January 1992, foreign investors were allowed to invest directly in the Korean stock market, albeit with a number of restrictions, including a limitation of 10 per cent of the share that non-resident investors as a group could hold in the total equity capital of listed companies. The limit was raised to 12 per cent in December 1994 and to 15 per cent in July 1995.

As a result of these measures, capital inflows, mainly in the form of portfolio investment, began to surge in 1991. Net foreign capital inflows in 1990 amounted to only $1.3 billion, but increased to $5.7 billion in 1991 and to $9.6 billion in 1993. Net foreign portfolio investment accounted for 51 per cent of the increase in total net foreign capital inflows in 1991 and 180 per cent in 1993 (a year with negative net direct investment). During this three-year period, the cumulative total of the current-account deficit was $12.9 billion, whereas foreign portfolio investment amounted to $21.9 billion. The surge in the capital inflow resulted in a large surplus in the overall account.

A sudden increase in foreign capital inflows on top of the improvement in the current account threatened the stability of both domestic financial markets and the economy in general. Several steps were taken to liberalize outward capital movements and, thus, to reduce the overall surplus. Domestic institutional investors such as securities firms, insurance companies and investment trust companies were allowed to invest in foreign securities without any restriction, and the mode of controlling outward direct investment was changed from a positive to a negative list system in February 1994.

Even though many controls on foreign exchange and cross-border capital transactions were removed or relaxed, the foreign-exchange system was still subject to severe criticism for being too restrictive. Among other things, the rigid controls were claimed to undermine the international competitiveness of domestic firms. In response to these complaints and foreign pressure for further deregulation, the government unveiled a new Plan for Foreign Exchange System Reform in December 1994. The plan attempts completely to liberalize current and capital account transactions (with a few exceptions) and to develop an efficient domestic foreign-exchange market over a five-year period divided into three stages. It espouses a gradual liberalization process, with the actual speed of liberalization adjusted to the state of the economy. A focal point of the reform is the adoption of the negative list system in more areas. Removal of restrictions on capital outflows is given a higher priority than liberalizing inflows. Capital account transactions closely related to investment in the real sector are deregulated prior to cross-border financial transactions (for more details, see Korea Ministry of Finance and the Economy, 1994; and Korea Institute of Finance, 1994).

The implementation of capital account liberalization began in February 1995, focusing on the deregulation of capital outflows. Among other things, the limit on the amount that domestic pension funds can invest in overseas securities was abolished, and domestic residents were for the first time allowed to hold overseas deposit accounts.

Korean policymakers have been reluctant to liberalize the capital account rapidly. There is considerable concern that macroeconomic stability would be jeopardized by a sudden opening-up of financial markets, while efficiency gains to the economy from liberalization are considered to be relatively small, possibly even insignificant, and would best be realized in the long run.

In a number of other countries, capital account liberalization has increased the volatility of financial markets, including the foreign-exchange market. Furthermore, little is known as to how a small, semi-open economy such as the Republic of Korea, in a disequilibrium characterized by a domestic interest rate twice as high as that in international financial markets, would move to a new equilibrium if restrictions on capital account transactions were removed suddenly and completely. At present, domestic financial markets are still underdeveloped and domestic financial institutions have little competitive advantage over their foreign counterparts.

Thailand, Malaysia and Indonesia

Unlike the Republic of Korea, these countries liberalized capital account transactions earlier and more aggressively. Given their low saving rates, they needed a large amount of foreign capital to promote economic growth. To attract more foreign capital, they actively deregulated inward FDI and cross-border financial transactions as capital inflows decreased sharply after the Latin American debt crisis in 1982.

Foreign Direct Investment

FDI flows to these countries have risen markedly since the late 1980s, attracted by strong economic performance and helped by the removal of restrictions and the introduction of incentives. While the cumulative inflow of inward FDI in Thailand was $2 billion during 1980–7, it increased to $12 billion during 1988–94. Total inward FDI in Malaysia was $21 billion between 1988 and 1994, compared to $7 billion between 1980 and 1987. For Indonesia, the numbers are $2 billion for 1980–7 and $10 billion for 1988–94.[4]

Thailand had lifted many restrictions on inward FDI during the 1970s, mainly through the Alien Business Law of 1972 and the Investment Promotion Act of 1977. These two acts basically espouse the negative list system. In the latter half of the 1980s, the Thai government broadened and accelerated the liberalization process in order to attract more foreign capital, thereby helping to sustain the country's rapid economic growth. While restrictions on inward FDI in import-substitution industries were largely lifted in the 1970s, the deregulation of inward FDI in the 1980s and 1990s focused on export industries, with the expectation that the expansion of labour-intensive export industries would boost employment and help reduce the current-account deficit.

In 1991, foreign investors were allowed to own 100 per cent of firms that exported all of their output. Additional incentives for FDI in export sectors, such as tax abatement or exemption, were introduced. The Thai government also introduced incentives for non-residents who invested in export-oriented activities outside of Bangkok. These included a five-year exemption from tariffs on imports of raw materials by foreign companies located in remote areas and exporting more than 30 per cent of their output. By contrast, companies located in the Bangkok area were granted an exemption only for one year.

Foreign companies establishing in provincial areas can receive exemption from the corporate income tax for up to eight years. The maximum import tariff was reduced from 100 per cent to 30 per cent as of 1 January 1995. With the help of these deregulatory measures, annual inward FDI in Thailand increased from \$0.4 billion in 1987 to \$2.4 billion in 1990, declining slightly thereafter.

In Malaysia, much of the liberalization of inward FDI took place during 1985–7. In 1985, as an incentive to encourage the transfer of advanced technology to domestic industries, the Malaysian government permitted non-residents to own more than half of the capital of companies considered 'high-tech'. The Promotion of Investment Act of 1986 provided various incentives for foreign investment in manufacturing, agriculture and tourism. These included simplification of the investment process and raising the limit on the percentage of a joint venture that non-residents could own. Since 1987, non-residents have been allowed to wholly own companies that export at least 80 per cent of their output and to purchase domestic real estate for business purposes with funds brought in from abroad.

Starting in 1989, foreign firms could issue corporate bonds in the domestic securities market. In the same year, legislation was passed to protect the copyright of non-residents for 25 years. These measures helped increase annual inward FDI from \$0.7 billion in 1988 to \$2.3 billion in 1990, and to \$6.1 billion in 1994.

In Indonesia, from the 1970s until the mid-1980s, the bulk of inward FDI was concentrated in the oil and gas sector. This meant ever-greater dependence of the economy on these industries. In an effort to develop a more balanced industrial structure and promote manufactured exports, Indonesia actively began to liberalize inward FDI in the non-oil-and-gas sector. In 1985, the approval process for inward FDI was considerably simplified and in the following year non-residents were allowed to establish joint ventures in the non-oil-and-gas export sector. Initially, the maximum non-resident ownership of joint ventures that exported all of their products was 80 per cent. The limit was raised to 95 per cent in 1987. More importantly, a negative list system was adopted in managing inward FDI in 1989. The minimum amount of inward FDI was gradually reduced from \$1 million and was entirely abolished in 1994.

In 1994, FDI was allowed in previously barred sectors such as telecommunications, ports, railways and nuclear power. During the early 1990s, most remaining restrictions on foreign ownership were removed so that 100 per cent ownership was possible in most industries by 1994. With the help of these measures, the amount of inward FDI increased from $0.6 billion in 1987 to $1.5 billion in 1991, and to $2.1 billion in 1994.

Portfolio and Other Investment

Along with the deregulation of FDI, the three countries also sped up the liberalization of cross-border financial transactions throughout the 1980s and early 1990s for the purpose of diversifying sources of foreign funds and encouraging the development of their domestic financial markets.

Thailand began to accelerate liberalization of cross-border financial transactions in the mid-1980s. The government created two funds for foreign investors in Thai securities, the Bangkok Fund in 1985 and the Thailand Fund in 1986, and allowed ten more funds during 1987–90. In 1987, in response to the foreign-ownership limit having been reached by so many companies, the Stock Exchange of Thailand established an Alien Board where foreign investors could trade such stocks among themselves. In general, foreign investors are restricted from holding more than 49 per cent of the total shares of a listed Thai company, but the limit varies by industry. In the banking sector, for example, a 25 per cent limit is applied.

The Bangkok International Banking Facilities (BIBF) were launched in March 1993 with the expectation that they would lower the cost of foreign borrowing and develop Thailand as a regional financial centre. BIBF is Thailand's version of an offshore financial market, in which commercial banks with BIBF licences are allowed to carry out lending (out–in) and other international and investment banking operations as well as traditional offshore banking (out–out). In 1993, BIBF licences were granted to 47 commercial banks. They included 32 foreign banks, 12 that had already been operating in Thailand and 20 newcomers (see Tivakul and Svetarundra, 1993; and Vichyanond, 1994).

Malaysia allowed foreign investors to participate directly in the domestic stock market in 1973, when the Kuala Lumpur Stock Exchange was established. Since 1995 foreign investors as a whole cannot hold more than 30 per cent of listed shares of any one company, and those wishing to hold more than 15 per cent or 5 million ringgit worth must obtain approval from the Foreign Investment Committee.

Since 1985 foreign securities companies have been allowed to open branches and, since 1986, to invest in local securities firms. In 1987, the maximum amount of residents' overseas borrowing in foreign currency that could be raised without approval by the central bank was increased from 100 thousand ringgit to 1 million ringgit.

In 1988, foreign stock brokerage firms were allowed to increase their equity shares in local brokerage firms from 30 per cent to 49 per cent. During 1987–9, three investment trust funds for foreign investors were established to promote foreign participation in the local stock market. Malaysia opened the Labuan International Offshore Financial Centre in 1990.

Indonesia, in an attempt to facilitate capital inflows, embarked on active liberalization of cross-border financial transactions in the mid-1980s. Foreign investor participation in the domestic stock market was first allowed in 1987, with ownership of companies limited to 49 per cent. The government allowed non-residents to establish joint-venture securities firms with residents in 1988.

In the same year, the government allowed the existing branches of foreign banks to open sub-branches in six major cities (Bandung, Semarang, Surabaya, Medan, Ujung Pandang and Denpasar) outside Jakarta and permitted foreign banks to establish joint ventures with domestic banks. While there had been only one joint-venture in 1988, their number increased to 30 by the end of 1994. During the same period the number of branches of foreign banks and joint-venture banks increased from 21 to 83. In 1989, the ceiling on foreign commercial borrowing by banks was removed. In 1992, the permissible purchase of bank shares by non-residents, initially banned, was raised to 49 per cent of equity, while domestic firms were permitted to list up to 30 per cent of their equity on foreign stock exchanges.

It should be noted, however, that more recently there have been changes in the capital account liberalization policies of South-East Asian countries. A number of measures have been adopted to reduce the volume and volatility of short-term flows as the massive inflow of foreign capital over a short period of time was considered to be destabilizing. Malaysia and Indonesia imposed quantitative restrictions on capital inflows, while Thailand sought to deregulate outflows.

Thailand chose to liberalize outflows rather than to restrict inflows. By liberalizing foreign-exchange controls in three stages from 1990 through 1994, most restrictions on outflows were removed. Previously, the outflow of capital was tightly controlled and there was almost no restriction on inflows. The first round of the liberalization process in

May 1990 focused on deregulation of current account transactions. The second (April 1991) and third (February 1994) rounds saw most of the controls on capital outflows lifted. For example, in 1991, the Thai Government allowed the free transfer of capital up to $5 million for direct investment and removed the requirement that repatriation of investment had to be approved. In 1994, it raised the maximum amount of capital that could be taken out of the country to Vietnam and bordering countries to 500 000 baht (about $20 000). Among the remaining restrictions, there is the need for approval by the Bank of Thailand for the purchase of foreign securities and real estate by residents.

In 1991, the Malaysian government made outstanding ringgit received through swap transactions with non-residents subject to a reserve requirement. In 1992, the total amount of borrowing in foreign currency from domestic banks by a resident was limited to $1 million; previously there had been no maximum. In early 1994, the government also implemented administrative controls to discourage the inflow of foreign capital, especially speculative short-term capital. These included prohibiting the sale of short-term money-market instruments to non-residents, commercial bank swaps, and forward transactions on the bid side with foreign customers. The first has proved to be most successful in curbing the inflow of short-term capital (IMF, 1995a).

Indonesia adopted several measures in 1991 to discourage overseas borrowing. Bank Indonesia, the central bank, reduced swap operations by lowering the limit for an individual bank from 25 per cent to 20 per cent of its capital, raising the swap premium by 5 percentage points, and announcing that future swap operations could be undertaken only at its initiative. Limits were imposed on offshore borrowing by state enterprises and commercial banks, and all state-related overseas commercial borrowing had to obtain prior approval from the government. In the same year, a debt management team was organized to supervise foreign loan transactions.

IV MACROECONOMIC ASPECTS OF CAPITAL INFLOWS AND POLICY RESPONSES

Inflation, the Real Exchange Rate and Financial Market Volatility: An Overview

The effects of capital inflows on the recipient country depend on the size and composition of the inflows, the foreign-exchange rate system, developments in domestic financial markets, and the availability and flexibility of economic policy measures. Usually, a surge in capital inflows causes the nominal and the real value of the currency to appreciate and the current account to deteriorate. It may also lead to an expansion of monetary aggregates, thus giving rise to increased inflationary pressure.

Figure 3.3 compares average consumer price inflation and the rate of real effective currency devaluation in the second half of the 1980s with those of the first half of the 1990s when these countries witnessed a surge in foreign capital inflow. Inflation increased in all four countries in the 1990s compared to the previous period. However, this was not necessarily a result of foreign capital inflows. Obviously, a more sophisticated and extensive econometric study is required to establish the causality between a higher rate of inflation and foreign capital inflow in these countries.

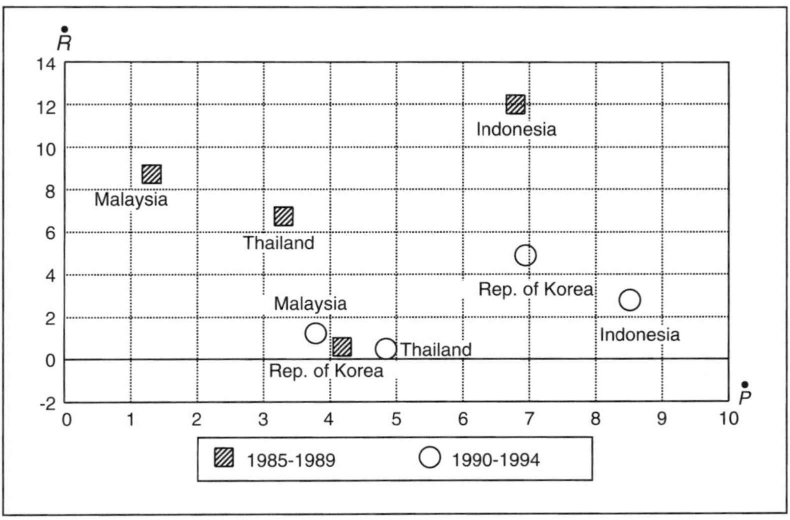

Figure 3.3 Rate of change in the consumer price index and rate of real effective currency devaluation, selected Asian countries, 1985–9 and 1990–4 (per cent)

Notes: $\dot{R}$ = Rate of real effective currency devaluation.
$\dot{P}$ = Rate of change in the consumer price index.

The real effective exchange rates for the Republic of Korea are estimates by the Korea Institute of Finance. Those of other countries are adopted from DRI's *World Market Executive Overview*. The wholesale price index has been used to calculate real effective exchange rates of all four countries.

The difference in the movement of real exchange rates is closely related to the composition of aggregate demand. In the Asian countries, investment as a share of GDP generally showed a rising trend during the period of capital inflows. In Latin America, investment fell and consumption rose, especially during 1990 and 1991. Differences in the behaviour of government consumption have also been a factor (Khan and Reinhart, 1995; Leiderman, 1995; and Calvo *et al.*, 1993). The Asian countries managed to maintain fiscal discipline in the face of rising capital inflows. Usually, public consumption is more oriented than private consumption towards non-traded goods.

The stability of these countries' real effective exchange rates in the 1990s has also been greatly affected by the steep nominal appreciation of the yen against the US dollar, coupled with stability of nominal exchange rates against the US dollar. This brought about a sharp nominal depreciation of their currencies against the yen. Given that Japan is a major trading partner, this generated substantial downward pressure on their real effective currency values. By contrast, these developments were only a minor influence on the real effective exchange rates of Latin American countries, as their trade with Japan is relatively less important.

The movement of foreign capital in massive amounts may increase the volatility of domestic financial markets, including the foreign-exchange market. To examine whether financial markets have become more volatile compared to the pre-capital-inflow period, GARCH variance has been estimated for exchange rates, stock returns and interest rates (see Appendix 3.1).

The results do not show clear evidence that exchange-rate volatility increased during the period of capital inflows compared to earlier periods. This is presumably due to the exchange-rate policies adopted: the policy response has been to maintain the international price competitiveness of exports by preventing a rapid nominal appreciation of the currency or even inducing depreciation through intervention in the local foreign-exchange market.

The fact that the movement of the won–dollar exchange rate has become more volatile since early 1995 could be explained by the fact that the Government of the Republic of Korea refrained from intervention in the foreign-exchange market, suggesting that volatility may have been suppressed by intervention until 1994.

The rupiah–dollar rate exhibited high volatility from the second half of 1990 through the first half of 1991, because the Indonesian government pursued depreciation of the rupiah more actively than before, as the current-account deficit increased rapidly during that period. The increased volatility of the ringgit–dollar rate in early 1994 was closely related to capital flows. The Malaysian government imposed several direct measures in early 1994 to curb the inflow of speculative short-term capital. This prompted foreign investors to withdraw investments from Malaysia. The result was a large depreciation of the ringgit over a short period of time.

Financial volatility may also arise in response to an increase in foreign participation in the stock market (Folkerts-Landau *et al.*, 1995; and IMF, 1995a). Domestic investors in emerging markets sometimes follow the strategies of foreign institutional investors who are considered to have more advanced skills in stock investment, thereby amplifying volatility. However, there is no strong evidence that the opening of stock markets or the inflow of capital during the 1990s resulted in increased volatility (see Appendix 3.1, Figure 3.A2). This is consistent with the results of Kim and Singal (1994) and the IMF (1995a). Indeed, the volatility of stock returns in the Republic of Korea tended to decrease after the opening of the stock market in January 1992, even though large swings remained.

However, the estimates do show that the presence of more foreign capital can weaken the stability of a stock market for at least a short period of time.[5] In late 1993 and early January 1994 massive capital inflows contributed to a rapid rise in stock prices on the Kuala Lumpur Stock Exchange, and in the first half of 1994 an outflow of foreign capital led to a rapid fall in stock prices. These flows thus resulted in increased volatility of stock returns in Malaysia. The Thai stock market saw a sudden outflow of foreign funds (related to the Gulf War) in the second half of 1990, and the Thai and Malaysian stock markets in early 1995 witnessed quick withdrawals of foreign investment prompted by the Mexican crisis. Such flows caused an increase in volatility of stock returns (see Appendix, Figures 3.A2b and c).

The volatility of weekly average interest rates in the Republic of Korea increased significantly in 1992 (see Appendix 3.1, Figure 3.A3), mainly related to domestic interest-rate liberalization. In Malaysia, interest rate volatility was very high in 1986. Subsequently, the volatility decreased considerably although it sometimes showed large swings. Large volatility increases in 1990 and early 1995 are partly attributable to sudden capital outflows prompted by the Gulf War and the Mexican crisis.

Faced with a surge in the inflow of foreign capital, the four countries sought to stabilize their exchange rates in order to protect their export sectors. Simultaneously, they have used monetary sterilization to absorb the excess liquidity resulting from the increase in net foreign assets. Strong fiscal discipline has also been maintained, especially in Thailand.

Macroeconomic Effects and Policy Responses

Republic of Korea

Since the mid-1960s, economic growth in the Republic of Korea has been propelled by the rapid expansion of exports and investment arising from increases in foreign demand. Reflecting this export-oriented development, the degree of openness (measured by exports plus imports as a percentage of GDP) has been very high since the mid-1980s.

Policymakers have been very careful not to allow the competitiveness of Korean products to fall behind. Between 1990 and 1993, the foreign-exchange rate policy was geared to maintaining a weak won-regardless of whether the overall balance was in surplus or deficit. As a result, the Korean won depreciated even when a large capital inflow generated an overall surplus.

The overall balance of payments account recorded deficits in 1990 and 1991 because of a large current account deficit (see Table 3.1). This was accompanied by a depreciation of the won against the US dollar. Since 1992, the won has been experiencing strong upward pressures as a result of large overall surpluses. Both a large increase in foreign capital inflows and the improvement in the current account have contributed to this. Despite the surpluses, the won continued to depreciate until the end of 1993, implying that the Bank of Korea actively intervened. The Bank of Korea's net foreign assets increased by $8.6 billion during 1992 and 1993, when the overall surplus was $11.4 billion.

Since 1994, the won has shown a steady appreciation against the US dollar. By the end of 1994 it had appreciated by 2.5 per cent compared to the end of the previous year. The appreciation was mainly because of the marked appreciation of the yen against the dollar, which led to a large depreciation of the real effective value of the won. Between 1992 and the second quarter of 1995, the real effective value of the won depreciated by 28 per cent, entirely accounted for by the appreciation of the yen. The strong yen has contributed to a sharp increase in Korean export earnings and this meant that the central bank could let the won appreciate to a certain extent without risking erosion of

Table 3.1 Republic of Korea: economic indicators, 1987–94 (per cent, unless otherwise indicated)

	1987	*1989*	*1990*	*1991*	*1992*	*1993*	*1994*
GDP growth	11.5	6.4	9.5	9.1	5.1	5.8	8.4
Inflation[a]	3.0	5.7	8.6	9.3	6.2	4.8	6.2
Money supply (M2)	18.8	19.8	21.2	18.6	18.4	18.6	15.6
Interest rate[b]	12.6	15.2	16.5	18.9	16.2	12.6	12.9
Nominal exchange rate							
(Korean won per $)[c]	822.6	671.5	707.8	733.4	780.7	802.7	803.5
Rate of change	−6.7	−8.2	5.4	3.6	6.5	2.8	0.1
Real effective exchange rate[d]							
(1990=100)	113.9	99.2	100.0	103.3	111.6	119.1	124.6
Rate of change	−0.4	−8.2	0.8	3.3	8.1	6.7	4.6
Investment/GDP	29.8	33.6	36.9	38.9	36.6	35.1	36.1
Saving/GDP	35.5	35.7	35.5	35.7	34.5	34.8	35.0
Fiscal balance/GDP	0.8	0.3	0.1	−1.01	−0.3	0.1	0.2
Current account balance ($ million)	9 854	5 055	−2 179	−8 728	−4 529	385	−4 531
Current account balance as a percentage of GDP	7.4	2.3	−0.9	−3.0	−1.5	0.1	−1.2
Capital account balance ($ million)	−5 843	−3 423	3 881	4 227	8 343	6 879	9 025
Capital account balance as a percentage of GDP	−4.4	−1.6	1.5	1.5	2.7	2.1	2.4
Overall balance ($ million)	5 202	2 453	−273.9	−3 741	4 898	6 542	2 822
Foreign exchange reserves ($ million)	3 566	14 978	14 453	13 306	16 640	19 704	25 032

a Rate of change of the consumer price index.
b Average annual yield on three-year bank-guaranteed corporate bonds.
c Annual average.
d Annual average; a rise in the index indicates a depreciation.

Source: Bank of Korea, *National Accounts*, various issues; Bank of Korea, *Monthly Bulletin*, various issues; IMF, *International Financial Statistics*, various issues.

the price competitiveness of Korean exporters. The large capital inflow and export expansion resulted in an overall balance of payments surplus of $2.8 billion in 1994. Although the surplus was large, so long as the yen remained strong the Bank of Korea did not consider it necessary to intervene in the foreign-exchange market.

As to monetary policy, it appears that the Bank of Korea resorted to active sterilization to counter the effects of foreign capital inflows on the money supply. Foreign-exchange market intervention increased the holdings of foreign assets by the central bank, thereby increasing the money supply – which is the most carefully monitored intermediate target of monetary policy. To offset the increase, the monetary authorities required financial institutions to purchase monetary stabilization bonds (MSBs). Kim (1991) calculates that the Bank of Korea sterilized about 90 per cent of the increase in net foreign assets during the 1980s.

Figure 3.4 shows considerable changes in the net domestic assets (NDA) and net foreign assets (NFA) of the Bank of Korea from 1986 to 1994, even after the market average exchange-rate system was adopted in 1990. This implies that the bank continued to intervene to stabilize the foreign-exchange rate. The intervention was most active during 1992–3 because of the large increase in foreign portfolio investment. The chart also shows that changes in NFA and NDA have been inversely related to each other, suggesting that the Bank of Korea has actively engaged in mopping up increases in the money supply resulting from its foreign-exchange interventions.

Due to sterilization, money supply growth in the Republic of Korea has been kept under control. It has been decelerating continuously since 1990 and inflation has also been falling (Table 3.1). While the Republic of Korea has avoided serious inflation, its interest rates have risen gradually since 1993 due to the crowding-out effect of the massive sterilization. The wide interest-rate gap between the Republic of Korea and the industrial economies continues to cause capital inflows.

Sterilization through sales of MSBs has other costs besides giving rise to higher interest rates: an increase in interest payments on MSBs is likely to produce inflationary pressure. Indeed, interest payments on MSBs explain about 78 per cent of the increase in the monetary base between 1990 and 1995. The Bank of Korea thus faces significant difficulties in further using sterilization to manage foreign capital inflows.

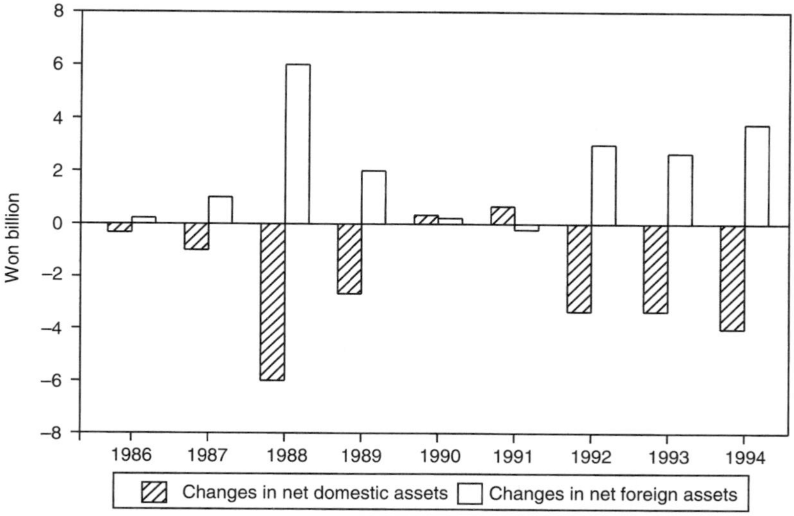

Figure 3.4 Republic of Korea: changes in net domestic assets and net foreign assets, 1986–94.
Source: Bank of Korea, *Monthly Bulletin*, various issues.

Thailand

Thailand has maintained fast economic growth since the late 1980s, with real GDP increases averaging 8.3 per cent annually during 1988–94. It is often stressed that the rapid growth of the Thai economy was largely due to the inflow of foreign capital beginning in 1988. The inflows played an important role in financing the high rate of investment when domestic savings were increasing slowly.

At the same time, Thailand had to deal with some adverse effects of the large capital inflow. High priority has been given to exchange rate stability (Nijathaworn and Dejthamrong, 1994; and Nijathaworn, 1995a). The baht–dollar rate has been more or less fixed since 1989. With Thailand's pursuit of export-led growth, maintaining price competitiveness for its exports has been crucial. A stable exchange rate has enabled the economy to continue to attract the foreign capital needed to maintain a high rate of domestic investment. However, the firm commitment of the government to keep the nominal exchange rate stable has added to the burden borne by monetary sterilization to mop up excess liquidity arising from the increase in foreign assets of the central bank as a result of foreign-exchange market intervention.

Since November 1984, the baht has been linked to a multiple-currency basket while previously it had been pegged to the US dollar. This change came partly as a response to the appreciation of the US dollar in the mid-1980s. Though the composition of the currency basket has not been disclosed, highest weights were likely given to the currencies of Thailand's major trading partners, the United States, Japan, and Germany.[6] The weights are known to be adjusted according to the developments in foreign-exchange markets.

At 8 a.m. on each business day, the Thai Exchange Equalization Fund (EEF) announces a basic exchange rate for the baht against the US dollar. The EEF will trade unlimited amounts of the dollar with the commercial banks within a 0.02-baht band around this rate until noon. In the afternoon, the dollar is traded only in the interbank foreign-exchange market, where the rate for the baht is largely dependent on expectations of the next day's basic rate.

In setting the basic rate every day, the EEF takes into account the current state and future prospects of exports, imports and domestic inflation, along with developments in the major currencies in international foreign-exchange markets. However, most observers conjecture that the current account balance plays a major role in deciding on the basic rate. This is reflected in the fact that the nominal rate has been extremely stable since the late 1980s. Between 1990 and 1994 the baht appreciated against the US dollar by only 0.3 per cent annually, despite the fact that the overall balance of payments showed a large surplus – attributable to a substantial inflow of foreign capital that more than offset the large current account deficit (see Table 3.2).

From the late 1980s onwards, the increase in net foreign assets was the major source of money supply growth. This increased liquidity was partly responsible for an increase in domestic demand and high domestic inflation. The rate of change of the consumer price index rose from 2.5 per cent in 1987 to 5.9 per cent in 1990. Greater domestic demand also contributed to a deterioration in the current account balance, which in turn reinforced Thailand's need for foreign capital. The current account deficit as a percentage of GDP widened to 8.5 per cent in 1990, from 0.7 per cent in 1987. Although it has since moderated, it has remained above 5 per cent throughout the first half of the 1990s.

Fiscal discipline has been of great importance in managing the inflow of foreign capital (Nijathaworn and Dejthamrong, 1994; and Nijathaworn, 1995a, 1995b). The government tightened fiscal policy in order to reduce domestic aggregate demand and inflationary pres-

Table 3.2 Thailand: economic indicators, 1987–94 (per cent, unless otherwise indicated)

	1987	*1989*	*1990*	*1991*	*1992*	*1993*	*1994*
GDP growth	9.5	12.2	11.6	8.1	7.6	8.9	8.5
Inflation[a]	2.5	5.4	5.9	5.7	4.1	3.5	5.3
Money supply (M2)	20.4	26.3	26.7	19.8	15.6	18.4	12.9
Interest rate[b]	9.50	9.50	12.25	13.67	8.88	8.63	8.46
Nominal exchange rate[c] (Thai baht per $)	25.72	25.70	25.59	25.52	25.40	25.32	25.15
Rate of change	−2.2	1.6	−0.5	−0.3	−0.5	−0.3	−0.7
Real effective exchange rate[d] (1990=100)	103.5	101.8	100.0	101.0	102.6	105.6	106.1
Rate of change	7.6	−4.9	−1.8	1.0	1.5	3.0	0.5
Investment/GDP	27.9	35.1	41.1	42.2	39.9	39.9	40.1
Saving/GDP	26.9	33.7	33.5	34.4	34.2	34.2	34.4
Fiscal balance/GDP	−0.7	3.5	4.9	4.0	2.5	1.8	1.87
Current account balance ($ million)	−366	−2 498	−7 281	−7 571	−6355	−7 047	−8 419
Current account balance as a percentage of GDP	−0.7	−3.5	−8.5	−7.7	−5.8	−5.6	−5.9
Capital account balance ($ million)	1 062	6 599	9 098	11 759	9 797	11 246	14 246
Capital account balance as a percentage of GDP	2.1	9.1	10.6	12.0	8.9	8.9	10.1
Overall balance ($ million)	945	5 029	3 235	4 618	2 925	3 907	4 169
Foreign exchange reserves ($ million)	3 906	9 641	13 247	17 287	20 012	24 078	28 884

[a] Rate of change of the consumer price index.
[b] Maximum rate offered by commercial banks on three-to six-month savings deposits (annual average).
[c] Annual average.
[d] Annual average; a rise in the index indicates a depreciation.

Source: IMF, *International Financial Statistics*, various issues; Bank of Thailand, *Annual Economic Report 1994*; DRI, *World Markets Executive Overview* (Fourth quarter 1995).

sures, as well as to lower the dependence on foreign capital by increasing national savings. The choice of fiscal policy is related to the ineffectiveness of monetary policy under a system of fixed exchange rates with free cross-border capital movements. It is also related, according to Nijathaworn (1995a, 1995b), to a policy bias (since the mid-1980s) towards strict fiscal discipline as the main medium-term means of macroeconomic stabilization. Actual government spending on investment is usually lower than budgeted expenditure, which enables the government to achieve a fiscal surplus more easily.

The government was able both to restrain its expenditure and improve tax revenue by enhancing the efficiency of tax collection and introducing new taxes, including a value-added tax of 7 per cent in 1992. As a consequence, the government was able to achieve a fiscal surplus in 1988 and every year since then. Between 1988 and 1994 the average surplus was about 3 per cent of GDP. As its fiscal position improved, the government repaid foreign debt in an effort to offset the inflow of foreign capital. The strong fiscal consolidation greatly contributed to a reduction in domestic inflationary pressure. In 1991, the fiscal surplus peaked at 4.9 per cent of GDP, absorbing more than 20 per cent of the increase in the money supply.

An important goal of monetary policy in the face of capital inflows has been monetary and interest-rate stabilization. The Bank of Thailand has used open-market operations in an attempt to control excess liquidity resulting from the increase in its net foreign assets and to reduce the volatility of domestic interest rates. This has been a tool of short-term management of excess liquidity, while fiscal policy has been used in a medium-and long-term perspective.

Frequent open-market operations have been necessary because under a system of fixed exchange rates with an open capital account as in Thailand, monetary tightening is only effective in controlling liquidity and interest rates in the short run (Schadler *et al.*, 1993). As a result, domestic interest rates were higher than those of the industrial economies throughout the 1990s, providing an ongoing incentive for foreign capital to flow in (see Figure 3.5).

Interventions in the repurchase market for government and state-enterprise bonds and issuing central bank securities have been the main tools of monetary sterilization, which has usually been accompanied by 'window guidance', through which the Bank of Thailand persuades commercial banks to restrain domestic credit. Thailand established a repurchase market in 1979 to encourage the develop-

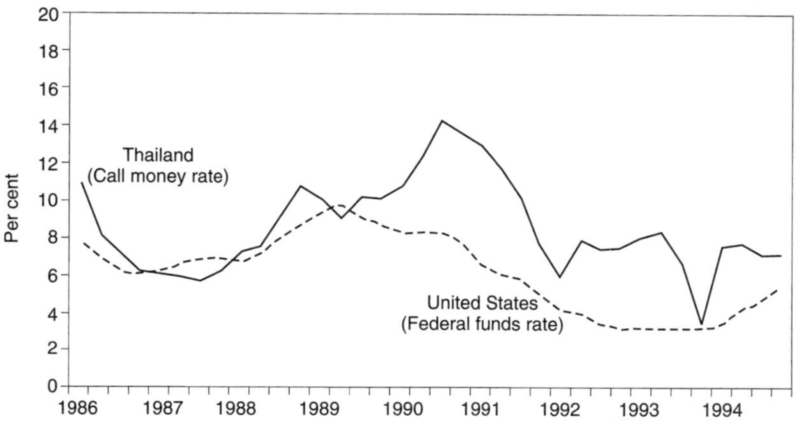

Figure 3.5 Interest rates in Thailand and the United States, quarterly, 1986–94
Source: IMF, *International Financial Statistics*, various issues.

ment of a money market and to provide the Bank of Thailand with a new instrument for open-market operations (see Kittisrikangwan *et al.*, 1994). In fact, open-market operations through the repurchase market in Thailand are effective only for very short-term liquidity management, as participants in this market prefer transactions with maturities of no more than two weeks. In general, financial institutions use the repurchase market for managing excess demand or the supply of funds with a very short time-horizon.

To overcome this, since 1987, the Bank of Thailand has issued central bank bonds with maturities between six and twelve months. It also established a short-term central-bank bond market in August 1995. Since then, it has also issued bonds with maturities ranging from one to six months on a weekly basis. This made the bank's injection or absorption of reserve money more effective.

The government has also dealt with the inflow of foreign capital by deregulating the outflow of capital. In three rounds of foreign-exchange liberalization since 1990 it removed all restrictions on capital outflows, except a few that are related to portfolio and property investment. This was also accompanied by tighter prudential requirements for the financial sector with respect to capital adequacy, loan-loss provisions, and exposure to foreign-exchange risk.

As a result of fiscal discipline, monetary tightening, deregulation of capital outflows and tighter prudential requirements, the growth of the money supply decelerated and inflation has been stable throughout the 1990s, despite increasing capital inflows. The growth rate of M2 fell from 26.7 per cent in 1990 to 15.6 per cent in 1992 and to 12.9 per cent in 1994. The consumer price index (CPI) increase went down from 5.9 per cent in 1990 to 3.5 per cent in 1993, but rose to 5.3 per cent in 1994. This rise was related to increased production costs. Continued inflows of FDI increased the demand for labour and caused the limited available infrastructure to be overcharged, leading to a rise in wages and the cost of infrastructure. The sharp appreciation of the yen against the US dollar was also a factor. The baht depreciated by 10 per cent against the yen during 1994.

Increased foreign portfolio investment exposes Thailand's financial markets to external shocks. Foreign acquisition of Thai stocks was a major factor in the 88 per cent increase in the Stock Exchange of Thailand (SET) index in 1993, following a 26 per cent increase in 1992. Foreign investors accounted for 19 per cent of the turnover on the SET in 1993 and 20 per cent in 1994.

Thailand experienced some turbulence in its stock and foreign-exchange markets because of the Mexican crisis. In mid-January 1995, a rumour that the government would be forced to devalue the baht due to the widening current account deficit led foreign investors to massive withdrawals of money from Thailand. On 12 January, they purchased about $5 billion in the local foreign-exchange market, driving the exchange rate against the US dollar in the interbank market down by 4.5 per cent, to 26.3 baht per dollar. The SET index fell by 5 per cent on 12 and 13 January.

The EEF began to intervene by selling unlimited amounts of US dollars at a fixed rate of 25.04 baht per dollar. A baht–dollar swap facility was also introduced by the Bank of Thailand in an attempt to gain the confidence of foreign investors. Ultimately, the panic subsided and the foreign-exchange and stock markets stabilized. A sustained crisis was avoided because Thailand's economic fundamentals were basically sound, especially as compared to Mexico. Nonetheless, careful attention should be paid to the fact that a rumour was able temporarily to destabilize the Thai economy.

Malaysia

Malaysia has maintained a real GDP growth rate of between 7 and 9 per cent since 1987. This rapid growth has been due largely to a rapid increase in investment, with foreign capital providing an important source of financing. According to the estimates by Bank Negara Malaysia (1995), a 1 per cent increase in real FDI and foreign borrowing resulted, respectively, in 0.111 per cent and 0.056 per cent growth in real GDP during 1970–93.

Faced with a substantial foreign capital inflow, until early 1994, the government mainly used sterilized intervention in the foreign-exchange market to avoid negative consequences for the economy.

Since 1975, the ringgit has been pegged to a basket of currencies of Malaysia's major trading partners – principally the United States, Japan, Singapore, Germany, the United Kingdom and the Netherlands. Bank Negara Malaysia has intervened frequently in the interbank foreign-exchange market to maintain the ringgit–dollar exchange rate within a target range. It is widely believed that the bank's target rate has been determined by the movement of an undisclosed multiple-currency basket.

During 1990–3, despite a large current account deficit, the overall balance-of-payments account maintained a surplus as a result of the huge inflow of foreign capital (see Table 3.3). In particular, during 1991–3, the interest-rate differential between Malaysia and the rest of the world began to widen (see Figure 3.6). At the same time, the market expected the ringgit to appreciate, as it was considered significantly undervalued; this resulted in a pronounced increase in the inflow of foreign capital during this period.

The overall surplus raised pressure on the ringgit, but Bank Negara Malaysia was able, except in 1992, to stabilize both nominal and real exchange rates by actively intervening in the local foreign-exchange market. In fact, the nominal value of the ringgit depreciated against the US dollar in 1991 and 1993 (Table 3.3). The bank is thought to have allowed the ringgit to appreciate in 1992 as the current account balance improved. Active intervention by the bank led to a substantial increase in its foreign-exchange reserves: they jumped from $7.4 billion at the end of 1989 to $10.4 billion at the end of 1991, and to $26.8 billion at the end of 1993. These reserves led to increased liquidity and raised inflationary pressures in the Malaysian economy.

To control excess liquidity, Bank Negara Malaysia, the central bank, has often relied on monetary sterilization. The main instruments during 1991 and 1992 were interbank-market operations and changes in the statutory reserve requirement. The bank tried to absorb excess liquidity by taking out loans with maturities of less than three months in the interbank market. To restrain lending by banks, it raised the reserve requirement from 6.5 per cent to 7.5 per cent in 1991, and to

Table 3.3 Malaysia: economic indicators, 1987–94 (per cent, unless otherwise indicated)

	1987	*1989*	*1990*	*1991*	*1992*	*1993*	*1994*
GDP growth	5.4	9.2	9.7	8.7	7.8	8.3	8.7
Inflation[a]	0.8	2.8	3.1	4.4	4.7	3.6	3.7
Money supply (M2)	7.2	16.1	12.8	14.5	19.1	22.1	14.7
Interest rate[b]	6.5	6.6	6.8	7.3	8.1	7.4	5.5
Nominal exchange rate[c] (Malaysian ringgit per $)	2.52	2.71	2.71	2.75	2.55	2.57	2.62
Rate of change	−2.4	3.4	0.0	1.7	−7.4	1.1	1.9
Real effective exchange rate[d]							
(1990=100)	89.6	98.7	100.0	104.4	98.0	102.1	105.4
Rate of change	9.2	−0.9	1.3	4.38	−6.1	4.2	3.2
Investment/GDP	23.2	28.6	31.3	35.9	33.5	35.0	38.5
Saving/GDP	31.1	29.0	29.1	26.8	30.1	30.8	32.0
Fiscal balance/GDP	−7.7	−3.3	−3.0	−2.0	−0.8	0.2	−0.5
Current account balance ($ million)	2 575	315	−870	−4 183	−2 167	−2 809	−4 147
Current account balance as a percentage of GDP	8.1	0.8	−2.0	−8.9	−3.7	−4.4	−5.9
Capital account balance ($ million)	−1 537	1 330	1 786	5 623	8 743	10 798	1 511
Capital account balance as a percentage of GDP	−4.9	3.5	4.7	11.9	15.1	17.4	2.1
Overall balance ($ million)	1 119	1 230	1 953	1 238	6 615	11 343	−3 157
Foreign exchange reserves ($ million)	7 055	7 393	9 327	10 421	16 784	26 814	24 888

[a] Rate of change of the consumer price index.
[b] Average annual yield on long-term government bonds.
[c] Annual average.
[d] Annual average; a rise in the index indicates a depreciation.

Source: IMF, *International Financial Statistics*, various issues; Bank Negara Malaysia, *Annual Report 1994*; DRI, *World Markets Executive Overview* (fourth quarter 1995).

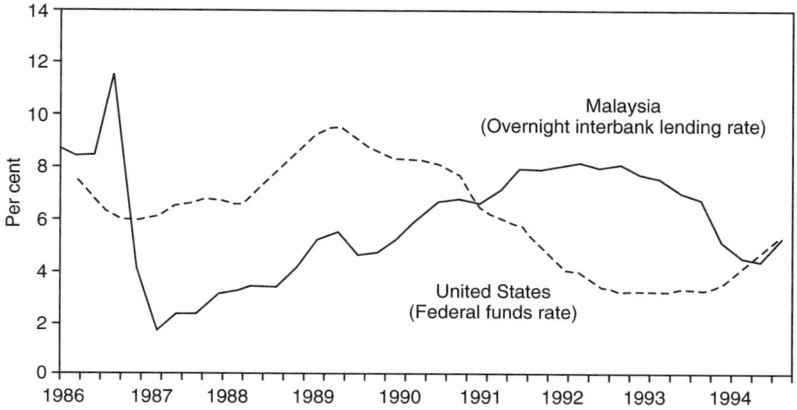

Figure 3.6 Interest rates in Malaysia and the United States, quarterly, 1986–94
Source: IMF, *International Financial Statistics*, various issues.

8.5 per cent in 1992. Additional measures were adopted to contain domestic credit expansion. In 1991, the bank added foreign loans related to swaps and foreign borrowing from offshore financial markets to the list of liabilities subject to reserve requirements. Also, it required deposits of the Employee Provident Fund, which holds about 20 per cent of financial assets in the country, and those of the government to be transferred from private banks to the central bank. Overall, Bank Negara Malaysia absorbed 24 billion ringgit from the banking sector through sterilization measures in 1992, equivalent to 90 per cent of the outstanding stock of reserve money.

However, monetary sterilization resulted in a rise in domestic interest rates until early 1993, leading to a widening gap between domestic and foreign rates (see Figure 3.6). The high interest-rate differential and the buoyant performance of the Malaysian stock market attracted additional foreign capital, especially in the form of portfolio investment, thus necessitating further sterilized intervention. In an effort to increase the coverage and effect of sterilization, Bank Negara Malaysia introduced the Bank Negara Bill and the Malaysia Savings Bond in 1993. During that year, it absorbed 6 billion ringgit and 1.4 billion ringgit, respectively, with these instruments. Nonetheless, the principal sterilization measure was still intervention in the interbank market, through which 27 billion ringgit, about 45 per cent of the outstanding reserve money, was absorbed in 1993.

Fiscal consolidation was also pursued to manage the expansion of the money supply resulting from the inflow of foreign capital. Efforts were made to restrain government spending. As a result, the fiscal deficit continued to decrease and, in 1993, the fiscal balance recorded a surplus. Regulation of the capital account was also reintroduced. For example, limits on non-trade-related transactions were imposed on commercial banks in 1992.

Despite monetary sterilization and fiscal restraint, the growth of monetary aggregates accelerated during 1990–3. The growth rate of M3, an intermediate target of the Malaysian monetary authorities, increased from 12.8 per cent in 1990 to 18.2 per cent in 1991, to 19.1 per cent in 1992, and to 23.5 per cent in 1993. The net increase in foreign assets held by Bank Negara Malaysia accounted for 64 per cent of the increase in M3 in 1992 and 75 per cent in 1993. M2 was also increasing (see Table 3.3).[7]

Prices rose faster in the early 1990s than in the 1980s. Between 1990 and 1993 the annual increase in the consumer price index averaged 4.0 per cent, although it began to moderate in 1993. The comparable figure for 1985–9 was only about 1.4 per cent. Given that the growth rate of the Malaysian economy had exceeded the potential rate, rapid monetary growth resulting from the inflow of foreign capital raised inflationary pressure further. While the potential growth rate is estimated by Bank Negara Malaysia (1995) to be 7 to 8 per cent, the Malaysian economy has actually grown by more than 8 per cent since 1988 (except in 1992). Also, the increase in inward FDI raised wages and the costs of other inputs, exacerbating inflationary pressures. In the first half of the 1990s Malaysia witnessed a sharp rise in asset prices. The stock market has been bullish, partly due to significant foreign portfolio investment. In 1993, the Kuala Lumpur Composite Index rose by 98 per cent, generating concern about the possibility of a speculative bubble.

The inflow of foreign capital destabilized the economy and led to a loss of monetary control by the central bank (Aziz, 1994). More importantly, the increase in the inflow of short-term speculative capital, especially in 1993, made the financial markets vulnerable to a reversal in the flow. All these effects prompted Bank Negara Malaysia to implement six administrative measures in January and February 1994 to contain the inflow, particularly of speculative short-term capital (see Table 3.4). These included the prohibition of short-

Table 3.4 Chronology of administrative measures to contain capital inflows in Malaysia in 1994

	Measures	*Date implemented*	*Date lifted*
(1)	Increase in statutory reserve requirement of commercial banks, finance companies and merchant banks		
	8.5 per cent → 9.5 per cent	3 January 1994	
	9.5 per cent → 10.5 per cent	16 May 1994	
	10.5 per cent → 11.5 per cent	1 July 1994	
(2)	Inclusion of all funds sourced abroad in the eligible base for computing statutory reserve requirement and liquidity requirement	16 January 1994	
(3)	Placement of limits on non-trade-related external liabilities of banking institutions[a]	17 January 1994	20 January 1995
(4)	Prohibition of sales of short-term monetary instruments by residents to non-residents[b]	24 January 1994	12 August 1994
(5)	Transfer of ringgit funds of foreign banking institutions held in commercial banks' non-interest bearing foreign nostro accounts to Bank Negara Malaysia	2 February 1994	16 May 1994
	Inclusion of nostro balances in the eligible liability base for reserve and liquidity requirement	16 February 1994	16 August 1994
(6)	Prohibition of commercial banks' swaps and outright forward transactions on the bid side with foreigners[c]	23 February 1994	20 January 1995

[a] Non-FDI-related external liabilities are also subject to ceilings.

[b] The restriction was applied to highly liquid instruments, including Bank Negara Bills, Treasury Bills, Malaysian Government securities, Cagamas Bonds and Notes, BA and negotiable instruments of deposit with a remaining maturity of one year or less. From 7 February 1994, private debt securities with a remaining maturity of one year or less (except convertible bonds) were also subject to the restriction.

[c] This measure was intended to prevent overseas investors from establishing a speculative long forward position of the ringgit when it was expected to appreciate.

Source: Bank Negara Malaysia, *Annual Report 1994*.

term money-market instrument sales to non-residents, a ban on commercial bank swaps unless trade-related, and tight restrictions on forward transactions with foreigners. Liabilities included in computing statutory reserves and liquidity requirements were expanded to cover foreign-currency deposits, foreign-currency borrowing from foreign banking institutions, and interbank borrowing. Also, the statutory reserve requirement was raised to 9.5 per cent (it was raised again in May and July 1995).

There was an immediate response from the foreign-exchange and stock markets. The ringgit depreciated rapidly due to an outflow of foreign capital. By the end of February 1994, it had depreciated against the US dollar by 3.3 per cent from the end of the previous year. The Kuala Lumpur Composite Index, after recording a new high of 1314 points on 5 January 1994, quickly fell below the 1000 level, falling to 954 points on 21 March 1994.

From the second quarter, however, the ringgit and stock prices began to stabilize. For the rest of the year, the ringgit displayed an upward trend against the US dollar and the Composite Index rose steadily. The markets reflected the improved soundness of the Malaysian economy rather than the inflow of speculative funds: high economic growth and fiscal consolidation continued.

The moderation of inflation in 1993 prompted Bank Negara Malaysia to reduce monetary sterilization in 1994. This led to a fall in domestic interest rates while international rates were rising, narrowing the differential between Malaysia and the industrial countries. Lower interest rates together with administrative measures discouraged the inflow of foreign funds and encouraged the outflow of foreign capital invested in Malaysian securities.

Finally, in the second half of 1994 a net outflow of foreign capital was recorded, as short-term speculative funds moved elsewhere. This resulted in a deceleration of the expansion of M3, which had grown by 23.5 per cent in 1993, to only 13.1 per cent in 1994. Consumer price inflation also moderated: it peaked at 4.4 per cent in February 1994, falling to 3.0 per cent in June 1994. Also, in the second half of 1994, as the economy showed signs of stabilization, Bank Negara Malaysia lifted some of the administrative measures (see Table 3.4).

The use of administrative measures is controversial. It is often argued that such measures should be used rarely and only temporarily, as they lead to distortions in the long run and damage a country's reputation. However, direct controls, coupled with a policy of low interest rates, were considered helpful in curtailing destabilizing short-term flows of foreign capital and restoring economic stability in Malaysia (IMF, 1995a). It should be noted, however, that this was possible only against the background of the sound economic fundamentals of the Malaysian economy.

Indonesia

Rapid economic growth of Indonesia in the 1990s benefited from the inflow of foreign capital. However, foreign capital inflow also created some adverse effects such as accelerating money supply growth. During 1990 and 1991, the economy showed signs of overheating due to a rapid expansion of demand caused by a substantial inflow of foreign capital (Bank Indonesia, 1994). Consumer price inflation rose from 6.4 per cent in 1989 to 7.8 per cent in 1990, and to 9.9 per cent in 1991. There was also a deterioration in the current account resulting from increasing imports: the deficit widened by $3.2 billion between 1989 and 1991, and the ratio of the deficit to GDP rose from 2.5 per cent to 4.4 per cent (see Table 3.5).

The inflow of foreign capital increased domestic liquidity and foreign-exchange reserves held by Bank Indonesia. As in the Republic of Korea and Malaysia, the government attempted to absorb the excess liquidity mainly through monetary sterilization. It also increased prudential requirements for commercial banks and imposed some direct controls on credit expansion. Despite the difficulties in macroeconomic management, the first priority has always been given to maintaining a weak rupiah in order to enhance the international competitiveness of exports (other than oil and gas which account for a quarter of total exports). The central bank has intervened in the interbank foreign-exchange market to maintain this policy.

Since 1978, the rupiah has been pegged to a basket of the currencies of Indonesia's major trading partners; previously, it had been pegged to the US dollar. Every business day at 3 p.m., Bank Indonesia announces a selling and a buying rate for the rupiah against the US dollar. The rates are applied to commercial banks' settlements on the same day as well as to swap transactions and export-draft rediscounting with the central bank. In 1994, the band was widened from 20 to 30 rupiahs. The market rate of the rupiah against the dollar is determined in the interbank foreign-exchange market, with its level reflecting expected changes in central bank rates. Normally, it fluctuates within the band set by the central bank the previous day.[8]

Table 3.5 Indonesia: economic indicators, 1987–94 (per cent, unless otherwise indicated)

	1987	*1989*	*1990*	*1991*	*1992*	*1993*	*1994*
GDP growth	4.9	7.5	7.2	7.0	6.5	6.5	7.3
Inflation[a]	9.3	6.4	7.8	9.4	7.5	9.2	8.5
Money supply (M2)	22.4	39.8	44.2	17.0	20.2	22.0	20.2
Interest rate[b]	17.50	18.58	18.53	21.18	21.13	16.35	12.99
Nominal exchange rate[c] (Indonesian rupiah per $)	1 643.9	1 770.1	1 842.8	1 950.3	2 129.9	2 087.1	2 160.8
Rate of change	28.2	5.0	4.1	5.8	4.1	2.8	3.5
Real effective exchange rated (1990=100)	100.0	100.8	100.0	104.7	108.4	111.5	114.3
Rate of change	34.1	−4.0	−0.8	4.7	3.5	2.9	2.5
Investment/GDP	31.4	35.2	36.1	35.5	35.9	33.2	34.3
Saving/GDP	28.1	32.7	31.7	31.1	33.4	31.5	31.8
Fiscal balance/GDP	−1.0	−2.1	0.4	0.5	−0.6	0.5	0.6
Current account balance ($ million)	−2 098	−1 108	−2 988	−4 260	−2 780	−2 016	−2 790
Current account balance as a percentage of GDP	−2.8	−1.2	−2.8	−3.7	−2.2	−1.3	−1.6
Capital account balance ($ million)	3 481	2 918	4 495	5 697	6 129	5 772	3 839
Capital account balance as a percentage of GDP	4.6	3.1	4.2	4.9	4.8	3.7	2.2
Overall balance ($ million)	630	495	2 251	1 528	2 070	594	784
Foreign exchange reserves ($ million)	5 483	5 357	7 353	9 151	10 181	10 988	11 820

[a] Rate of change of the consumer price index.
[b] One-year time deposits rates in commercial banks (end of period).
[c] Annual average.
[d] Annual average; a rise in the index indicates a depreciation.
Source: IMF, *International Financial Statistics*, various issues; Bank Indonesia, *Indonesian Financial Statistics*, various issues; DRI, *World Markets Executive Overview* (fourth quarter 1995).

The main factor that Bank Indonesia considers in setting its official rate has been the inflation differential between Indonesia and its major trading partners (Bank Indonesia, *Annual Report, 1992/1993*; and Euromoney, 1995). Given that inflation has been persistently high in Indonesia relative to the industrial economies, the nominal value of the rupiah has persistently depreciated even when the overall balance was recording a surplus due to the large inflow of foreign capital (see Table 3.5). The nominal value of the rupiah showed a steady depreciation of about 4.0 per cent annually against the US dollar between 1990 and 1994, while the inflation differential between Indonesia and the United States was 4.8 percentage points. Also, the rupiah depreciated sharply against the Japanese yen in the same period. Consequently, the real effective value of the rupiah was fairly stable.

The policy of stabilizing the real exchange rate has been aimed at containing short-term capital inflows. A persistent depreciation of the rupiah's nominal value was able to keep the domestic effective interest rate (interest rate minus expected depreciation rate of the rupiah) lower than it would have been if the currency had appreciated. This policy helped reduce the incentive for foreign capital inflows.

However, the policy aimed at maintaining exchange-rate stability in the face of a massive inflow of foreign capital led to an increase in the money supply, making the change in net foreign assets an important determinant of the change in money supply. This outcome led Bank Indonesia to pursue monetary sterilization continuously. To absorb excess liquidity, Bank Indonesia relies mainly on sales of short-term central bank securities, Bank Indonesia Certificates (Sertifikat Bank Indonesia, henceforth SBI). These were first issued in February 1984. Initially such certificates were issued with maturities of six months or less, but since February 1991 longer maturities have also been issued. The bank issues SBIs in daily auctions, with maturities ranging from seven to 360 days, depending on the state of domestic liquidity. The bank also absorbs liquidity by selling money-market securities (Sural Berharga Pasar Uang, SBPU) to commercial banks. SBPUs are short-term private securities traded in the money market, including promissory notes issued by banks and their customers and bills of exchange. Bank Indonesia sells SBPUs from its portfolio in auctions whenever there is a need to withdraw liquidity.

Monetary sterilization was stepped up as the money supply increased dramatically in 1990. This led to an increase in the sales of SBIs and SBPUs in the following two years. Net sales of SBIs increased to 9.4 trillion rupiahs in 1991 and 9.6 trillion rupiahs in

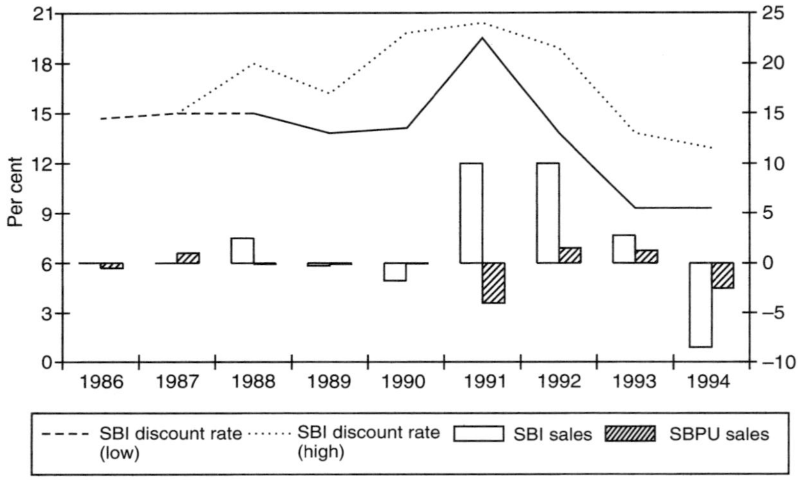

Figure 3.7 Indonesia: net sales of SBI and SBPU, and the SBI discount rate 1986–94 (trillion rupees)
Source: Bank Indonesia, *Indonesian Financial Statistics*, various issues.
Notes: SBI discount rate: left scale. SBI and SBPU sales: right scale; for further explanation, see text.

1992, compared to net repayments during 1989 and 1990 (see Figure 3.7). As a result, the ratio of outstanding SBIs to money supply (M1) increased from 6 per cent in 1990 to 42 per cent in 1991, and to 72 per cent in 1992. Net sales of SBPUs also began to rise in 1992. The sterilization helped moderate the growth rate of 'broad' money supply. M2 growth fell from 44.6 per cent in 1990 to 17.0 per cent in 1991.

Bank Indonesia used several additional methods to control excess liquidity. It raised the discount rate on export drafts, and imposed direct controls on banks to contain credit expansion. For example, a portion of state-enterprise deposits in commercial banks was transferred to the central bank in 1991. Several measures to restrict the inflow of foreign capital were also implemented in the course of 1991, as discussed earlier.

These measures and monetary sterilization were more or less successful in moderating domestic demand in 1992. The consumer price index rose by only 7.5 per cent during the year, almost 2 percentage points less than in 1991, and the current account deficit was reduced by $1.4 billion. However, the inflation rate rose again to 9.2 per cent in 1993, and to 8.5 per cent in 1994. One factor was the decision by the government to reduce industrial subsidies, which led to the rise in administered prices of a number of commodities produced by state enterprises. These included cement, fertilizers and oil-based fuels.

Rapid growth of the money supply was also an important source of inflation (Asian Development Bank, 1995). Since 1993, Bank Indonesia has done less sterilization in order to reduce the burden of interest payments on SBIs (see Figure 3.7). Higher inflation can also be attributed to the persistent depreciation of the nominal value of the rupiah. The sharp depreciation of the rupiah against the Japanese yen resulting from the steep appreciation of the yen in international foreign-exchange markets, together with Indonesia's policy of maintaining a weak rupiah, caused prices of imported goods from Japan to balloon. From the end of 1992 till the end of 1994, the rupiah depreciated by 33 per cent against the yen, but the share of Japanese goods in Indonesia's total imports remained at approximately 30 per cent. This implies that exchange-rate stabilization had some destabilizing macroeconomic effects.

Increased issues of central bank securities in the early 1990s tended to raise their discount rates, thus leading to higher interest rates in the Indonesian economy and to a further widening of the gap between domestic and international rates. In March 1992, the government permitted foreign investors to purchase up to 49 per cent of the shares of domestic private and state-owned commercial banks listed on the Indonesian stock markets. Previously, they had not been allowed to buy shares of banks. The larger interest-rate differential, coupled with the development and deregulation of the domestic capital market, provided a strong incentive for foreigners to invest in Indonesian securities. As a result, the inflow of foreign portfolio investment – which is presumed to be short-term and speculative – rose sharply.

In an attempt to reduce the inflow of short-term capital, Bank Indonesia began to lower the discount rates of SBIs in 1992 and continued to maintain nominal depreciation of the rupiah. Nonetheless, Indonesia's effective rate of return (domestic interest rate minus depreciation rate of the rupiah) remained high relative to returns available in industrial countries (see Figure 3.8). In addition, institutional investors' worldwide rush into emerging markets contributed to a flood of foreign portfolio investment, especially after mid-1993. The proportion of foreign ownership of shares on the Jakarta Stock Exchange rose from 24.0 per cent in fiscal year 1992/1993 to 31.0

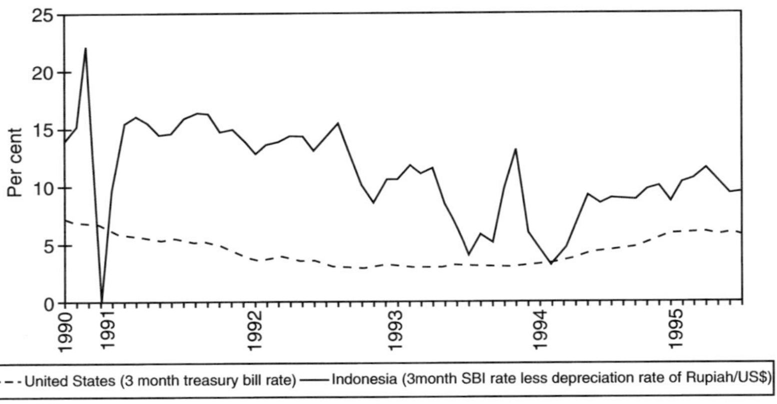

Figure 3.8 Interest rates in Indonesia and the United States, monthly, 1990-5
Source: Bank Indonesia, *Indonesian Financial Statistics*, various issues.

per cent in fiscal year 1993/1994.[9] Accordingly, the economy became vulnerable to a sudden outflow of foreign capital.

The Mexican crisis in December 1994 shook Indonesia's foreign-exchange and capital markets. Rumours of rupiah devaluation linked to the size of Indonesia's large foreign debt (about $87 billion in 1994, the equivalent of about eight times the value of foreign-exchange reserves at the end of 1993) triggered a withdrawal of funds. On 22 December, two days after the Mexican government devalued its currency by 15.3 per cent, strong demand for the US dollar caused the rupiah to depreciate rapidly against the dollar in the interbank market. On 13 January 1995, the value of the rupiah rose to 2223 against the US dollar, 5 rupiah above Bank Indonesia's selling rate. Compared to 22 December 1994, the rupiah had depreciated by 1.7 per cent. In the eleven months before the crisis, the average rate of depreciation had been only 0.3 per cent a month.

To restore exchange-rate stability, Bank Indonesia intervened by selling $580 million in spot, forward and squaring transactions. Simultaneously, it raised its official discount rate by 50 basis points. These measures helped restore confidence that the rupiah would not be devalued further, so that demand for the dollar subsided.

The Indonesian stock market suffered a net outflow of foreign investment and falling stock prices in early January 1995. By the end of January 1995, these had reversed, but the net inflow was slower than prior to the Mexican crisis. Ownership by non-residents of shares listed on the Jakarta Stock Exchange fell from 31.8 per cent at the end of March 1994 to 28.9 per cent a year later. A bearish sentiment has continued since the crisis. Moreover, interest rates have shown a rising trend as Bank Indonesia increased the discount rate for SBIs, in part to prevent another major exodus of capital.

V POLICY ALTERNATIVES FOR MANAGING CAPITAL INFLOWS

To mitigate negative effects of surges of capital inflow, it is essential to enhance the soundness and robustness of the economy. Still, such sudden surges can threaten the stability of financial markets and the economy at large, so that policy measures, at least on a temporary basis, are required.

The key policy measure, especially in response to sustained large inflows, to stabilize both the exchange rate and the money supply has been sterilized intervention. However, sterilization through issuing central bank securities or increases in reserve requirements has shortcomings, particularly when used over longer periods. It results in quasi-fiscal costs as long as the interest rate on central bank securities is higher than that on foreign-exchange reserves.[10] Also, interest payments on these securities increase the money supply and, as a result, can contribute to inflation, which in turn causes a real appreciation of the currency. In addition, sterilization may produce a vicious circle, as further capital inflows may be caused by the widening differential between domestic and international interest rates. Thus, in the long run, it is not capable of dealing with a continued large capital inflow.

A surge in capital flows – a sharp change in the direction and level of liquid speculative capital – has a potential for destabilizing domestic financial markets. In the current world financial environment, the distinction between short-term and long-term capital has partly lost its meaning. Rather, it is the speed and ease with which capital in various forms can flow that is relevant. This is partly a function of the type of asset (or liability) and partly a matter of the controls and rules applied to it by regulators in a specific market, such as restrictions on the movement of certain types of capital. In liberalized financial markets, portfolio investment is generally quite liquid. The Republic of Korea,

Thailand, Malaysia and Indonesia have experienced substantial inflows of this kind of foreign capital since the early 1990s.[11]

This section takes up policy measures that have been used or considered to deal with undesired consequences of continued capital inflows. These include both macroeconomic policy measures and direct capital controls.

Macroeconomic Policies

Flexible Exchange Rates

In the face of capital inflows, all four countries have acted to maintain, or even depreciate, their currencies in order to help the price competitiveness of their exports. They have largely succeeded: their currencies have been stable or, in the case of Indonesia, even depreciated against the US dollar. At the same time, they have experienced a large current account deficit (see Tables 3.1–3.3 and 3.5).

A policy of flexible exchange rates implies that the exchange rate is allowed to fluctuate according to market conditions. Given that the four countries studied here have a large overall surplus due to the massive inflow of foreign capital, a flexible-exchange-rate policy would result in an appreciation of their domestic currency. By allowing appreciation, they can reduce the burden of sterilization discussed earlier. Also, unless appreciation is not expected to be persistent, the magnitude of capital inflows might be reduced through a rise in the expected rate of depreciation.

Flexible exchange rates would also help reduce inflation by lowering import prices. Because these countries depend heavily on Japanese-produced industrial equipment and intermediate goods, the appreciation of the yen against the dollar resulted in higher domestic prices through simultaneous depreciation of the domestic currency against the yen. Although by the end of 1995 the yen had weakened against the dollar from its record levels in early 1995, the problem of having a principal market for exports (the United States) different from a principal source of imports (Japan) remains. In an effort to mitigate the effect of the yen rate on domestic prices, the Malaysian Government allowed an appreciation of about 4 per cent against the US dollar during the second quarter of 1995 (Wuchikomi *et al.*, 1995).

When the capital inflow is fully absorbed through nominal appreciation of the currency, the real value of the currency also appreciates, and this can lead to a large current-account deficit. If a country adopts a single policy variable such as the money supply or the exchange rate to absorb the impact of capital inflows, it is likely to experience side effects that are considered undesirable. It is thus better to employ both monetary and exchange-rate policy to maintain sustainable growth with price stability. In any case, the integration of the domestic economy into the world economy makes it more difficult to manage exchange rates and the money supply separately.

Fiscal policy is also a useful tool in dealing with capital inflows. Increasing the budget surplus can mitigate both inflationary pressure and real appreciation of the currency. Moreover, because a reduction in government expenditure has the same effect as a decrease in demand for loanable funds, it can lower interest rates. Thailand provides an example for the successful use of this approach.

However, due to the heavy demand on the government for investment in infrastructure and social services it is very difficult to have a large budget surplus in these countries. Furthermore, fiscal policy is generally designed on the basis of medium- and long-term considerations, which makes it too slow to allow timely intervention in dealing with short-term speculative capital inflows.

Encouraging Capital Outflows

Increasing capital outflows can play an important role in dealing with inflows. All the countries under consideration have lifted restrictions on capital outflows to reduce, directly and indirectly, the volume or the potential adverse effects of the capital inflow. However, the size of outflows is still negligible relative to that of inflows in all four countries. The main reason is the reluctance of domestic residents to invest abroad. This is particularly true for portfolio investment, because of lower returns and lack of requisite investment skills by domestic financial institutions.

However, central bank swap arrangements could be used to provide additional incentives for domestic residents to make portfolio investments abroad. When the accumulation of foreign reserves exceeds a desired level, the central bank sells a part of the reserves to domestic financial institutions in exchange for domestic currency. The buyers are required to invest the acquired funds abroad for a specified period. At the end of the period, the central bank reimburses the buyers for any loss resulting from the interest-rate differential between the domestic and foreign markets, as well as any loss from changes in the exchange rate. Germany used this method to stabilize the money supply in the 1970s, and the Philippines, Malaysia, and Singapore have also used it. Since pressure on the money supply from the foreign sector is transferred abroad during the swap period, a swap can contribute to stabilizing the domestic money supply and interest rates without new issues of central bank securities.

Direct Management of Capital Inflows

Employing a mix of monetary, fiscal, and exchange-rate policies, together with encouraging capital outflows, may not always be sufficient to counter surges in capital inflows. The authorities may then consider the introduction of a tax on foreign-exchange transactions or direct control measures such as limitations on the amount of domestic currency foreigners can purchase, restrictions on external borrowing by banks, and an increase in the reserve requirements.

Variable Deposit Requirement

Imposing variable deposit requirements (VDR) on incoming capital, i.e. differentiating reserve levels according to the specific type of a capital inflow and particular circumstances, reduces the volume of inflows. VDRs are similar to compensatory balances on loans as a way of raising effective interest rates. More specifically, they work as an implicit levy on capital transactions which, by increasing their cost, decreases demand.

A VDR is more market-efficient than quantitative restrictions but, because it limits domestic firms' access to international financial resources, it has to be implemented carefully. To the extent that FDI is a long-term investment in real productive capacity and contributes to economic development it should not normally be discouraged. VDRs on portfolio investment are difficult to impose for practical reasons. This leaves only foreign borrowing by residents as an area where a VDR might be used.

The reserve ratio can be adjusted according to the volume of capital inflows, but should be kept constant across maturities. It is also straightforward to determine the ratio that fully absorbs the interest-rate differential between home and abroad via the following relationship:

$$R' = \frac{R_f}{1 - D} + E_x$$

where R' is the effective interest rate on foreign borrowing, R_f the foreign interest rate, D the reserve ratio, and E_x the expected rate of currency depreciation during the borrowing period. Substituting the domestic interest rate for the effective rate, i.e. making it as expensive to borrow abroad as domestically, allows the equation to be solved for the reserve ratio (D). Required reserves would be deposited in non-interest-bearing foreign-currency accounts at the central bank until the loan is repaid.

Because a VDR hinders access to foreign financial resources that can enhance the competitiveness of domestic banks and firms, its use should be limited to periods of heavy capital inflow caused by a substantial increase in interest-rate differentials or associated with a rapid appreciation of the currency. In such cases, VDRs have been shown to be effective, at least in the short run.

Australia used this method when experiencing a surplus in its overall account coupled with a current-account deficit in the early 1970s. A rapid rise in domestic interest rates due to a restrictive monetary policy generated expectations of a currency appreciation and thus led to massive capital inflows. When the government imposed a non-interest-bearing reserve requirement on all foreign borrowing exceeding A$10 000, inflows were reduced. The reserve ratio, initially 25 per cent, was adjusted depending on the size of inflows.

Equally, Malaysia made an effort in January 1995 to curb the inflow of short-term capital by making foreign-currency borrowing from foreign banking institutions subject to a reserve requirement. This is a variant of the VDR, with a single reserve ratio being imposed, regardless of the volume of foreign borrowing. The requirement, coupled with other restrictions on capital inflows implemented in early 1994, contributed to reducing the amount of incoming foreign capital.

In the Republic of Korea, the legal framework for imposing a VDR is in place, but it has never been applied in practice. Its effects on capital inflows would undoubtedly be quite small because foreign borrowing by residents has not been important compared to FDI and foreign portfolio investment. The government continues directly to restrict borrowing from abroad by domestic firms and financial institutions. However, when this restriction is relaxed, the volume of such borrowing is expected to rise rapidly.

On the other hand, a VDR would be fairly effective in curtailing capital flows into Indonesia and Thailand, where foreign borrowing by residents has accounted for a large portion of capital inflows. However, the Thai government would probably be reluctant to use a VDR because Thailand has promoted itself as a regional financial centre, and such a move might jeopardize such a development.

A Levy on Foreign-Exchange Transactions

Transaction taxes are used in a number of financial markets: for example, by stock exchanges in the Republic of Korea and Japan, although the rates are very low. Foreign-exchange transaction taxes, both explicit and implicit, as a means of deterring short- term speculative capital flows, have been extensively analysed (Dornbusch, this volume; Eichengreen and Wyplosz, 1993; Eichengreen *et al.*, 1995; Felix, 1995; Garber and Taylor, 1995; and ul Haq *et al.*, 1996). An explicit levy on foreign-exchange transactions has been widely debated within the industrial economies and international organizations such as the United Nations and the IMF. The case for or against a global tax is beyond the scope of this study. In this section, only the practicality as well as desirability of imposing the tax unilaterally by an individual country is examined. There is also the question of whether the tax should be imposed on foreign-exchange transactions related to the current account. Such a tax increases costs for those trading goods and services, and thus might cut into the competitiveness of exports. To avoid this problem, the tax should perhaps be confined to capital account transactions, in particular, non-resident investments in domestic stocks, bonds and other short-term financial instruments. The tax also would have to include financial derivatives because they can mimic conventional financial instruments.

In general, the tax could be levied when foreign investors buy and sell domestic currency in connection with their trading in these financial instruments. Since foreign investors have to exchange foreign currencies for domestic currency at domestic financial institutions, administration of the tax would not be as difficult as it might appear. Moreover, in many countries, including the Republic of Korea, foreign investors have to register and invest through designated financial institutions, and hence find it much more difficult to avoid the tax than otherwise. It should be noted, however, that a tax that may be effective in some countries may not work in others because of differences in the financial and foreign-exchange system.

There are several ways to handle a transaction tax: it can be imposed on the seller or the purchaser of the domestic currency, or both. For foreign-exchange transactions, round-trip taxes are more effective. The tax rate can be varied according to the degree of capital-market openness and the level of short-term capital flows. It should be noted that the impact of such a tax is related to the length of the investment period. For example, when a 2 per cent round-trip tax is imposed (1 per cent for each buy and sell), the annualized decrease in return on investment is around 0.2 per cent over a 10-year period, but for a day-trade the decrease is about 124 600 per cent at an annual rate.

An implicit levy requires foreign investors to make non- interest-bearing deposits at the central bank when they sell foreign currencies for domestic currency. Examples of the use of such levies include Italy during the 1970s and Spain in 1992.[12] Unlike an explicit tax, an implicit tax hampers long-term investments if the deposit period is as long as the investment period. This can be mitigated by having the same deposit period for all transactions, one just long enough to decrease the returns on short-term investments to the point where they become unattractive. Care must be taken in deciding the reserve ratio, as it will discourage long-term investment if it is too high, while too low a reserve ratio will not accomplish the purpose.

Even if a comprehensive and clean currency transaction tax system is introduced, financial markets sooner or later are likely to find ways to evade the tax. One of the most likely ways to do so is to increase cross-border transactions that do not go through the local foreign-exchange market. To prevent this, a tax system in which cross-border payments as well as the purchase or sale of foreign exchange are taxed can be implemented, as suggested by Dornbusch in this volume. However, the cost of administering such a system may be too high to make it realistic. As Dornbusch points out, it will also increase offshore clearing of inflows and outflows, which lowers the effectiveness of the tax system. Moreover, even this system cannot prevent financial markets from evading the tax by developing complicated derivatives.

A foreign-exchange transaction tax increases transaction costs, which in theory should discourage the movement of short-term speculative capital. However, many observers doubt its effectiveness in this respect. It is sometimes argued that empirical studies have failed to demonstrate a relationship between transaction costs and volatility in domestic financial markets. This implies that a foreign-exchange transaction tax would not decrease the volatility of exchange rates or security prices (Schwert, 1993; Hakkio, 1994; and IMF, 1995b).

Even if it works, the tax has shortcomings. By decreasing the return on domestic securities, it makes them less attractive to foreign investors, and, to the extent that the tax reduces liquidity (the volume of transactions), it could make the foreign-exchange market more volatile. In addition, it raises equity problems if it is applied only to transactions by non-residents. A foreign-exchange transaction tax is also inconsistent with the aim of countries like the Republic of Korea, Thailand and Malaysia to become international financial centres, something that requires liberalization and internationalization of the domestic financial market.

Nonetheless, a transaction tax might have positive effects if applied flexibly, with the tax rate being adjusted to the amount of short-term capital flows. It could help lengthen the investment horizon of foreign investors and shift foreign participants in domestic financial markets from trading to investing. Even though it may not be able to reduce the volatility of stock or bond prices, it can at least influence the pace of capital flows. The revenue can be used to enhance the stability of the foreign-exchange market.

The use of a foreign-exchange transaction tax could mitigate the reluctance of developing countries to open their financial markets (Dornbusch, this volume). The Korean government plans to liberalize capital account transactions more aggressively in the future. With a tax in place, albeit at a zero rate in normal times, it could tell opponents of liberalization that it has a potential weapon against speculators.

Malaysia implemented direct controls on capital inflows in 1994 as the increased inflow of short-term speculative capital undermined the stability of its economy and financial markets. These might not have been necessary if a currency transaction tax had been available.

As was explained in Section IV, Thailand and Indonesia experienced turbulence in their financial markets due to a sudden outflow of foreign capital prompted by the Mexican crisis. They seem reluctant, however, to impose a transaction tax because they feel it would reduce the amount of capital available for their economic development. In these countries, the need for foreign capital to finance a high rate of domestic investment will continue for some time into the future. Rather than inviting difficulties in external financing, Thailand and Indonesia are willing to accept some volatility in capital movements as long as foreign capital, whether short-term speculative or not, is contributing to economic development. These countries also feel that imposing a currency transaction tax will cause damage to their financial markets, which are still in an infant stage of development, and may lead to retaliation by industrial countries which are major investors in these countries.

VI CONCLUSIONS

The Republic of Korea has gradually headed into capital account liberalization and its progress is expected to accelerate. This process, if well managed, will contribute to the development and globalization of the domestic economy as well as to greater efficiency of the domestic financial market. The inflow of foreign capital has been crucial to supporting a high rate of investment and output in Indonesia, Malaysia and Thailand. It appears that all three of these East Asian countries, unlike the Republic of Korea, are prepared to accept all types of foreign financing, regardless of their maturities, as long as foreign capital is needed to sustain rapid growth.

The ongoing liberalization of capital account transactions, the growing need for foreign capital, and favourable growth, are likely to combine in attracting a large amount of capital to the East Asian economies. However, at times, such a growth-oriented policy may suffer from an increase in the volatility of short-term capital flows, which may disturb domestic financial markets and macroeconomic stability, as it has in Malaysia. Faced with the instability problem, Malaysia had to resort to direct control measures to dampen short-term capital movements.

Maintaining the soundness and robustness of the domestic economy may be the most efficient way to offset any negative effects of speculative short-term capital, but when there is a surge of capital inflows, governments of all four countries are likely to consider measures to influence the level and characteristics of capital inflows, such as taxes on short-term bank deposits and other financial assets, reserve requirements against foreign borrowing, prudential limits on banks' offshore borrowing, and limits on consumption credit as suggested by the IMF (1995a). While it has shortcomings, the currency transaction tax would certainly be one of the most effective measures in reducing volatile short-term speculative capital movements.

Appendix 3.1 Estimates of financial market volatility in the Republic of Korea, Thailand, Malaysia and Indonesia, 1985–95

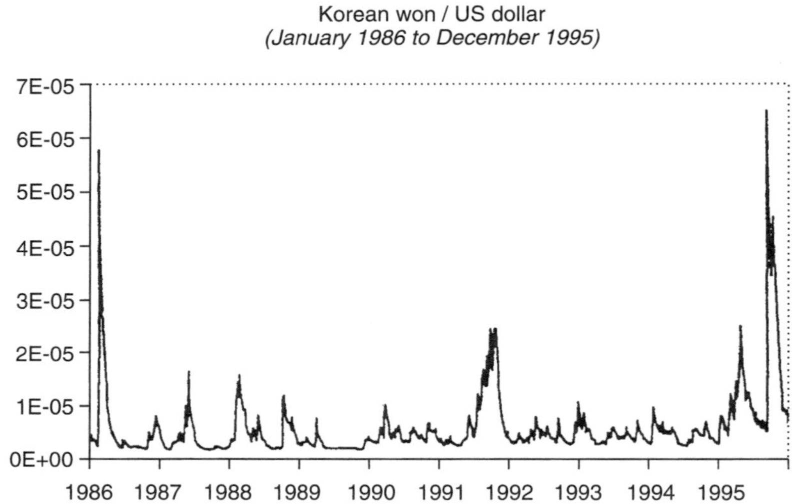

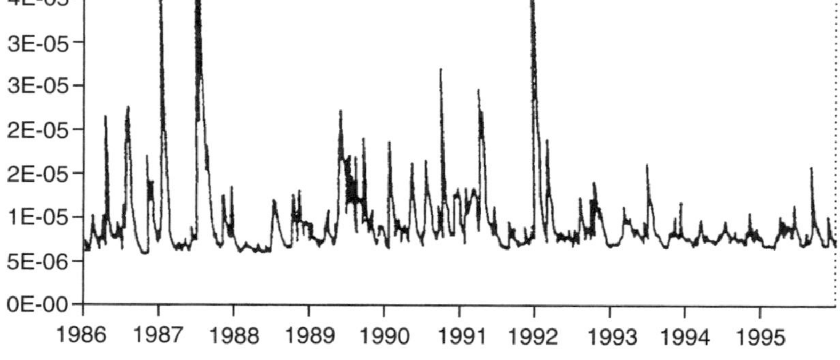

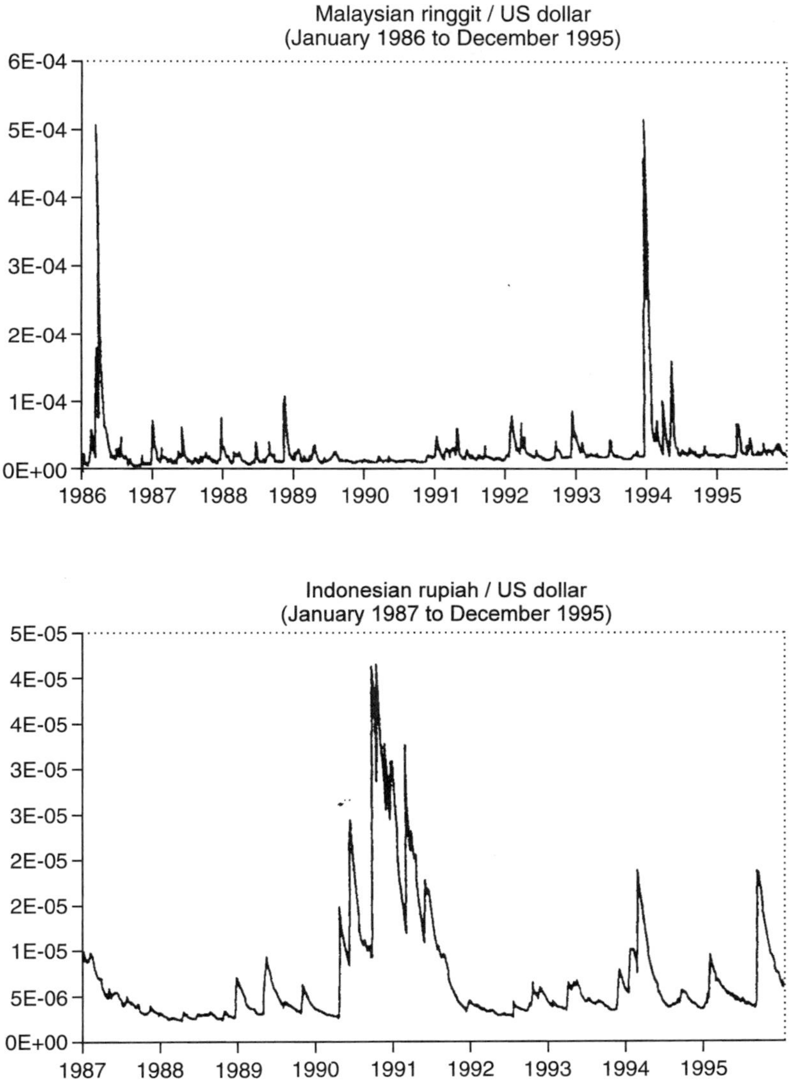

Figure 3.A1 GARCH variance of weekly exchange rates, 1986–95
Notes: The GARCH variance (h_1) of the rate of change in the weekly average exchange rate of the local currency against the United States dollar (R_1) is estimated as follows:

$$R_t = a + bR_{t-1} + u_t$$

where $u_t \,/\, \Omega_{t-1} \; - N(0, h_t)$, and

$$h_t = w + \alpha\, u_{t-1}^2 + \beta\, h_{t-1}$$

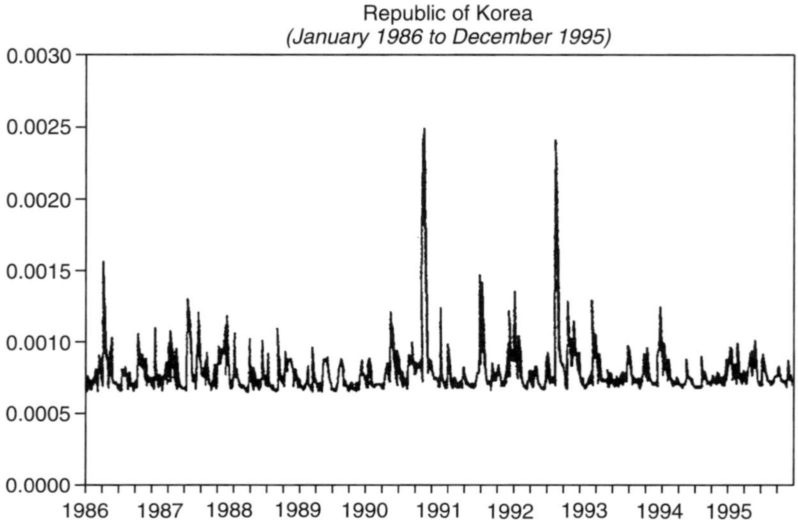
Republic of Korea
(January 1986 to December 1995)
0.0030
0.0025
0.0020
0.0015
0.0010
0.0005
0.0000
1986
1987
1988
1989
1990
1991
1992
1993
1994
1995

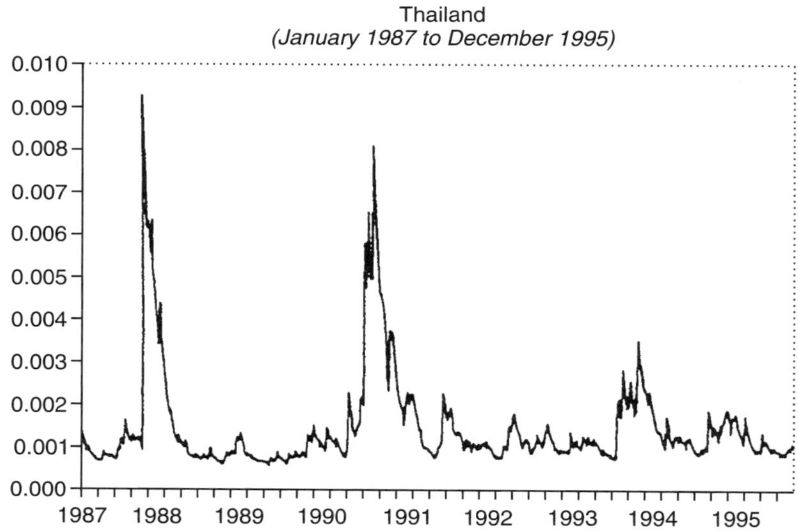
Thailand
(January 1987 to December 1995)
0.010
0.009
0.008
0.007
0.006
0.005
0.004
0.003
0.002
0.001
0.000
1987
1988
1989
1990
1991
1992
1993
1994
1995

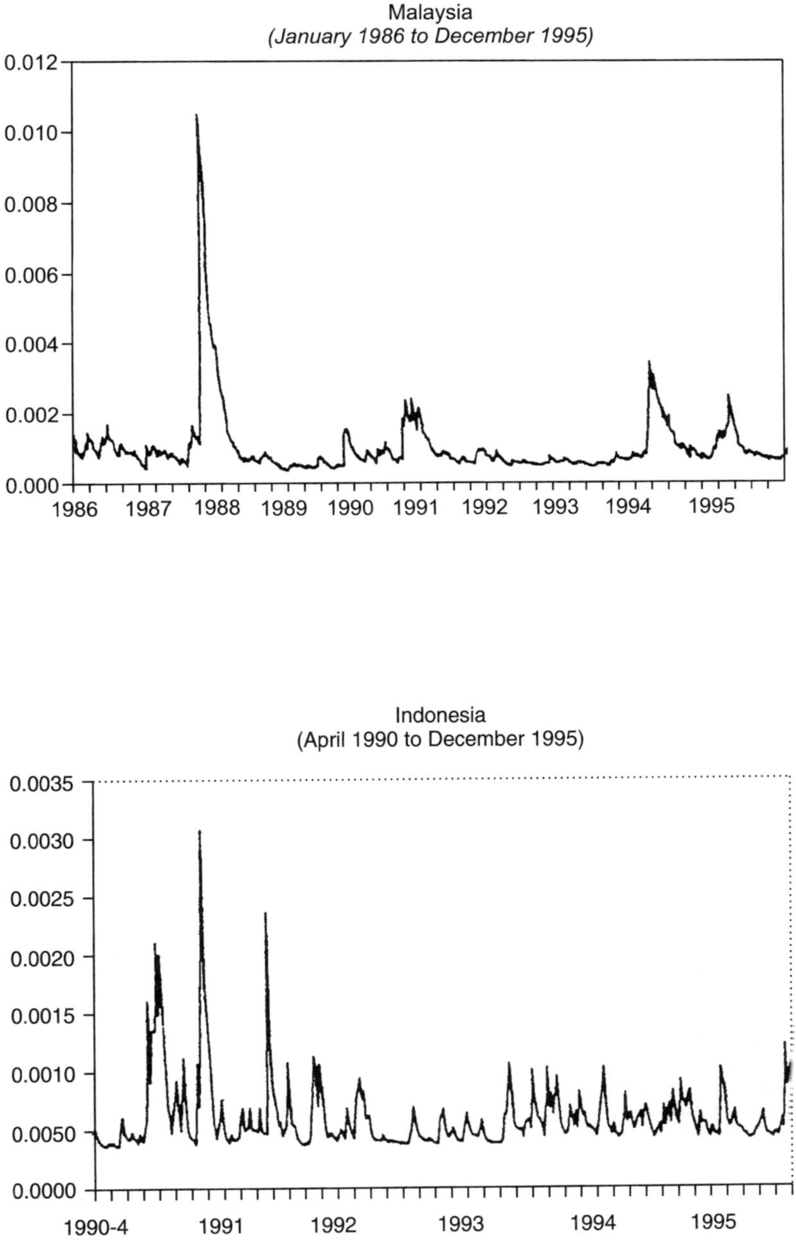

Figure 3.A2 GARCH variance of weekly stock returns, 1986–95

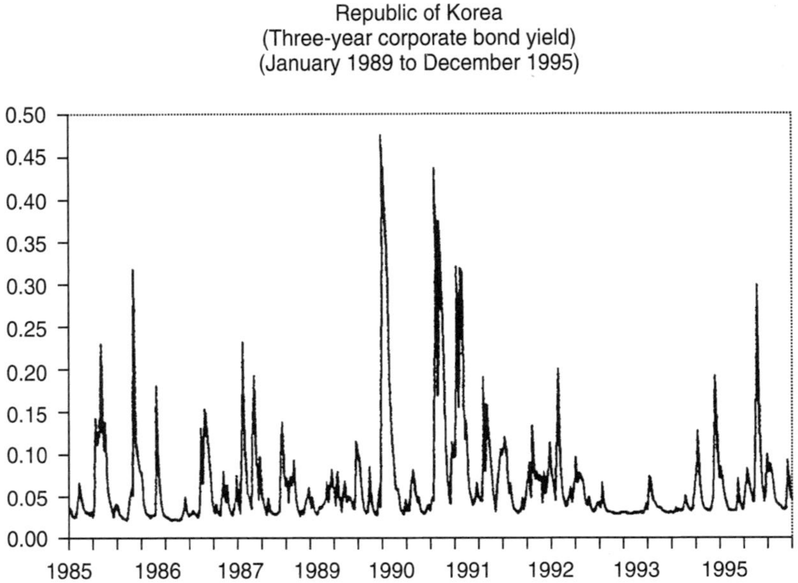

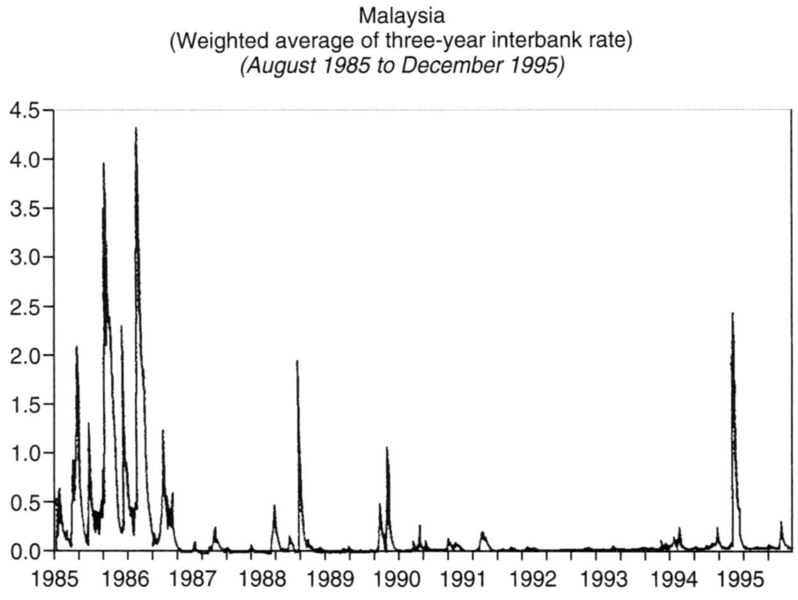

Figure 3.A3 GARCH variance of interest rates, 1985/9 to 1995

Notes

1. The authors would like to thank Gerry Helleiner, Yilmaz Akyüz and participants in the Conference on Global Capital Flows in Economic Development (organized by UNCTAD and the Jerome Levy Institute of Bard College) for their helpful comments. The authors are alone responsible for all remaining errors.
2. Asian developing countries include Asian newly industrializing economies (NIEs), the Association of South-East Asian Nations (ASEAN) and other Asian countries except Japan.
3. The Korea International Trust was the first fund designed specifically for foreign investors. It was established in 1981 by the Hankuk Investment Trust Corporation. The Korea Fund, organized under United States law and listed on the New York Stock Exchange, was launched in 1984. Others followed, including the Korea Europe Fund (based in Guernsey and listed in London) in 1987 and the Korea Asia Fund (based in the Cayman Islands and listed in Hong Kong and London) in 1991.
4. Japanese firms have been the most active foreign investors in these countries. The sharp appreciation of the yen *vis-à-vis* other major currencies after the Plaza Accord in 1985 drove many Japanese firms to move production facilities to South-East Asian countries to take advantage of their lower wages and natural resource costs. Japan accounted for 40 per cent of total inward FDI in the three countries during 1990–2.
5. Foreign investors held 10.0 per cent of listed stocks in the Republic of Korea by the end of 1995, 13.0 per cent in Malaysia by the end of 1994, and 28.9 per cent in Indonesia in March 1995. In Thailand, foreign investors accounted for about 20 per cent of the total turnover in 1994.
6. According to Euromoney (1995), the weights are 80–85 per cent for the US dollar, 8–15 per cent for the yen, and 4–10 per cent for the Deutschmark.
7. M3 in Malaysia is M2 plus all private sector deposits with finance companies, merchant banks and discount houses.
8. As of April 1995, the Indonesian foreign-exchange market was composed of 112 foreign-exchange banks and nine brokerage companies. Commercial banks are subject to limits on their foreign-exchange position. As of early 1996, a bank's overall position is limited to a weekly average of 25 per cent of its paid-up capital.
9. The Indonesian fiscal year ends on 31 March.
10. For Latin American countries these costs have been estimated by Lederman (1995) to amount to between 0.25 and 0.50 per cent of GDP.
11. UNCTAD (1995) pointed out that one important factor in determining vulnerability to sudden swings in capital flows is the extent to which residents issue and hold foreign-currency-denominated assets at home. It appears that the four countries studied in this paper are not very much exposed to this kind of vulnerability since they still apply strong restric-

tions on issuing and holding such assets. Furthermore, since domestic markets for foreign-currency-denominated assets are not well developed in these countries, acquisition of such assets by residents is very limited. Thus, residents of these countries obtain most foreign-currency-denominated assets abroad rather than at home.

12. When the September 1992 European currency crisis hit, Spain, in an attempt to avoid a realignment of the peseta, imposed an implicit levy on the purchase of foreign currencies by domestic financial institutions. (This is in the opposite direction from the levy considered here.)

References

Asian Development Bank (1995) *Asian Development Outlook* (New York: Oxford University Press).

Aziz, Z. (1994) 'Capital Flows and Monetary Management: the Malaysian Experience', paper presented at the Eleventh Pacific Basin Central Bank Conference, Hong Kong, 31 October–4 November.

Bank Indonesia, *Annual Report*, various issues.

Bank Indonesia, *Indonesian Financial Statistics*, various issues.

Bank Indonesia (1994) 'Indonesia's Experience in Managing Capital Inflows', Research Department, mimeo.

Bank of Korea, *National Accounts*, various issues.

Bank of Korea, *Monthly Bulletin*, various issues.

Bank of Korea, *Balance of Payments*, various issues.

Bank Negara Malaysia (1995) *Annual Report 1994.*

Bank of Thailand (1995) *Annual Economic Report 1994.*

Calvo, G., L. Leiderman and C. Reinhart (1993) 'Capital Flows and Real Exchange Rate Appreciation in Latin America: The Role of External Factors', *IMF Staff Papers*, vol. 40, no. 1 March, pp. 108–51.

DRI (1995) *World Markets Executive Overview*, Fourth Quarter.

Eichengreen, B. and C. Wyplosz (1993) 'The Unstable EMS', *Brookings Papers on Economic Activity*, no. 1.

Eichengreen, B., J. Tobin and C. Wyplosz (1995) 'Two Cases for Sand in the Wheels of International Finance', *Economic Journal*, vol. 105, pp. 162–72.

Euromoney (1995) *The 1995 Guide to Emerging Currencies*, London.

Felix, D. (1995) 'The Tobin Tax Proposal', *Futures*, vol. 27, no. 2, pp. 195–208.

Folkerts-Landau, D., G. Schinasi, M. Cassard, V. Ng, C. Reinhart and M. Spencer (1995) 'Effects of Capital Flows on the Domestic Financial Sectors in APEC Developing Countries' in M. Khan and C. Reinhart (eds) 'Capital Flows in the APEC Region', *IMF Occasional Paper*, no. 122.

Garber, P. and M. Taylor (1995) 'Sand in the Wheels of Foreign Exchange Markets: A Special Note', *Economic Journal*, vol. 105, pp. 173–80.

Hakkio, C. (1994) 'Should We Throw Sand in the Gears of Financial Markets?', *Federal Reserve Bank of Kansas City Economic Review*, vol. 79, no. 2, pp. 17–31.

IMF (1995a) 'Financial Transaction Taxes', mimeo.

IMF (1995b) *International Capital Markets: Developments, Prospects, and Policy Issues* (Washington, DC: International Monetary Fund).

IMF, *Balance of Payments Statistics*, various issues.

IMF, *International Financial Statistics*, various issues.

Khan, M. and C. Reinhart (1995) 'Macroeconomic Management in APEC Economies: The Response to Capital Inflows', in M. Khan and C. Reinhart (eds) 'Capital Flows in the APEC Region', *IMF Occasional Paper*, No. 122, pp. 15–30.

Kim, E. H. and V. Singal (1994) 'Opening Up of Stock Markets: Lessons from and for Emerging Markets', *Papers on Policy Issues*, no. 6, Korea Institute of Finance.

Kim, K. (1991) 'A Study on the Effectiveness of the Sterilization Policy in an Open Economy: The Case of Korea', *Studies in Financial and Monetary Economics*, vol. 28 [in Korean].

Kittisrikangwan, P., M. Supapongse and J. Jantarangs (1994) 'Monetary Policy Management in Thailand', *Papers on Policy Analysis and Assessment*, Economic Research Department, Bank of Thailand.

Korea Institute of Finance (1994) *Foreign Exchange System Reform in Korea* [in Korean].

Korea Ministry of Finance and the Economy (1994) *The Plan for Foreign Exchange System Reform* [in Korean].

Leiderman, L. (1995) 'Policy Lessons from Latin America's Experience with Capital Inflow' in R. Dornbusch and Y. C. Park (eds) *Financial Opening: Policy Lessons for Korea* (Seoul: Korea Institute of Finance and International Center for Economic Growth).

Mathieson, D. J. and L. Rojas-Suarez (1993) 'Liberalization of the Capital Account: Experiences and Issues', *IMF Occasional Paper*, no. 103 (March).

Nijathaworn, B. (1995a) 'Central Banking Policies in Thailand', paper presented at the Sixth APEEM Meeting, Bangkok, Thailand, 17–18 August.

Nijathaworn, B. (1995b) 'Capital Flows, Policy Response, and the Role of Fiscal Adjustment: The Thai Experience', paper presented at a World Bank Seminar on Managing Economic Reform under Capital Flow Volatility, Washington, DC, 30 May–2 June.

Nijathaworn, B. and T. Dejthamrong (1994) 'Capital Flows, Exchange Rate and Monetary Policy: Thailand's Recent Experience', *Papers on Policy Analysis and Assessment*, Economic Research Department, Bank of Thailand.

Park, Y. C. (1995) 'Korea's Experience with Managing Foreign Capital Flows', paper presented at the UNDP Meeting on Proposals for an International Currency Transaction Levy, New York, 10 October.

Schadler, S., M. Carkovic, A. Bennett and R. Kahn (1993) 'Recent Experiences with Surges in Capital Inflows', *IMF Occasional Paper*, no. 108.

Schwert, G. (1993) 'Stock Market Volatility', *Journal of Financial Services Research*, vol. 46, pp. 23–4.

Tivakul, A. and P. Svetarundra (1993) 'Financial Innovation and Modernization of the Thai Financial Market', paper presented at the OECD Workshop on Financial Innovation and Modernization of Financial Markets, Paris, 2–3 December.

ul Haq, M., I. Kaul and I. Grunberg (eds) (1996) *The Tobin Tax: Coping with Financial Volatility* (New York and Oxford: Oxford University Press).

UNCTAD (1995) *Trade and Development Report 1995* (New York and Geneva: United Nations).

Vichyanond, P. (1994) *Thailand's Financial System: Structure and Liberalization*, Research Monograph no. 11 (Bangkok: Thailand Development Research Institute).

Wuchikomi, S., M. Murakami and Y. Hagiwara (1995) 'Foreign Exchange Rate Policy and the Role of the Yen in East Asian Countries', *Bank of Tokyo Quarterly* (Autumn) [in Japanese].

4 Capital Inflows and Macroeconomic Policy in Sub-Saharan Africa

Louis Kasekende, Damoni Kitabire and Matthew Martin[1]

I INTRODUCTION

During the last three years, there has been an expanding literature on private capital inflows to developing countries. In 1992 and 1993, attention focused on the rise in such inflows, their causes and nature. Gradually, it moved to their potential macroeconomic impact and the policy implications. In 1994 and 1995, following events in Mexico, it has concentrated on the sustainability of the inflows, and the policy implications of potential reversal.

Virtually all of the studies have focused on Latin America, though some authors have also examined East Asian experiences. Analysis of Eastern Europe is extremely rare (Calvo, Sahay and Vegh, 1995; Griffith-Jones, 1995), and that of Africa is virtually non-existent (with the notable exception of the excellent study by Asea and Reinhart, 1995). Even the most comprehensive recent analysis and survey of the literature (Fernandez-Arias and Montiel, 1995) has concluded that there is only impressionistic evidence of private capital inflows to sub-Saharan Africa, where 'capital inflows have not materialized'. Africa has continued to be analysed from the point of view that most of its capital inflows causing 'Dutch Disease' effects are aid inflows (see, for example, Younger, 1992).

The key areas examined in the literature have been the scale and composition of private capital inflows, their causes and sustainability, their effects on macroeconomic stability, and their responsiveness to policy measures. This chapter analyses the characteristics of capital inflows to sub-Saharan Africa in each of these areas, showing the similarities and differences with other regions of the developing world. A debate is also developing as to the nature of capital Africa *should* attract. Scholars have warned that short-term capital inflows, subject to abrupt reversal, will be very disruptive to the domestic financial sector, in particular in the presence of existing weaknesses in that sector (Lipumba, 1994; Calvo, Sahay and Vegh, 1995). Some argue for foreign direct investment (FDI) which is less susceptible to transient financial shocks. But counter-arguments have also been made to the effect that FDI is equally volatile, as dividends and retained earnings will be quickly repatriated during a financial crisis.

It is important to emphasize at the outset that both national and international data on capital inflows to Africa are extremely unreliable. Data issues in other regions have centred on distinguishing between private and official inflows; gross and net inflows; short-and long-term capital; bank and non-bank flows; and between debt and non-debt-creating flows. It has been necessary to rely fairly extensively on data from either the IMF (*International Financial Statistics*), OECD (*Financing and External Debt of Developing Countries*) or the World Bank (*World Debt Tables*) (Fernandez-Arias and Montiel, 1995). For many countries in sub-Saharan Africa the data problems are more fundamental: they have poor recording systems for virtually all capital inflow data, and many inflows are recorded in the current account or under errors/omissions.[2] In addition, even superficial comparison of global and country data indicates huge underestimates and unreliable categorizations of inflows in global data and particularly for those for sub-Saharan Africa.

Because of data and other limitations, the scope of this chapter is limited. It focuses on six countries for which reasonably reliable data are available (Kenya, South Africa, Tanzania, Uganda, Zambia and Zimbabwe), with particular emphasis on the experiences of Uganda, Zambia and Tanzania. The last country witnessed one of the largest surges in capital inflows in the early 1990s with dramatic macroeconomic effects.[3] A brief summary of the liberalization process in the above mentioned countries is given in Appendix 4.1.

It also has to be recognized that there are diverse experiences in Africa, not least in the speed and sequencing of countries' policy reforms (Kasekende and Martin, 1995). The policy regime in a number of countries in the region is nevertheless now more conducive to both domestic and foreign investment than it recently was. Foreign-exchange markets have been extensively liberalized to a point where even the capital account has been highly decontrolled. Some countries are currently receiving inflows which are significant relative to GDP, and the less desirable effects of such inflows are emerging. In the recent past, Kenya, Uganda and Zambia are among those that have experienced disruptive effects originating from capital inflows. The reform of the policy regime has frequently been credited for the resurgence in capital inflows to selected countries in Africa, especially by the IMF and World Bank. While domestic policy reforms have, without doubt, contributed to the marked improvement of capital inflows to Africa, they cannot fully account for the varied country experiences.

II SCALE AND COMPOSITION OF PRIVATE CAPITAL INFLOWS

In absolute terms, the scale of private capital inflows to other developing regions dwarfs inflows to sub-Saharan Africa (SSA). According to the latest World Bank estimates, based on capital account and equity–debt flows, inflows to all developing countries averaged more than $131 billion a year during 1990–4, peaking at about $190 billion in 1993 (Table 4.1). Of this amount about $2.1 billion a year went to SSA countries, peaking at about $3.4 billion in 1990. Even in relation to macroeconomic variables such as GDP or exports, inflows to SSA based on capital account recordings were much lower than those to Latin America, East or South Asia. However, when private transfers are included in these flows, they are comparable with or even higher than those to other developing countries in Asia and Latin America.

The main reason for the underestimates of inflows to SSA in published global databases (apart from the fact that they do not show the most recent information) is the specific composition of inflows to many SSA countries, which makes them much harder to measure, and the absence of recording systems for the main types of inflows.[4]

Firstly, the main inflows to SSA have been difficult to record or classify. With the loosening of borrowing restrictions, short-term bank loans to the private sector for trade financing have grown considerably. At the same time, because private inflows have not historically been important, virtually no country in SSA has adequate recording systems for monitoring private sector debt, especially short-term debt. Most countries do not even attempt to record inflows, believing that such 'intrusion' may be seen and prove to be counter-productive to the spirit and intent of liberalization. Moreover, large amounts of capital inflows by residents and non-residents are misrecorded in the current account under a residual item, 'private transfers'.[5]

Table 4.1 Capital flows to developing countries and sub-Saharan Africa, 1990–4 ($ billion)

	1990	*1991*	*1992*	*1993*	*1994*
All developing countries					
FDI	24.10	34.40	45.20	68.50	78.20
Portfolio investment	2.80	7.10	13.90	45.80	34.50
Long-term private flows	5.80	10.30	19.10	23.10	20.40
Private flows (minimum)	32.70	51.80	78.20	137.40	133.10
Short-term flows	17.00	20.90	39.30	33.60	23.70
Private non-guaranteed flows (PNG)	9.30	8.40	20.70	19.80	27.40
Private flows (maximum)	59.00	81.10	138.20	190.80	184.20
Long-term official flows	28.40	27.60	23.20	23.40	16.80
Grants	25.10	32.50	27.10	23.60	22.80
IMF credit	0.05	3.20	1.20	0.70	1.60
Total all flows	112.55	144.40	189.70	238.50	225.40
Profits on FDI	−17.70	−18.50	−21.20	−23.10	−25.10
Interest on long-term private debt	−32.50	−30.40	−26.90	−23.80	−28.00
Private transfers (minimum)	−17.50	2.90	30.10	90.50	80.00
Interest on PNG	−4.90	−5.60	−5.90	−6.40	−7.60
Interest on short-term debt	−15.50	−17.60	−15.30	−16.70	−18.10
Private transfers (maximum)	−11.60	9.00	68.90	120.80	105.40
Interest on long-term official debt	−20.40	−22.10	−22.10	−24.20	−26.20
IMF charges	−2.50	−2.50	−2.40	−2.30	−1.80
Total net transfers	19.05	47.70	95.90	142.00	118.60
Sub-Saharan Africa					
FDI	0.90	1.90	1.80	1.90	2.30
Portfolio investment	0.00	0.00	0.00	0.20	0.90
Long-term private flows	−0.03	0.04	−1.40	0.30	−0.40
Private flows (minimum)	0.87	1.94	0.40	2.40	2.80
Short-term flows	2.30	−0.50	1.20	0.80	−1.90
PNG (to private sector)	0.20	0.04	0.10	0.02	−0.20
Private flows (maximum)	3.37	1.48	1.70	3.22	0.70
Long-term official flows	4.70	4.00	4.90	4.10	4.00
Grants	10.40	9.60	9.60	8.50	8.50
IMF credit	−0.30	−0.03	0.00	−0.20	0.45
Total all flows	18.17	15.05	16.20	15.62	13.65
Profits on FDI	−1.70	−1.60	−1.70	−1.70	−1.80
Interest on long-term private debt	−1.30	−1.40	−1.50	−0.60	−0.80
Private transfers (minimum)	−2.13	−1.06	−2.80	0.10	0.20

Interest on short-term debt	−0.70	−0.60	−0.60	−0.50	−0.50
Interest on long-term official debt	−2.40	−2.90	−1.80	−2.10	−2.40
Private transfers (maximum)	−2.73	−5.02	−3.90	−1.68	−4.80
Interest on PNG	−0.30	−0.30	−0.30	−0.30	−0.20
IMF charges	−0.20	−0.20	−0.20	−0.10	−0.10
Total net transfers	11.57	8.05	10.10	10.32	7.85

Note: A large portion – but not all – of short-term and private non-guaranteed inflows are private. The private inflows/transfers are shown excluding (minimum) and including (maximum) short-term and private non-guaranteed flows.
Source: World Bank IECIF Database, January 1995.

These transfers have risen dramatically since SSA countries liberalized their foreign-exchange systems, by introducing, first, 'own-funds' imports, where no questions were asked about the source of the funds, and later, foreign-exchange bureaux, where all current-account transactions could be conducted. Originally, it was assumed that the sources of funds for the bureau system were unrecorded exports and workers' remittances. However, more recently it has become clear that, because of inadequate monitoring and supervision of bureaux transactions, virtually any capital account transaction could be conducted through the bureaux.[6] In other words, the current account is entirely porous and the capital account has effectively been liberalized. In some countries, large amounts of flight capital have returned (or left) through the bureaux; and non-residents are thought to conduct frequent, albeit small, capital account transactions there. However, inadequate recording procedures make it impossible to separate out the proportion of bureaux inflows which are capital-related, let alone to distinguish among types of capital-related inflows. In short, inflows related to the current account produce 'capital inflows' whose scale in relation to the economy is comparable to, and in some cases exceeds, that of other regions.

The more easily measurable inflows to SSA have fallen since the early 1990s, from around \$5 billion a year to under \$1.2 billion. The composition of these inflows evolved somewhat differently from that in other regions (see Table 4.2):

- Medium- and long-term commercial lending to both the public and the private sector collapsed after the debt crisis, as it did in Latin America, but to an even more dramatic degree. In 1978–82, such lending accounted for around half of total inflows, but in 1990–3 outflows virtually offset all non-debt inflows.

- Short-term bank loans have always accounted for a larger proportion of inflows than in other regions and became even more pronounced in 1990–3; they were only around 20 per cent of inflows in 1978–82.
- FDI rose sharply as a proportion of total inflows over the period 1990–3, but remained relatively small (at around $1.6 billion a year, lower in real terms than in the early 1980s) and confined largely to six SSA countries.
- Portfolio investment has grown recently, with booms in most regional stock markets and the launching of several new regional portfolio funds, but (with the exception of South Africa) still remains relatively small; in 1990–3 it did not exceed $120 million a year.

Table 4.2 Composition of private capital inflows to developing regions, 1978–82 and 1990–3 (per cent of total)

	1978–82			*1990–3*		
	Latin America	*Asia*	*Sub-Saharan Africa*	*Latin America*	*Asia*	*Sub-Saharan Africa*
FDI	15.1	15.0	9.8	33.0	37.5	140.3
Portfolio investment	4.9	3.6	0.0	68.1	14.2	10.9
Long-term bank loans	63.6	53.9	53.9	−32.1	21.7	−143.5
Short-term loans	16.4	27.5	36.3	30.5	27.0	92.3

Source: IMF, *International Financial Statistics*, various issues; and World Bank, *World Debt Tables*, various issues.

Aggregate net private capital inflows to the six countries in our sample were greatly influenced by the experience of South Africa. This country was a net exporter of capital in the period 1986–9. The huge outflow of private capital from South Africa resulted in the sample countries recording a total net export of private capital of $6195.6 million in the period 1986–9. However, the direction of flow was reversed in the period 1990–3 to a net inflow of $2072.6 million. Excluding South Africa, the five remaining countries received private capital inflows amounting to $851.4 million in 1986–9, decreasing slightly to $868.6 million in 1990–3 (see Table 4.3).

The experience of Zambia shows a unique (in our sample) trend in private capital inflows. Net private capital inflows amounted to $714

Table 4.3 Capital flows to selected countries in sub-Saharan Africa, 1986–9 and 1990–3 ($ million)

	Including private transfers			*Excluding private transfers*		
	1986–9	*1990–3*	*1986–93*	*1986–9*	*1990–3*	*1986–93*
Kenya	647.7	779.6	1427.3	327.0	252.0	579.0
South Africa	−6655.0	1243.0	−5412.0	−7047.0	1204.0	−5843.0
Tanzania	765.2	943.9	1709.1	−214.0	−8.0	−222.0
Uganda	450.0	586.7	1036.7	31.0	−20.0	11.0
Zambia	597.0	200.0	797.0	714.0	240.0	954.0
Zimbabwe	−97.7	471.2	373.5	−6.6	404.6	398.0
Total	−4292.8	4224.4	−68.4	−6195.6	2072.6	−4123.0

Note: A minus sign indicates a net outflow.
Source: IMF, *International Financial Statistics*, various issues; and World Bank, *World Debt Tables*, various issues.

Table 4.4 Private capital flows to selected countries in sub-Saharan Africa, 1986–9 and 1990–3 (per cent of GDP)

	Including private transfers			*Excluding private transfers*		
	1986–9	*1990–3*	*1986–93*	*1986–9*	*1990–3*	*1986–93*
Kenya	1.71	2.75	2.15	0.86	0.89	0.87
South Africa	−2.44	0.29	−0.77	−2.59	0.28	−0.83
Tanzania	5.50	9.05	7.02	−1.54	−0.08	−0.91
Uganda	3.21	4.69	3.91	0.22	−0.16	0.04
Zambia	6.00	1.69	3.66	7.18	2.03	4.38
Zimbabwe	−0.44	2.01	0.82	−0.03	1.72	0.87
Total	−1.16	0.81	−0.01	−1.67	0.40	−0.46

Note: A minus sign indicates a net outflow.
Source: IMF, *International Financial Statistics*, various issues; and World Bank, *World Debt Tables*, various issues.

million in the period 1986–9 (see Table 4.3). Subsequently, they declined significantly to $240 million. By contrast, the remaining countries in the sample experienced sizeable growth in net inflows during 1990–3 compared to the period 1986–9.

It is estimated that net private capital flows of the six countries as a ratio to GDP moved to an inflow of 0.8 per cent in 1990–3, from a net outflow of 1.2 per cent in 1986–9. Zimbabwe and Uganda recorded an increase in net private capital flows from −0.4 and 3.2 per cent in 1986–9 to 2.0 and 4.7 per cent in 1990–3, respectively. Similarly,

Kenya and Tanzania experienced an increase in net private capital inflows from 1.7 and 5.5 per cent to 2.8 and 9.1 per cent of GDP, respectively, in the two reference periods (Table 4.4).

By contrast, private capital inflows as a ratio to GDP fell markedly in Zambia, from 6.0 per cent in 1986–9 to 1.7 per cent in 1990–3. One factor distinguishing Zambia from the other five countries is that macroeconomic instability was much greater in 1990–3 compared to 1986–9. In particular, inflation increased from an average of about 50 per cent in 1986–9 to an average of 149 per cent in 1990–3. In the cases of Kenya and Zimbabwe, the moderate increase in inflation between the two periods did not discourage private capital inflows.

Overall, trends in inflows to SSA are similar to those for other small countries relying predominantly on short-term bank loans and FDI rather than medium-and long-term loans or portfolio inflows. In terms of their sustainability, it is significant that the less volatile medium- and long-term bank loans and FDI virtually cancel each other out, leaving SSA economies excessively dependent on short-term bank inflows, which could be unsustainable (Table 4.5).

As indicated above, South Africa dwarfs the other five countries as it accounts for about 58 per cent of total net private capital inflows to the six countries in the sample. Apart from the size of inflows, the nature of inflows to South Africa is quite different from those of the remaining countries in the sample. South Africa received significant resources under the categories of private long-term debt and portfolio

Table 4.5 Composition of private capital inflows to sub-Saharan Africa,[a] 1986–9 and 1990–3

	$ million			*Per cent share in total private capital inflows*
	1986–9	*1990–3*	*1986–93*	*1990–3*
FDI	279.8	475.2	755.0	11.2
Short-term debt, net	−3061.0	1379.0	−1682.0	32.6
Long-term debt, net	−2235.0	−1502.0	−3737.0	−35.5
Portfolio investment	−1179.4	1720.4	541.0	40.7
Private transfers	1902.8	2151.8	4054.6	50.9
Total	−4292.8	4224.4	−68.4	100.0

[a] Kenya, South Africa, United Republic of Tanzania, Uganda, Zambia, and Zimbabwe.

Source: IMF, *International Financial Statistics*, various issues; and World Bank, *World Debt Tables*, various issues.

investments, equivalent to 0.8 per cent and 0.4 per cent of GDP, respectively, in the 1990–3 period. Of the remaining five countries, it is only Zimbabwe that received (still meagre) inflows under these two categories . The surprising finding is that even for countries that have had stock markets for a relatively long period, e.g. Zimbabwe and Kenya, investors are yet to be significantly attracted to shareholding in domestic investment.

The other interesting finding revealed by the data is that investor confidence has greatly improved in South Africa. In the period 1990–2, South Africa received substantial resources under the category of short-term inflows (net), amounting to $2181 million with a peak in 1991. But since 1992 there has been a shift in favour of portfolio investment and private long-term debt.

Short-term capital inflows have exhibited a very high degree of volatility. In a number of instances countries have recorded high inflows in one year followed by a net outflow in the subsequent recording period. For example, in 1987, Kenya received net inflows under this heading amounting to 2.6 per cent of GDP, but this was followed by an outflow equivalent to –0.8 per cent of GDP. The experience was repeated in 1990–1, when Kenya allowed holders of foreign-exchange certificates to negotiate premiums in secondary market trading. As a result, Kenya received net short-term inflows amounting to about $300 million (equivalent to 3.2 per cent of GDP) in 1990, but, following the reversal of the policy, Kenya experienced an outflow of $273 million (equivalent to 3.6 per cent of GDP) in 1991. Similarly, Zambia has recorded wide swings in net short-term capital inflows. Net inflows equivalent to 4.2 per cent of GDP were recorded in Zambia in 1988; these were followed by outflows in 1989 and 1990 equivalent to 2.4 and 3.3 per cent of GDP, respectively.

FDI has been mainly directed to Zambia in the period 1986–93, equivalent to 3.6 and 2.9 per cent of GDP in 1986–9 and 1990–3, respectively. This reflects investments in the mining industries. Kenya, Tanzania and Zimbabwe have also benefited from FDI, but the inflows as a percentage of GDP have only been between 0.16 and 0.3 per cent. For the six countries aggregated, FDI amounted to $279.8 million in 1986–9, increasing to $475.2 million in 1990–3, equivalent to 0.09 per cent of GDP (Table 4.6).

The other development that distinguishes South Africa and Zambia from the remaining four countries is that the latter countries received substantial resources recorded as private transfers. If such transfers are included in the broad category of private capital flows, the six

Table 4.6 Composition of capital flows to sub-Saharan Africa, by country, 1986–9 and 1990–3

	FDI		*Short-term debt, net*		*Long-term debt, net*		*Portfolio investment*		*Private transfers*		*Total*		
	1986–9	*1990–3*	*1986–9*	*1990–3*	*1986–9*	*1990–3*	*1986–9*	*1990–3*	*1986–9*	*1990–3*	*1986–9*	*1990–3*	*1986–93*
In $ million													
Kenya	138.0	84.0	87.0	115.0	102.0	53.0	0.0	0.0	320.7	527.6	647.7	779.6	1427.3
South Africa	–171.0	–26.0	–3416.0	1241.0	–2376.0	–1760.0	–1084.0	1749.0	392.0	39.0	–6655.0	1243.0	–5412.0
Tanzania	1.0	31.0	–215.0	–39.0	39.0	205.0	0.0	0.0	979.2	951.9	765.2	943.9	1709.1
Uganda	3.0	7.0	28.0	–27.0	...	...	0.0	0.0	419.0	606.7	450.0	586.7	1036.7
Zambia	360.0	342.0	354.0	–102.0	...	...	0.0	0.0	–117.0	–40.0	597.0	200.0	797.0
Zimbabwe	–51.2	37.2	101.0	191.0	...	...	–95.4	–28.6	–91.1	66.6	–97.7	471.2	373.5
Total	279.8	475.2	–3061.0	1379.0	–2235.0	–1502.0	–1179.4	1720.4	1902.8	2151.8	–4292.8	4224.4	–68.4
As per cent of GDP													
Kenya	0.36	0.30	0.23	0.40	0.27	0.19	0.00	0.00	0.85	1.86	1.71	2.75	2.15
South Africa	–0.06	–0.01	–1.25	0.29	–0.87	–0.40	–0.40	0.40	0.14	0.01	–2.44	0.29	–0.77
Tanzania	0.01	0.30	–1.54	–0.37	0.00	0.00	0.00	0.00	7.04	9.12	5.50	9.05	7.02
Uganda	0.02	0.06	0.20	–0.22	0.00	0.00	0.00	0.00	2.99	4.85	3.21	4.69	3.91
Zambia	3.62	2.90	3.56	–0.86	0.00	0.00	0.00	0.00	–1.18	–0.34	6.00	1.69	3.66
Zimbabwe	–0.23	0.16	0.46	0.81	0.18	0.87	–0.43	–0.12	–0.41	0.28	–0.44	2.01	0.82
Total	0.08	0.09	–0.83	0.26	–0.60	–0.29	–0.32	0.33	0.51	0.41	–1.16	0.81	–0.01

Source: IMF, *International Financial Statistics*, various issues; and World Bank, *World Debt Tables*, various issues.

countries exported just over $4292.8 million in 1986–9 but received over $4224.4 million in 1990–3. Excluding South Africa, the region was a net recipient of private capital during both of the two sub-periods; private capital inflows increased from $2363 million in 1986–90 to $2981 million in 1990–3. In the latter period private transfers accounted for over 50 per cent of total private capital inflows, equivalent to about 0.5 per cent of GDP. Most of the private transfers were accounted for by Kenya, Uganda and Tanzania. These three countries recorded receipts of private transfers equivalent to 2.0, 4.9 and 9.1 per cent of GDP, respectively. Zimbabwe also recorded a marked increase in private transfers during the 1990s, especially in 1992 when it recorded receipts equivalent to 0.6 per cent of GDP.

It has not been possible to collect data on costs or maturity of inflows, particularly of bonds, or on the sources of inflows (especially the division between domestic and foreign investors). This is unfortunate because these variables could be expected to have major implications for the sustainability or volatility of inflows and the resulting policy response (see IMF, 1995a; and Ffrench-Davis and Griffith-Jones, 1995).

III CAUSES OF CAPITAL FLOWS

Having discussed the main features of the capital flows, we now examine the factors that have led to the increase in inflows. The factors underlying capital inflows to developing countries tend to be divided into external or 'push' factors, on the one hand, and domestic or 'pull' factors, on the other.

The 'pull' factors include:

- political and economic reforms boosting confidence in the economy;
- debt restructuring to reduce the debt overhang and enhance the sustainability of foreign-exchange inflows;
- liberalization of foreign-exchange markets and the current or capital account of the balance of payments;
- proliferation of specific incentives and simplification of procedures for direct and portfolio investment (Gooptu, 1994);
- liberalization of restrictions on private sector foreign borrowing;
- very high real domestic interest rates (including the effect of changes in the exchange rate).

The major 'push' factors have been identified as:

- the decline in international interest rates;
- the cyclical downturn in developed countries, which reduced economic activity and demand for investment funds;
- the trend towards diversification of assets by portfolio investors, until attainment of the maximum stock of investments in emerging markets that such investors wish to hold;
- changes in regulations in developed countries which made investment in emerging markets easier and more profitable.

Overall, the literature has concluded that both factors were involved, with some stressing 'push' factors, especially interest-rate differentials (Calvo, Leiderman and Reinhart, 1993a and 1994; Asea and Reinhart, 1995; Chuhan *et al.*, 1993; Fernandez-Arias, 1994), and others stressing 'pull' factors (Hernandez and Rudolph, 1995; Niehans, 1994).

One of the problems with much of the literature on causes of capital inflows is that it tends to rely on econometric analysis of price influences (notably interest-rate differentials), taking too little account of the influence on inflows of structural factors in individual countries or of the subjective 'sentiment' factors influencing international capital markets (Fernandez-Arias and Montiel, 1995). Some of the literature has attempted to judge the influence of different 'pull' factors by trends in the stock markets of the recipient countries, or in their secondary market debt prices, as if these trends were objective measures of the credibility of the recipient country. This is a particularly dubious method to use for SSA countries, where there are large subjective 'risk premia' in all such prices, and where country-level distortions in market behaviour, based on speculative information, can influence prices.

With the exception of Asea and Reinhart (1995), there has been little econometric analysis of the causes of capital inflows to SSA countries. No doubt this is partly because of lack of data. It seems, however, that 'push' factors, notably United States short-term interest rates, have had much less of an impact on private flows in Africa than in other regions (Asea and Reinhart, 1995), suggesting that inflows might be more sustainable; on the other hand, African interest rates were highly significant (ibid.).

As a result of the poor sequencing of adjustment reforms, it seems likely that several transitory 'pull' factors were particularly important in SSA countries, notably:

- Extremely high real domestic interest rates on treasury bills and central bank bills were a significant factor in capital inflows to Zambia, Kenya, Uganda and Zimbabwe during the initial stages of financial liberalization (see also Asea and Reinhart, 1995). In a number of countries in SSA, financial liberalization was launched at a time when the government budget still depended heavily on bank financing. Efforts to manage liquidity and at the same time mobilize resources to finance the fiscal deficit through the sale of government and/or central bank paper resulted in high discount rates and caused a self-sustaining cycle through currency appreciation and even higher interest rates, attracting further capital inflows (see also Galbis, 1993; Montiel, 1995; and Roe and Sowa, 1994). In addition, private sector borrowers were pushed to seek foreign loans in order to avoid high domestic interest rates.
- Temporary booms in export prices attracted large export pre-financing loans and speculative capital inflows (as in earlier periods – see Hadjimichael *et al.*, 1995). This was particularly the case in Kenya and Uganda in 1994–5.

Spillover effects from Mexico on SSA, with the exception of South Africa, are not thought to have been great, having been overruled by regional factors. A review of South Africa's international borrowing, however, reveals that delayed entry of South Africa into the international capital markets was to a great extent due to the Mexican crisis. A global bond issue by South Africa in December 1994 did not perform well, as investors shifted to higher quality bonds at the time. Interest in South African bonds was only regained in the second half of 1995, influenced by their high yield and the stable South African exchange rate. Capital inflows to Kenya and Uganda have varied sharply with perceptions of their relative economic prospects and arbitrage opportunities from divergent (regional) trends in interest and exchange rates. Similarly, there is growing evidence that capital inflows to South Africa have influenced the entire Southern African region, partly because South African companies are borrowing for investment in neighbouring countries.

A deeper analysis of the numbers in the sample countries in the study reveals that most short-term borrowing is in the form of trade credit. Following the liberalization of foreign-exchange markets in these countries, exporters and importers found it cheaper to access short-term trade financing externally since foreign interest rates were far lower than interest rates prevailing in these countries

Table 4.7 Real lending rates in selected countries of sub-Saharan Africa, 1986–94[a] (per cent per annum)

	1986	*1987*	*1988*	*1989*	*1990*	*1991*	*1992*	*1993*	*1994*
Kenya	10.1	8.8	6.7	6.6	2.4	0.2	−9.5	9.2	–
South Africa[b]	10.0	15.0	18.0	18.0	18.0	17.0	14.0	13.0	13.0
Tanzania	−20.4	−20.9	−3.0	0.4	10.3	8.7	8.9	15.6	–
Uganda	−128.0	−238.0	−143.6	−40.2	−119.0	−12.9	−20.9	13.9	–
Zambia	−23.8	−22.0	−38.0	n.a.	−72.0	n.a.	−142.4	−76.0	–
Zimbabwe	−1.3	−0.5	5.6	0.1	−5.4	−7.3	−7.1	8.4	–

[a] Real lending rates are equivalent to nominal interest rates net of inflation.
[b] Figures are for the nominal bank rate.
Source: IMF, *International Financial Statistics*, various issues.

(see Table 4.7). (In addition, foreign export creditors have an advantage as it is common for foreign governments to guarantee such lines of credit. This substantially reduces the risk borne by the creditor agency. The ECGD Export Credit Guarantee Department of the United Kingdom and the equivalent agency – COFACE – of France have actively participated in guaranteeing credit to SSA.) In the case of Kenya, this is evidenced by the change in external short-term debt which shifted from an outflow of about \$70 million in 1988 to an inflow of about \$350 million in 1989–90. Similarly, short-term debt in Zimbabwe shifted from a net outflow of \$8 million in 1986–8 to an inflow of \$290 million in 1989–90.

Further analysis of the data on private capital inflows reveals that recent developments, especially in the policy environment, are critical in accounting for the inflows to the six countries in our sample. In the case of South Africa, political factors influenced capital flows to the extent of reversing the outflows that occurred in the 1980s to inflows in the 1990s. In particular, the reforms initiated by De Klerk in 1989 and the release of Nelson Mandela in 1990 improved the credit rating of South Africa, resulting in a resurgence of short-term trade financing. Further, investor risk assessment improved following successful abolition of the Financial Rand in March 1995.[7] The liberalization of the foreign-exchange markets, permitting residents to hold foreign exchange in the domestic banking system, has also played a catalytic role in the return of flight capital and increasing remittances by nationals working abroad in the countries in our sample, excluding South Africa.

The presence of sizeable private transfers in the overall private capital inflows complicates judgement on the volatility of inflows. Private transfers represented mainly returning flight capital, workers' remittances and misreported capital account transactions, usually short-term inflows, mainly on account of trade financing. If these private transfers are transformed into holding of real assets, they will be less susceptible to volatility. There are chances that private transfers may be sustained as long as attractive policies are maintained, such as allowing residents and/or non-residents to open foreign-exchange denominated accounts in the domestic banking system.

As countries reduce their debt burden, improve on import cover and maintain a track record of private sector inflows such as private transfers, their credit rating in international capital markets will improve. This is likely to trigger increased (primarily short-term) capital inflows. One interesting observation from the numbers is that FDI and private short-term debt can be quite sensitive to the macroeconomic environment.

All indications are that it is difficult fully to assess whether inflows to the region are of a temporary nature. This makes it difficult to design an appropriate policy response. To the extent that the assessment of private capital inflows is subject to misjudgement, countries in the region should design policy responses, mindful that the inflows may be temporary. Given that the financial sectors of countries in the region are inefficient and that the effectiveness of monetary policy remains weak, the countries are faced with a big challenge of absorbing such inflows without excessive appreciation in the domestic currency.

IV SUSTAINABILITY OF CAPITAL INFLOWS

The balance of international opinion on the sustainability of private capital inflows has undergone a virtual U-turn in the last two years. Though some authors (Devlin, Ffrench-Davis and Griffith-Jones, 1994; UNCTAD, 1994) had been warning of problems for some time, opinion in the multilateral financial institutions and the financial community was that capital inflows were sustainable because they reflected a fundamental revival of confidence in emerging markets, though it was acknowledged that their magnitude might decline over time. Even at the end of 1994 Washington sources were suggesting that a 'soft landing' (i.e. a gradual decline in net inflows) was possible, unless there was a sharp rise in international interest rates or collapse in recipient country economies (Fernandez-Arias, 1994; World Bank, 1994). In 1995, opinion moved more towards the 'hard landing' (i.e. large fall in net inflows) and 'crash' (i.e. large net outflows) scenarios (see Fernandez-Arias and Montiel, 1995, p. 28), with organizations such as the IMF (1995a) and the Bank for International Settlements (1995a) suggesting, with the benefit of hindsight, that the inflows were unsustainable. Opinions in African countries have undergone a similar evolution, largely in response to actual trends in inflows.

The composition of inflows to SSA makes them *a priori* less sustainable. It is generally accepted that short-term and portfolio inflows are highly volatile (Griffith-Jones, 1995; IMF, 1995a; Reisen, 1993b). It has also been shown that FDI exhibits some measure of volatility (Claessens *et al.*, 1995). If we add private transfers, the most volatile type of inflows in SSA, according to the volatility ranking of Turner (1995), capital inflows to Africa would seem to have been highly volatile.

Nevertheless, until inflows actually declined sharply, opinion in some quarters was euphoric about the prospects for continued inflows, on the (untested) assumption that permanent 'pull' factors were at work. Without a doubt, as in the Mexican case, there will soon be many sources telling African governments that the inflows were 'obviously' unsustainable, and identifying previously ignored economic 'fundamentals' which should have indicated to anyone with reasonable intelligence that the inflows could not continue.

The key requirement for African governments is to avoid euphoria and retrospective judgements, and to focus on objective measures of the sustainability of inflows. The most convincing suggestion so far has been by Dadush *et al.* (1994), to the effect that net liabilities ought not to be more than 200 per cent of exports or, in dynamic form, that the change in net liabilities (measured as the ratio of the current account deficit to exports) ought not to be more than twice the change in exports (averaged over a period of four years). This measure has been criticized for its assumption of equal weighting for all types of inflows, ignoring the higher volatility of short-term and portfolio inflows. Moreover, it would be inappropriate for many SSA countries because it includes the current-account 'private transfer' inflows. A more accurate measurement for SSA countries would be the change in net liabilities (measured as the current account deficit excluding private transfers) compared to the change in exports. In addition, to take account of different levels of volatility, it would be desirable to measure short-term and portfolio inflows as a proportion of total inflows and in relation to GDP and exports. Sustainability also ought to be judged against the fact that nowadays domestic investors can far more easily denominate their holdings in foreign exchange, thereby increasing vulnerability to outflows.

Finally, SSA governments should be mindful of the large volume of literature indicating that inflows to developing countries (and financial inflows in general) are intrinsically volatile, having produced six crises in Latin America in the last 150 years (see Griffith-Jones, 1995). Perhaps the most prudent guideline has been provided by Williamson (1994): to regard all positive shocks as temporary, and all negative shocks as permanent. As Griffith-Jones has pointed out, if a country bases policy action on assuming that inflows are permanent, they are more likely to become temporary, as in the case of Mexico, while, if it more prudently assumes they are temporary, they are more likely to be permanent, as in the case of Chile.

V MACROECONOMIC IMPACT OF PRIVATE CAPITAL INFLOWS

Many of the economies in SSA have over the past decade or so implemented wide-ranging policies intended to promote efficiency and growth. It then becomes difficult to assess whether capital inflows are a cause or an effect of macroeconomic stabilization. In particular, ODA inflows have played a critical role in the reform process of a number of countries in the region. Because of such inflows, with the associated domestic financing of the budget, member countries have been able to increase both the current account and budget deficits as a percentage of GDP without threatening macroeconomic stability.

As indicated earlier, all countries in the sample, with the exception of Zambia, received much higher private capital inflows in 1990–3 than in the period 1986–9. Private capital inflows have until recently often been seen as having largely positive effects; namely overcoming foreign-exchange and import constraints; supplementing domestic savings and investment; smoothing national expenditure by compensating for negative terms-of-trade shocks; raising the microeconomic efficiency of production, especially by reducing financial intermediation spreads and by supplying technology and skills through FDI. However, more recently, developing countries have come to realize that private capital inflows can also have negative effects, especially on macroeconomic stability, linked closely to the above positive effects. For example:

- While easing foreign-exchange constraints, capital inflows can lead to sharp currency appreciation.
- If capital inflows are spent on imports, they can lead to rising current account deficits.
- If spent on consumption, capital inflows may have no effect on the size or productivity of investment, and can even discourage domestic savings.
- If financial markets are underdeveloped and performing poorly, large external inflows can reduce their intermediation efficiency still further, causing loss of monetary control and greater volatility.
- Overall, if capital inflows are procyclical, they can exaggerate all the destabilizing effects of terms-of-trade changes.

This section focuses on each of these effects in turn.

Effects on the Exchange Rate

The single most important effect of private capital inflows has been on the exchange rate. They have led to sharp currency appreciation in some instances and thus undermined efforts to improve export competitiveness. Changes in private inflows have also undermined exchange-rate stability, with negative effects on long-term growth (Ghura and Grennes, 1993). Their effects are hard to disaggregate from those of stabilization measures, terms-of-trade changes and official capital inflows. However, Elbadawi and Soto (1994) have found that all types of inflows can have large short-term destabilizing effects on the exchange rate, even though short-term and portfolio inflows have no long-term effect on the exchange rate;[8] and longer-term direct investment inflows have effects largely consistent with macroeconomic equilibrium.

Private capital inflows, predominantly short-term, have led to short-term currency appreciations in almost all countries in our sample (Table 4.8). Kenya and Uganda experienced very sharp appreciation of their currencies in 1993–4 and 1994–5 at a time when private transfers and access to short-term trade credits increased markedly. The appreciation in real effective terms in both Uganda and Kenya was well over 20 per cent in 1994. Zambia experienced a depreciation in real effective terms in 1991 which was followed by an appreciation

Table 4.8 Nominal and real exchange rates of selected countries in sub-Saharan Africa, 1986–94 (1985 = 100)

		1986	*1987*	*1988*	*1989*	*1990*	*1991*	*1992*	*1993*	*1994*
Kenya	N	98.8	100.6	107.9	125.6	139.6	167.7	196.3	353.7	342.1
	R	...	...	...	...	103.5	108.1	100.7	128.0	100.0
South	N	...	92.8	103.0	119.5	118.0	126.0	130.0	149.0	n.a.
Africa	R	...	96.1	102.0	101.3	98.4	95.0	91.3	93.4	92.6
Tanzania	N	186.9	367.4	567.4	819.4	1114.9	1252.6	1701.0	2316.0	2912.0
	R	...	...	...	...	396.0	382.0	438.0	497.0	497.0
Uganda	N	209.0	639.0	1584.0	3330.0	6401.0	10955.0	16922.0	17835.0	14717.0
	R	...	...	...	...	155.8	217.0	227.0	230.0	179.0
Zambia	N	251.6	283.9	264.0	416.0	932.0	1990.0	5042.0	14026.0	24813.0
	R	...	...	...	...	70.0	81.0	75.0	70.0	79.0
Zimbabwe	N	106.2	106.2	113.0	137.0	150.0	212.0	319.0	406.0	506.0
	R	...	...	...	...	100.7	126.0	128.0	132.0	139.0

Note: R denotes real exchange rates and N denotes nominal exchange rates. An increase in the index represents a depreciation.
Source: United Nations Economic Commission for Africa, *Economic and Social Statistics on Africa*, various issues; and IMF, *International Financial Statistics*, various issues.

in 1992 and 1993 and a depreciation in 1994. Similarly, South Africa has experienced marked movements in both directions in its real effective exchange rate. In the period 1986–9, when South Africa was a net exporter of capital, the real effective value of the currency depreciated. In 1990–2 it appreciated again as the country became a net recipient of capital. Unlike other countries in the sample, Zimbabwe has experienced a depreciation in the real value of the currency throughout the period 1990–4. This was a result of deliberate policy to guard against an appreciation in real effective terms.

Effects on the Balance of Payments

A second key issue is the balance-of-payments effect: increases in expenditure on imports (increasing the current account deficit) or reserves accumulation. This is important for sustainability because, to the degree that capital inflows increase the current account deficit through higher imports (though they will also increase fiscal revenue from tariffs), they will automatically decline again, perhaps abruptly, if these flows decline; on the other hand, accumulation of reserves should increase inflows by boosting confidence. Spending on imports has often been found to lag well behind the receipt of capital inflows.

Table 4.9 External reserves of selected countries in sub-Saharan Africa, 1986–93 (months of imports)

	1986–9	*1990*	*1991*	*1992*	*1993*
Kenya	1.6	0.9	0.6	0.4	2.2
South Africa	1.8	1.4	1.7	2.1	1.5
Tanzania	0.5	2.8	2.8	4.5	2.7
Uganda	0.6	0.7	1.0	1.5	2.1
Zambia	0.8	1.4	1.4	n.a.	n.a.
Zimbabwe	1.5	1.3	1.3	3.3	...

Source: IMF, *International Financial Statistics*, various issues; and World Bank, *World Debt Tables*, various issues.

Calvo and Reinhart (1995) suggest that small capital-receiving countries in Latin America have seen more reserves accumulation than increased import expenditure.

The experience of the countries in our sample with respect to reserve accumulation has been mixed, making it difficult to identify a single factor accounting for observed changes therein. From Table 4.9 it can be seen that some countries have consistently built reserves over the period. However, some of them lost reserves due to a decrease in medium-term loans, especially following a scale-down in donor financial support. Zimbabwe lost reserves due to the prolonged drought period in 1992. The loss of reserves in Kenya and South Africa was due to a decline in official transfers, while in Zambia and Tanzania this was accounted for by the decline in medium-term capital inflows. In Uganda and Zambia the drop in medium- and long-term loans was more than offset by the increase in grants. In addition, some of these countries lost reserves because of the increase in the level of imports. One key factor which has to be recognized is that private transfers have so substantially increased in Kenya, Uganda and Tanzania that donor disbursement for balance-of-payments support has been used for building up reserves.

Effects on Investment, Savings and Consumption

The third main group of effects is on investment, savings and consumption, and thereby on GDP growth. In this context, it is important to note that greater expenditure on consumption is likely to cause the real value of the currency to appreciate more rapidly, whereas investment will slow appreciation through imports of capital goods (Calvo,

1994; Khan and Reinhart, 1995). This is particularly true of investment expenditures related to FDI transactions: because these are not intermediated through the domestic financial system, they will have less effect on the real exchange rate or the financial markets. Beyond the initial division into investment and consumption, the key variables determining the GDP-effect are the type and productivity of investment, and the proportion allocated to the production of tradables.

Unfortunately, reliable savings and investment data are extremely rare in sub-Saharan African countries; those that exist are usually derived as residuals from national accounts. Equally, data on import composition which might be used as a proxy are usually somewhat outdated; and data on the current account which might indicate a savings–investment gap are also misleading because they include some capital account inflows.[9] Preliminary calculations based on 1986–93 data indicated ambiguous results on savings and investment behaviour in the six countries.

Zambia managed to increase the rate of gross domestic investment (GDI) to GDP. This was mainly financed by ODA (see Table 4.10). Similarly, Zimbabwe was able marginally to increase the GDI/GDP ratio. For the remaining countries, the GDI/GDP ratio fell between the two periods.

Savings as a ratio to GDP have generally decreased in the countries of our sample, with the exception of Tanzania. Zimbabwe suffered the biggest decline of close to 12 per cent. The trends in gross domestic savings as a share of GDP indicate that growth in these countries has been financed mainly by foreign savings. To the extent that private capital inflows are volatile and uncertain, growth is not sustainable. There is an urgent need to mobilize domestic savings to support the growth process, especially in Tanzania and Uganda, where savings rates are lowest.

The numbers in Table 4.10 also reveal that imports in relation to GDP increased in the countries in the sample, with the exception of South Africa, and especially so in Kenya, Zambia and Zimbabwe. Trade liberalization combined with increased capital inflows to the six countries to generate this result.

Monetary and Financial Effects

A potential risk of attempts to prevent currency appreciation through accumulation of reserves is loss of monetary control, leading to an acceleration of inflation. The appropriate policy response is to

Table 4.10 Selected countries in sub-Saharan Africa: macroeconomic indicators, 1986–9 and 1990–3

	Current-account balance[a] *(% of GDP)*		*Gross domestic savings (% of GDP)*		*Fiscal deficit*[a] *(% of GDP)*		*Gross domestic investment (% of GDP)*		*Inflation (%)*		*Debt service (% of exports)*	
	1986–9	*1990–3*	*1986–9*	*1990–3*	*1986–9*	*1990–3*	*1986–9*	*1990–3*	*1986–9*	*1990–3*	*1986–9*	*1990–3*
Kenya	(4.8)	(1.7)	19.9	19.5	(5.7)	(5.8)	24.0	18.0	7.0	28.0	39.0	36.0
South Africa	2.9	0.2	2.7	2.2	(2.4)	(4.7)	20.0	16.0	15.6	14.5	...	...
Tanzania	(1.5)	(16.0)	(1.4)	4.0	(5.3)	(3.9)	21.6	21.4	31.0	22.0	47.0	105.3
Uganda	(3.0)	(3.5)	3.8	0.2	(2.3)	(4.1)	16.8	14.8	170.0	30.1	55.0	77.0
Zambia	(9.4)	(10.5)	16.0	14.3	(8.0)	(5.0)	16.9	24.3	50.0	149.0	33.0	69.0
Zimbabwe	0.8	(5.8)	23.2	11.1	(6.2)	(6.0)	21.0	22.0	11.8	27.6	29.0	29.0

[a] Including grants.

Source: IMF, *International Financial Statistics*, various issues; and World Bank, *World Debt Tables*, various issues.

sterilize the liquidity injection through open-market operations. Depending on the magnitude of the liquidity injection and depth of the financial sector, there is a great likelihood that successful sterilization can only be attained at very high interest rates. Further, the appreciation of the domestic currency, in both nominal and real terms, may not be avoided.

Increased volatility in financial markets has certainly occurred in SSA countries, but less in the stock markets than in markets for treasury bills and central bank bills where high interest rates have been attracting private capital inflows, characterized by speculative bubbles, with knock-on negative consequences for the performance of the banks' lending portfolios (Asea and Reinhart, 1995; Calvo, Sahay and Vegh, 1995; Griffith-Jones, 1995; IMF, 1995a). These can be magnified by the imbalances in the structure of assets and liabilities produced by capital inflows. The financial system acquires liquid liabilities in foreign exchange, integrated into a volatile international capital market (to add to its volatile domestic liabilities which may be made more volatile by foreign capital inflows), while its assets are neither externally protected nor liquid (Rojas-Suarez and Weisbrod, 1995).

It is difficult to separate the effects of private capital inflows from those of the wider distortions and underdevelopment of the financial sector: capital inflows only exacerbate the moral hazard and adverse selection already prevalent, by adding to the volume of funds requiring intermediation (Calvo, Leiderman and Reinhart, 1993b). However, it is reasonable to assume that the negative effects of capital inflows on the financial system will be more pronounced in countries where the financial sector is in poor shape. If prudential regulations are binding in such circumstances, then few banks would be able to hold open foreign-exchange positions overnight. This could easily trigger instability in the market, as banks make efforts to reduce over-bought positions or else central banks have to remain active participants in the foreign-exchange market to promote stability, risking a loss of control over domestic liquidity.

Overall, there is strong evidence that private capital inflows to some SSA countries, in contrast to Latin America (Ffrench-Davis and Griffith-Jones, 1995), have been procyclical rather than countercyclical, following terms-of-trade booms (Kenya and Uganda) and exaggerating all of their destabilizing effects.

The detrimental effects of capital inflows may be even worse in SSA countries than in other regions, because of their high degree of aid dependence: private capital inflows can reduce the capacity of SSA countries to mobilize aid inflows, especially for balance-of-payments support. In the context of liberalized foreign-exchange markets, private inflows have reduced private-sector demand for donor-funded import support, leading donors to cut new pledges (Zambia and Zimbabwe). Similarly, accumulation of reserves and the apparently more healthy balance-of-payments position leads donors to question the whole rationale of fast-disbursing balance-of-payments support and to move funds to much slower-disbursing project support. This may not be appropriate, given the low absorptive capacity of the project-implementing agencies and the continuing budget constraints which would be better resolved by programme aid. The negative implications may become clear if private capital inflows reverse themselves, leading to a fall in international reserves and precipitating a foreign-exchange crisis as the currency depreciates rapidly. A useful alternative to balance-of-payments financing is direct budget support and debt relief. The local currency equivalent of such disbursements is used to support the budget at the same time as the foreign exchange boosts reserves. Direct budget support has effects broadly similar to those of import support. It may be equally difficult to sustain donor budget support if such inflows are seen as adversely affecting economic growth.

In the context of its aid relationships, we therefore prefer to call the recent strengthening of the Uganda shilling a 'Uganda Disease' rather than a 'Dutch Disease' (for more details of this argument, see Kasekende and Martin, 1995).

VI POLICY MEASURES

The potential negative economic effects of private capital inflows discussed in the previous section show the need for policy measures to influence their scale and composition. The literature has concluded that no single policy measure can influence them decisively. Not surprisingly, the effectiveness of individual measures depends on the scale, nature and purpose of the capital inflows and the characteristics of the recipient economy. It is relatively easy to specify theoretical policy rules: for example, short-term volatile portfolio inflows could require some offsetting policy intervention to smooth any destabilizing effects, even though their long-term effects on equilibrium might be minimal; while long-term direct investment might be entirely consistent with long-term macroeconomic equilibrium and therefore require no corrective measures (Corbo and Hernandez, 1994; Elbadawi and Soto, 1994). However, given the problems with data and monitoring, many SSA governments have had extreme difficulty in identifying capital inflows (especially their scale, composition and permanence) and therefore in deciding appropriate policy responses.

The crucial question for African countries has been whether to resist currency appreciation and, if so, how. The scope for change in exchange-rate policy has become much more limited due to the extreme degree of liberalization (to a free float) implemented in most non-CFA countries, compared to the 'basket pegs', administered devaluations or band mechanisms used in other developing countries. This makes many of the conventional recommendations irrelevant, such as those for moves towards more exchange-rate flexibility, administered appreciations or depreciations, or deliberate introduction of exchange-rate uncertainty/noise to deter speculators. Some Washington-based authors have even suggested that exchange-rate policy is no longer relevant or feasible in SSA circumstances. However, given the central role of currency depreciation in the few successful adjustment programmes in SSA – notably in promoting export competitiveness – most African governments have preferred to treat any appreciation as a major problem and to take measures to reverse or reduce it. (For a powerful argument of the case for making the exchange rate a key element of development policy, see Williamson, 1995.)

Furthermore, the policy response to the large capital inflows has been complicated by the current fiscal stance. With the exception of South Africa, the countries have faced budgetary problems of varying degrees. Budget deficits have varied between 1 and 13 per cent of GDP. In the case of Kenya and Zimbabwe, these have remained high throughout the first half of the 1990s. Uganda and Zambia have achieved significant success in controlling the budget since 1992. In the case of Uganda, the government has made substantial repayments to the banking system. This has been achieved through strict control of government expenditure combined with efforts to boost revenue mobilization. The countries in the sample mostly rely on the sale of financial instruments (mainly treasury bills) to sterilize liquidity injections. In cases where fiscal policy is expansionary, open-market operations are used to promote macroeconomic stability; similarly, liquidity injections arising from the foreign-exchange market are sterilized mainly by the sale of financial instruments. As pointed out earlier, this instrument suffers from limitations arising from the lack of depth in the financial sector. In situations where budgetary restraint is difficult and effectiveness of monetary policy instruments limited, the policy of absorbing the inflows through intervention may cause macroeconomic instability. In particular the risk of inflationary pressure is high.

In the following, three types of policy measures will be examined that have been used by countries receiving large capital inflows:

- measures to increase the demand for foreign exchange, including central-bank intervention in foreign-exchange markets; liberalization of the current account; and liberalization of the capital account;
- measures to reduce aggregate demand and offset the inflationary effects of the capital inflows or of interventions in the foreign-exchange market;
- measures to reduce the scale of capital inflows or to influence their composition in favour of those associated with investment.

Measures to Increase Demand for Foreign Exchange

Unsterilized intervention in the foreign-exchange market leads to reserve accumulation and increases the money supply. This can have secondary positive effects by reducing interest rates and making inflows less likely – but (in the absence of an accommodating increase in money demand) it may also raise inflation and thereby increase the real appreciation of the currency further. Nevertheless, in the absence of monetary tools which can sterilize such large inflows, this has often been the first line of defence for low-income SSA countries.

One recommendation in the literature is for greater current-account liberalization in order to increase demand for foreign exchange. As already discussed, current account transactions have been fully liberalized in the anglophone SSA countries which have been experiencing capital inflows. The only additional liberalization which could occur is a reduction of import tariffs. It is unlikely that this would have much effect on increasing import demand, given the existing high level of import dependence of low-income SSA countries and the low level of enforcement of tariff collection. In addition, a reduction in tariffs could be undesirable, given the dependence of the budget on tariff revenue. In any case, an increase in imports could be undesirable, given the already high import dependence of SSA countries and the failure of adjustment programmes to effect any rationalization of import composition. (These issues have been discussed in greater detail in Martin and Mistry, 1995.) Thus, further current-account liberalization would not be a priority tool for most SSA countries.

Capital account liberalization is seen as a third method of increasing demand for foreign exchange. Suggestions include full capital account liberalization to allow capital outflows which would offset inflows; the reduction or elimination of subsidies on any inflows (e.g. incentives for foreign investment, deposit insurance or subsidized forward cover on foreign-exchange transactions); gradual liberalization designed to encourage certain types of inflows or outflows (see Fischer and Reisen, 1992).

In some SSA countries, such measures might well be ineffective at this time, given the relative unimportance of inflows subject to capital account controls or subsidies and other incentives, and the predominance of inflows coming through the porous current account and the foreign-exchange bureaux. However, Kenya announced far-reaching such measures in October 1994, intended to offset capital inflows. Residents were permitted to invest abroad and to hold accounts overseas. In South Africa and Zimbabwe there are currently active debates about capital account liberalization. The recent trend towards capital account liberalization calls for a critical analysis (see, for instance, Ffrench-Davis and Griffith-Jones, 1995) that takes into account the risk that liberalization may well increase inflows (Hanson, 1992; Mathieson and Rojas-Suarez, 1993; Williamson, 1994), and/or may also undermine the effectiveness of sterilized intervention by making domestic and foreign bonds fully substitutable.

Correct sequencing of capital account liberalization with other measures (especially stabilization and internal financial sector strengthening and liberalization) is crucial. The only consistent sequencing recommendation in the adjustment literature is that capital-account liberalization should be one of the last steps in adjustment policy (see Kasekende and Martin, 1995); thus it should not be undertaken prematurely in countries with weak domestic financial systems, merely in order to influence private capital inflows.

Measures to Reduce Aggregate Demand

Sterilization through Open-Market Operations

Such sterilization has been the most popular policy in SSA countries. It has two main risks, which has provoked debate over whether sterilization is 'easy' (Reisen, 1993a) or 'hard' (Calvo, Leiderman and Reinhart, 1993 and 1994).

One risk is that it will perpetuate interest-rate differentials and accelerate capital inflows. Frankel (1994) concludes that sterilization will increase interest rates, but to a much larger degree if the source of the problem is higher export receipts or higher money demand rather than capital inflows. The degree of increase will depend on the substitutability of government paper and other assets, on the behaviour of the demand for money (especially its sensitivity to interest rates), and on the interest elasticity of aggregate demand. However, Fernandez-Arias and Montiel (1995) argue that the higher interest rate effect should be only temporary. Another risk is that sterilization will increase the fiscal/quasi-fiscal burdens of government or central bank paper, both through larger issues of such paper and through higher interest rates than the central bank can obtain on its reserves (Calvo, Leiderman and Reinhart, 1994; Corbo and Hernandez, 1994). For these reasons, it has been suggested that a more realistic target than complete sterilization is to maintain the pre-inflow growth rate of real balances, as has been achieved by Chile.

As a result of the over-reliance on the treasury bill instrument both to sterilize large capital inflows and to finance wide budget deficits, interest rates have increased sharply in some countries. Kenya, Zambia and Tanzania have suffered from this problem at different times during the early 1990s with discount rates increasing to well over 50 per cent per annum. To ease the problem, fiscal policy should be tight. Uganda offers a good example in this respect. The discount rate on treasury bills in that country has fallen from 40 per cent in 1990 to the current levels of between 9 and 15 per cent. The recent experience of Zambia also supports the need for fiscal restraint. Zambia has managed to reduce the discount rate on treasury bills from over 70 per cent in 1993 to about 20 per cent in 1994 through fiscal discipline.

Other Methods of Sterilization

There is a variety of other methods of sterilization, including an increase of the reserve requirement on bank deposits and shifting government deposits to the central bank.

Increasing the reserve requirement on bank deposits (or particular types of deposits) is equivalent to a tax on the banking system (because reserve requirements are not remunerated). This can be a highly effective prudential measure to narrow spreads in financial intermediation, to reduce the money multiplier and to limit credit to the private sector (Reinhart and Reinhart, 1995). It can work particularly effectively on individual types of inflow (e.g. offshore borrowing or uncovered foreign-exchange exposure) and if used countercyclically to target the source of a boom. However, over the medium term, there is a risk that the efficiency of the financial system is reduced, as borrowers may be pushed towards less efficient lenders in order to avoid the effects of reserve requirements. In addition, it requires a balanced judgement about the possible negative effects on key elements of finance such as trade finance. Kenya and Tanzania have used the policy of varying reserve requirements in liquidity management. However, given the current weakness in the financial sector, this policy measure tends to raise intermediation costs further. For that reason, Uganda has avoided increasing reserve requirements. Efforts have been made to reduce costs to commercial banks by treating a portion of vault cash as eligible reserves in addition to reducing the reserve requirement to the current level of 8 per cent. The difference in reserve requirements policy may offer a partial explanation for the far higher lending rates in Kenya and Tanzania compared to Uganda.

Moving government deposits (or postal savings, social security and public enterprise funds) from commercial banks to the central bank or into government paper (see Fischer and Reisen, 1992; Reisen, 1993a; Khan and Reinhart, 1995) has also proven to be a highly effective means of sterilization. However, depending on the interest rates paid by the central bank, this could have the effect of reducing the rates paid to savers or of increasing interest-rate costs to the central bank.

Fiscal Measures

Many authors see fiscal measures as the only long-term policy option (Corbo and Hernandez, 1994, Schadler *et al.*, 1993). Similarly, the main recommendation in SSA adjustment programmes has been to tighten fiscal policy, first to guard against the inflationary impact of a possible reversal of capital inflows, and secondly to offset the effects of sterilization by reducing interest rates through lower government borrowing, thereby discouraging capital inflows. Moreover, it has been suggested that expenditure cuts are more effective than tax rises in reducing aggregate demand (Calvo, Leiderman and Reinhart, 1993b).

The policy of fiscal restraint has been used with measurable success in Uganda. The recent positive experience in Zambia and the difficulties in promoting macroeconomic stability in Kenya, Zimbabwe and Tanzania lend further support to fiscal restraint. Uganda has managed to absorb the large inflows without losing control over inflation and interest rates.

However, many authors have also cautioned against the possible distortion of long-term fiscal plans in order to offset potentially temporary capital inflows. This could be especially important in those SSA countries where expenditure is already at critically low levels and the potential to increase revenue is limited. They have also indicated that fiscal measures may increase capital inflows by reducing the perceived prospect of liquidity problems for the government and freeing funds for domestic borrowing linked to some types of capital inflows.

Measures to Increase Domestic Savings

Such measures are sometimes seen as a means to reduce aggregate demand, and sometimes as measures to influence the make-up of capital inflows. Similarly, targeted sterilization measures (reserve requirements on particular types of capital inflows or borrowing) may be used to reduce aggregate demand and to influence the composition of inflows.

Most SSA adjustment programmes have recently begun to include drastic measures to boost private savings by reform of the financial sector. The principal mechanisms proposed have been greater competition in the financial sector via more open entry for new financial institutions, and liberalization of interest rates. There is little evidence from Africa or elsewhere, however, that such measures have had a dramatic positive effect on private savings, and there is a high risk that other financial sector reforms may undermine prospects for higher private financial savings rates (especially the disappearance of rural bank branches and savings networks). Finally, some of the key factors in mobilizing private-sector savings in other countries, such as improved postal savings banks, more productive social security funds, or private pensions, have barely been considered in Africa. Given the current design of financial sector reform, it seems unlikely that measures to increase domestic financial savings will have effects large enough to counteract the effects of private capital inflows.

Measures to Influence the Scale and Composition of Inflows

There has been heated debate over the desirability and feasibility of capital controls and taxes, with some (Dornbusch, in this volume; Griffith-Jones, 1995; Williamson, 1994) believing they are an essential part of the policy arsenal; and others (Corbo and Hernandez, 1994, Schadler *et al.*, 1993; Mathieson and Rojas-Suarez, 1993) seeing them as temporary and largely ineffective measures, which are quickly dodged through over-and under-invoicing of trade or through parallel financial and foreign-exchange markets. However, even conservative sources (Bank for International Settlements, 1995b; IMF, 1995a) have recently acknowledged the positive role played in the Latin American and Asian cases by such measures as:

- extra reserve requirements on particular inflows, especially on foreign borrowing by companies or banks or open foreign-exchange positions of the banks;
- quantitative restrictions on inflows, for example on foreigners buying treasury bills (in Malaysia) or domestic bonds (Colombia);
- taxes on short-term inflows, aimed at reducing the dollar returns of investments (in Brazil, Chile and Colombia);
- minimum stay periods on FDI (Chile and Colombia).

Some have tried to distinguish among measures which are good for short periods (taxes and bans) and those which are desirable for longer periods (prudential regulations such as reserve requirements), but the consensus appears to be growing that many forms of controls on capital inflows are an essential weapon in the policy arsenal, provided that they are accompanied by measures directed at demand for foreign exchange and domestic aggregate demand, and the pursuit of 'sound macroeconomic fundamentals'.

Given the absence of data on capital inflows in many SSA countries, it is hard to see how governments could design or implement appropriate controls or taxes on capital inflows. Any such measures attempted in the current low-information context would only risk exacerbating current distortions or speculative bubbles. In addition, the arguments used about evasion in middle-income countries with better recording systems would presumably apply more strongly in SSA countries, making effective implementation doubtful. The same would apply to any SSA participation in a global tax. However, once more information is available, it may be possible to design carefully targeted controls and taxes.

VII CONCLUSIONS

Where does the above analysis leave African policymakers in deciding which policy measures to use to react to capital inflows? As in any other country, the need for policy intervention depends on the size and composition of inflows, their causes, and the perception and objective analysis of their sustainability. We have shown that the key first step for all sub-Saharan countries must be to improve recording and monitoring of inflows. For some, this means starting virtually from scratch with disaggregating data on inflows through the bureaux and monitoring private sector borrowing; for others, it is a more sophisticated process of improving the coverage of monitoring, especially of uses of inflows. However, for those countries which have abandoned all monitoring, there is concern that any attempt to record inflows would be perceived by the markets as an attempt to control and would undermine the credibility of liberalization, driving the capital inflows away or back into the parallel markets.

In order to facilitate proper analysis of capital inflows and their macroeconomic effects and to attempt to influence these through appropriate policy measures, authorities must seek to improve recording and monitoring systems both in their own countries and in international organizations. The most intractable problem may be how to introduce national recording and monitoring systems without driving capital inflows back to the parallel market.

Nevertheless, pending improvements in the data, it is possible to see that:

- contrary to the message of global databases, several sub-Saharan countries have experienced sizeable private capital inflows which are larger compared to the size of their economies than those of Latin American and Asian countries;
- the composition of those inflows (in so far as it is known) indicates that important elements (private transfers and short-term bank inflows) could be volatile; however, the prospects of maintaining private transfers are high, given an attractive macroeconomic environment;
- the causes of the inflows have been predominantly 'push' factors and only transitory 'pull' factors, together with some regional spillover effects in Southern African countries, rather than permanent 'pull' factors, again indicating their likely unsustainability;

- perceptions and objective analyses of sustainability indicate that the inflows could be temporary but, as indicated, lack of information on the nature of investment may render them permanent; the potential volatility of the inflows makes a strong case for action to monitor them and to minimize their destabilizing macroeconomic effects.

The type of policy action to be taken in response to the inflows depends on their macroeconomic effects and on the objectives of the government. Flows to sub-Saharan countries have consistently caused real currency appreciation, either through nominal appreciation, where stabilization policies have been tightly pursued, or through inflation, where they have not. They have sustained high import levels and permitted reserves accumulation in the countries analysed. They have caused protracted financial instability and undermined financial sector reform programmes, and they have been procyclical and have complicated aid mobilization efforts.

The current situation and objectives of the governments are remarkably similar. All the countries studied share the objectives of improving competitiveness and reducing inflation; yet, with the possible exception of South Africa and the CFA franc zone (among those not studied), none of them would wish to use a stable exchange rate as an inflation anchor. All have relatively recently embarked on financial sector reform programmes, and are anxious to raise domestic savings from current low levels. (Again, South Africa is the exception, with much higher initial savings levels.)

Given the need to balance the objectives of competitiveness and stability, the desirable policy mix for SSA countries would be a pragmatic one, drawing on the maximum number of policy levers, as in Chile, rather than relying exclusively on sterilized intervention or fiscal compression (Fernandez-Arias and Montiel, 1995; Williamson, 1995). However, as with small nations in other continents, fewer policy options are currently open to most SSA governments (Calvo and Reinhart, 1995) because of the following factors:

- their complete exchange-rate flexibility, and highly open current account and (through a porous current account) capital account;
- their slow progress with structural reforms, notably development of the domestic financial sector, which makes sterilization methods less effective and formal capital account opening less desirable, for fear of exacerbating the poor health of domestic banks;

- the poor fiscal position (in some countries), which makes sterilization costs unsustainable, or the need for prior fiscal adjustment (in others), which makes further fiscal adjustment to temporary capital inflows undesirable and politically problematic;
- the poor quality of data and of enforcement mechanisms for taxes and controls of any kind, and the unconventional nature of much of the capital (in the form of private transfers) which will make capital taxes and controls (whether national or global) less effective.

Given these factors, the priority policy measures would appear to be:

- sterilized intervention in order to minimize inflation and to accumulate reserves to guard against reversal of capital inflows;
- application of selective reserve requirements, especially on offshore borrowing and foreign borrowing by the private sector;
- fiscal tightening; despite its shortcomings, this is consistent with promoting macroeconomic stability in countries faced with high capital inflows given the relative ineffectiveness of monetary policy;
- transfer of government and other public-sector deposits from commercial banks to the central bank (although this may undermine financial stability, given current weaknesses of the financial sector);
- measures to limit foreign purchases of treasury bills and domestic bonds;
- removal of incentives for capital inflows and selective gradual opening of the capital account (where justified, based on analysis of motives for inflows/outflows and on adjustment sequencing considerations);
- convincing donors to maintain levels of balance-of-payments and/or fiscal support in order to increase reserves and guard against future outflows.

Even this seemingly specific and limited list looks long for a typical sub-Saharan policymaker faced with many other demands for monitoring, research, and policy design and implementation. Yet, as strikingly put by Calvo and Reinhart (1995, p. 35): 'While sound macroeconomic policies are advisable, policymakers in small countries are advised to be extra cautious in protecting the domestic financial system against the vagaries of international capital inflows.'

Most sub-Saharan countries are very small. Thus the problem of large unsustainable capital inflows is one they should take very seriously, devoting resources to urgent further analysis of its scale and causes, and the policy measures they can take to minimize its negative effects.

Appendix 4.1 Review of the Liberalization Process in Selected Countries in Southern Africa

Zimbabwe

The experience of Zimbabwe in liberalizing its economy is fully described by Ncube *et al.* (1996). The first phase of the liberalization process was started in 1990 with the objective of moving the economy from a highly regulated status to market-orientation. Imports were substantially liberalized, while surrender requirements remained in force. The current account deficit deteriorated from $147 million in 1990 to $500 million in 1991. In the following year, Zimbabwe devalued its currency to eliminate overvaluation. Unfortunately, the economy was hit by a drought in 1992 which further widened the current-account deficit. The deficit was financed by external borrowing, enabling the government to maintain a high level of reserves. The cover of imports increased from 4.1 months in 1993 to 5.5 months by end-December 1994 and 7 months by June 1995. The controls in foreign-exchange dealing were gradually eased in the period 1992–4, and the government allowed foreign investors to freely invest in the stock exchange and remit both capital and dividends, beginning July 1993. Foreign-exchange surrender requirements were also gradually eased.

Between January and July 1994, exporters were required to surrender 40 per cent of their earnings at the official rate while 60 per cent could either be sold in the interbank market or held in a foreign-currency account. The surrender requirement was abolished on 1 July 1994. The currency was gradually depreciated from Zim.$2.8 in 1990 to Zim.$8.2 per US dollar in 1994. An interbank foreign-exchange market was set up in January 1994, though the Reserve Bank of Zimbabwe (RBZ) remained an active participant in the market, especially during the first six months of its operation. The RBZ initially retained an official window rate but the two-tier exchange rate was finally abolished on 1 July 1994. In order to increase competition in the interbank market, the government permitted the setting up of foreign-exchange bureaux. In February 1995 Zimbabwe took on the obligations of Article VIII of the IMF Articles of Agreement (current account convertibility).

A key outcome of financial reform in Zimbabwe has been the surge in domestic interest rates, both nominal and real, from about 10 per cent in 1990 to 30 per cent by 1994. As a result, some private sector borrowers resorted to cheaper credit lines from external sources precipitating a real appreciation of the Zimbabwean dollar.

Zambia

Zambia gradually moved its foreign-exchange regime from a controlled to a market-based system over the period 1992 to 1995. As a first step, Zambia established a foreign-exchange bureaux system in October 1992, which operated simultaneously with the official window managed by the Bank of Zambia. The dual system was eliminated in December 1993, with the setting up of the interbank system. Since then, the foreign-exchange system has been fully market-based.

In January 1994, all forms of exchange control on both capital-and current-account transactions were eliminated. The nominal value of the currency depreciated by over 80 per cent from Kwacha 177 per dollar in 1992 to about K942 in September 1995. However, with the very high rate of inflation experienced during the period, the real value of the currency actually appreciated. Zambia's reserves rose from import cover of one month in 1991 to two and a half months by 1994.

Interest rates were liberalized in September 1992 at a time when the requirements for fiscal accommodation were still high. As a result, the nominal discount rate on short-term government paper increased sharply from 182 per cent in 1993 to 591 per cent in July 1993. The rates have since dropped to around 40 per cent. Such high interest rates undoubtedly attracted short-term capital inflows. Beginning in 1994, non-residents were allowed to participate in treasury bill and government bond markets without restriction.

Tanzania

As in Zimbabwe and Zambia, significant progress has been achieved in decontrolling prices in Tanzania. The exchange and trade regimes have been extensively liberalized. Import licensing has been eliminated and exporters are currently permitted to retain 100 per cent of their foreign-exchange receipts. In order to promote dealings in foreign exchange, Tanzania established an interbank foreign-exchange market in June 1994, and the bureaux which were set up in 1992 were permitted to participate in the interbank foreign-exchange market. This was intended to promote competition in the foreign-exchange market since only two banks were registered by then. The participation by bureaux in the interbank foreign-exchange market is to be reviewed with a view to limiting their operations only to 'over-the-counter' transactions.

Tanzania has made significant progress in its privatization programme. By the end of 1994, about 95 out of 371 parastatals had been divested, and 50 had been targeted for restructuring or divestiture in 1995. In a further effort to provide financial support to the economic development process, Tanzania is preparing the groundwork for the establishment of capital markets. However, foreign investors are not yet permitted to participate. Capital transfers to all countries are still subject to approval by the authorities.

Kenya

Kenya made substantial progress in liberalizing its trade regime during the late 1980s. However, insufficient adjustment of the exchange rate made the liberalization process unsustainable. Whenever import demand outpaced supply of foreign exchange, import licensing would be tightened.

The failure to sustain the reform process continued to characterize macroeconomic management in the first three years of the 1990s. In the foreign-exchange market, holders of foreign-exchange certificates were permitted to negotiate premiums in secondary market trading, creating a dual system. This was followed by a revaluation and foreign-exchange rationing system which caused substantial losses to holders. Additionally, the economy was characterized by rising inflation, from 13 per cent in 1989 to a peak of 46 per cent in 1993. Furthermore, efforts to finance the widening budget deficit through sale of government paper pushed interest rates to very high levels.

Since mid-1993, Kenya has moved very fast in stabilizing the macroeconomic environment and liberalizing the economy. Inflation was brought down to single digit levels. An interbank foreign-exchange system was started in October 1993. By end-1993, all restrictions on remittances of dividends and expatriate earnings had been lifted. In addition, residents were permitted to borrow abroad up to $1 million. In February 1994, further efforts to eliminate controls on the capital account were announced. Exporters were allowed 100 per cent retention of export proceeds, the limit on resident borrowing from abroad was removed, foreigners were allowed to open foreign-currency accounts in domestic banks and the restrictions on domestic borrowing by foreign-controlled companies was removed. By June 1994, Kenya accepted the obligations of Article VIII (Sections 2, 3 and 4) of the Articles of Agreement of the IMF.

In the financial year 1994–5, Kenya made further progress in reforming the foreign-exchange market and liberalizing the capital account. The Central Bank of Kenya started licensing foreign-exchange bureaux in October 1994. In addition, residents were permitted to invest funds abroad including the retention of overseas accounts. Additionally, foreign investors were allowed to participate in the Nairobi Stock Exchange. In 1994, offshore borrowing by residents was allowed without limit, provided that the interest rate did not exceed the London inter-bank offer rate (LIBOR) plus 2 percentage points and that such borrowing was not guaranteed by the government.

Uganda

The liberalization of the foreign-exchange and trade regime in Uganda has been extensively discussed by Kasekende *et al.* (1994). The new government that came into power in January 1986 took almost one and a half years to develop an appropriate policy package to address the numerous economic problems that affected Uganda. During that time, the policy regime was characterized by a high degree of uncertainty, an overvalued currency and very high inflation.

Following the launch of the Economic Recovery Programme in May 1987, insufficient exchange-rate adjustment and inefficient budget management undermined the reform programme. However, since June 1990, Uganda has moved reasonably quickly to correct macroeconomic distortions. The government implemented very tight monetary and fiscal measures, sanctioned the establishment of foreign-exchange bureaux in July 1990, launched a foreign-exchange auction system in January 1993, and replaced it with an interbank system in November 1993. Under the interbank system, all surrender requirements on exports or any other foreign-exchange inflows were removed. In addition, residents were permitted to operate foreign-currency accounts. In the period since 1990, the government pursued an aggressive policy of attracting foreign investment. As part of this process, Uganda enacted a new Investment Code with highly liberal provisions on repatriation of capital and dividends. Since early 1993, both nominal and real currency values appreciated markedly, in part reflecting higher private capital inflows and improved terms of trade. In 1994, Uganda acceded to Article VIII Sections 2, 3 and 4 of the IMF's Articles of Agreement; the capital account was fully liberalized in mid-1997.

South Africa

South Africa has experienced structural disruptions since 1970 that have had a profound impact on investment and the overall economic performance of the country. The Angolan War, oil price shocks in the 1970s, the worldwide recession towards the end of the 1970s, sanctions and political instability all combined to disrupt the long-run growth performance of the country.

In 1980 there was a sharp upsurge in the gold price which restored investors' confidence and paved the way for major policy transformations. By then, the political situation in South Africa had deteriorated to such an extent that foreign creditors were reluctant to extend further credit to domestic enterprises and other financial institutions. Disinvestment campaigns emanating mainly from Western nations, accompanied by stricter trade and financial sanctions, forced the government to declare a moratorium on foreign debt in 1985. Disinvestment together with the repayment of foreign debt contributed to net capital outflows of around R5 billion per annum from 1985 onward.

In addition, before 1985, the balance of payments followed a clear cyclical pattern. During an upswing in the business cycle, increased demand for imports caused the current account to move into a deficit, which in turn was financed by direct and indirect capital inflows. During a downswing, imports declined, and the current account moved into a surplus that enabled the repayment of loans. This pattern was disrupted by net capital outflows which occurred after 1985. Whereas, in the past, current-account deficits were financed by capital inflows, net outflows since 1985 implied that the current account had to be transformed into a surplus.

The consequent balance-of-payments constraint had important implications for investment in South Africa since 1985. Real growth declined to a mere 0.6 per cent per annum between 1985 and 1993. Gross domestic investment declined sharply, from an average annual rate of 28.6 per cent of GDP in the period 1970–84 to 21.2 per cent in the period 1985–93, with private investment falling from 15.3 to 13.6 per cent of GDP and public investment declining from 13.3 to 7.6 per cent of GDP.

With the breakdown of the Bretton Woods system in 1971, South Africa began to experiment with various exchange-rate systems to accommodate floating exchange rates. Following the recommendations of the 1978 Interim Report of the Commission of Inquiry into the Monetary System and Monetary Policy, South Africa opted for a dual managed floating exchange-rate system in 1979, with substantial intervention by the South African Reserve Bank. The high gold price during the 1970s and early 1980s contributed to an overvaluation of the currency.

In 1983 the Reserve Bank allowed the exchange rate to be more market-determined. A direct attempt was made to drain the economy of excess liquidity with the liberalization of exchange control through the abolition of the Financial Rand mechanism in February 1983. Coupled with declining gold prices since 1981, political unrest and disinvestment, this contributed to a sharp depreciation of the currency. Capital outflows since 1983 necessitated the reinstatement of the Financial Rand in 1985. The depreciation of the currency effectively increased the cost of imported capital and subsequently depressed investment.

Political uncertainty and the concomitant macroeconomic instability that prevailed during the 1970s, and particularly after 1985, increased the risk for potential investors and consequently reduced investment.

South Africa formally accepted the obligations of Article VIII, Sections 2, 3 and 4, of the IMF's Articles of Agreement in September 1973, and finally unified its exchange rate in 1996.

Notes

1. The views expressed in this paper are those of the authors and do not reflect the views of the Bank of Uganda or the Ministry of Finance and Economic Planning of Uganda in any way. The authors are grateful to Andrew Bvumbe, Ibrahim Elbadawi, Stephany Griffith-Jones, Richard Ketley, Mohsin Khan, Polycarp Musinguzi, Stuart Kufeni, Benno Ndulu, Carmen Reinhart, Charles Ojwiya, Jonathan Leape, Allister Moon, Tim Lamont, Carlene Francis and Daudi Sajjabi for supplying their valuable time, opinions, data and materials during the preparation of this paper; and to the Swedish and Danish governments for funding earlier work on capital flows to Africa. However, we remain responsible for any errors and misinterpretations in the paper.
2. Refer to Kasekende, Katarikawe and Rweikiza (1995) for a full discussion of problems relating to the compilation of balance-of-payments statistics in Uganda.
3. The study does not cover the experience of the franc zone area. Following the change in parity of the common currency in January 1994, some investors evidently expected a further devaluation and this triggered capital outflows. Nor does the study cover the experiences of Zaire and Nigeria, both of which are rich in natural resources. It would be interesting to analyse capital movements to and from these two countries, given recent developments in their economic and political environments.
4. Of course, factors noted for other developing countries may also be partly responsible, particularly: discrepancies between source and recipient country data due to on-lending through intermediary countries; and inadequate data coverage in source countries. On the latter, see also Ffrench-Davis and Griffith-Jones (1995).

5. Similar recording of capital flows as current account transactions has been noted in El Salvador by Calvo and Reinhart (1995).
6. It is also likely that there is substantial under-recording of the scale of the bureaux transactions.
7. See *Centre for Research into Economics and Finance in South Africa, Quarterly Review,* London, October 1995, pp. 2–10.
8. These tend to be magnified by weaknesses in the financial sector. Uganda, for example, experienced turbulence in the foreign-exchange market in August 1994, partly due to panic in a very thin dealer market.
9. As noted above, in a number of countries in the region, bureaux transactions are not properly categorized. Certain capital account transactions are misreported as current account transactions under the line 'private transfers'.

References

Asea, P. K. and C. M. Reinhart (1995) 'Real Interest Rate Differentials and the Real Exchange Rate: Evidence from Four African Countries', paper presented to an African Economic Research Consortium Workshop, Nairobi, June.

Bank for International Settlements (1995a) *Annual Report 1994/95* (Basle: BIS).

Bank for International Settlements (1995b) *International Banking and Financial Market Developments* (Basle: BIS).

Calvo, G. A. (1994) 'The Management of Capital Flows: Domestic Policy and International Cooperation' in UNCTAD, *International Monetary and Financial Issues for the 1990s*, vol. IV (New York and Geneva: United Nations).

Calvo, G. A., L. Leiderman and C. M. Reinhart (1993a) 'Capital Flows and Real Exchange Rate Appreciation in Latin America: the Role of External Factors' *IMF Staff Papers*, vol. 40, no. 1, March.

Calvo, G. A., L. Leiderman and C. M. Reinhart (1993b) 'The Capital Flows Problem: Concepts and Issues', *IMF Paper on Policy Analysis and Assessment*, PPAA/93/10.

Calvo, G. A., L. Leiderman and C. M. Reinhart (1994) 'Inflows of Capital to Developing Countries in the 1990s: Causes and Effects', *Economic Perspectives* (September).

Calvo, G. A., R. Sahay and C. A. Vegh (1995) 'Capital Inflows in Central and Eastern Europe: Evidence and Policy Options', *IMF Working Paper 95/57* May.

Chuhan, P., S. Claessens and N. Mamingi (1993) 'Equity and Bond Flows to Latin America and Asia: the Role of Global and Country Factors', *World Bank IECIF Policy Research Working Paper*, no. 1160 (July).

Claessens, S., M. Dooley and A. Warner (1995) 'Portfolio Capital Flows: Hot or Cold?', *World Bank Economic Review*, vol. 9, no. 1 (January).

Corbo, V. and L. Hernandez (1994) 'Macroeconomic Adjustment to Capital Inflows: Latin American Style versus East Asian Style', *World Bank IECIF Policy Research Working Paper*, no. 1377 (November).

Dadush, U., A. Dhareshwar and R. Johannes (1994) 'Are Private Capital Flows to Developing Countries Sustainable?', *World Bank Working Paper*, WPS 1160.

Devlin, R., R. Ffrench-Davis and S. Griffith-Jones (1994) 'Crescimentos dos fluxos de capital e desenvolvimento: Uma visao geral dos questoes de política econômica' [with English summary], *Pesquisa e Planejamento Econômico*, vol. 24, no. 3 (December).

Elbadawi, I. A. and R. Soto (1994) 'Capital Flows and Long-term Equilibrium Exchange Rates in Chile', *World Bank PRD Working Paper*, no. 1306, (June).

Fernandez-Arias, E. (1994) 'The New Wave of Private Capital Inflows: Push or Pull?', *World Bank IECIF Policy Research Working Paper*, no. 1312 (June).

Fernandez-Arias, E. and P.J. Montiel (1995) 'The Surge in Capital Inflows to Developing Countries: Prospects and Policy Response', March, mimeo.

Ffrench-Davis, R. and S. Griffith-Jones (1995) *Coping with Capital Surges* (New York: Lynne Rienner).

Fischer, B. and H. Reisen (1992) 'Towards Capital Account Convertibility', *OECD Policy Brief*, no. 4 (Paris: OECD).

Frankel, J. A. (1994) 'Sterilisation of Money Inflows: Difficult (Calvo) or Easy (Reisen)?', *IMF Working Paper 94/159*, December.

Galbis, V. (1993) 'High Real Interest Rates Under Financial Liberalisation: Is There a Problem?', *IMF Working Paper 93/7*, January.

Ghura, D. and T. J. Grennes (1993) 'The Real Exchange Rate and Macroeconomic Performance in Sub-Saharan Africa', *Journal of Development Economics*, vol. 42, pp. 155–74.

Gooptu, S. (1994) 'Are Portfolio Flows to Emerging Markets Complementary or Competitive?', *World Bank IECIF Policy Research Working Paper*, no. 1360 (September).

Griffith-Jones, S. (1995) 'Capital Flows to Latin America and Asia: Lessons for Eastern Europe', Institute for Development Studies, Sussex, June, mimeo.

Hadjimichael, M. T., D. Ghura, M. Mühleisen, R. Nord and E. M. Uçer (1995) 'Sub-Saharan Africa: Growth, Savings and Investment 1986–93', *IMF Occasional Paper*, no. 118 (Washington, DC).

Hanson, J. A. (1992) 'Opening the Capital Account: A Survey of Issues and Results', *World Bank FPS Working Paper*, no. 101 (May).

Hernandez, L. and H. Rudolph (1995) 'Sustainability of Capital Flows to Developing Countries: Is a Generalised Reversal Likely?', *World Bank Working Paper*, WPS 1518 (October).

IMF (1995a) *International Capital Markets: Developments, Prospects and Policy Issues* (Washington, DC).

IMF (1995b) *World Economic Outlook* (Washington, DC).

IMF, *International Financial Statistics*, various issues.

Kasekende, L., M. Katarikawe and R. Rweikiza (1994) 'The Impact of Imports on Development in Low Income Africa. Uganda Final Report',

External Finance for Africa Project (Oxford: Oxford International Associates).

Kasekende, L. and M. Martin (1995) 'Macroeconomic Policy Research Issues: The Sequencing, Credibility and Consistency of Adjustment in Africa', paper presented to an African Economic Research Consortium Senior Policy Seminar, Nairobi (April).

Khan, M. S. and C. M. Reinhart (1995) 'Capital Flows in the APEC Region', *IMF Occasional Paper*, no. 122.

Lipumba, N. (1994) *Africa Beyond Adjustment* (Washington, DC: Overseas Development Council).

Martin, M. and P. S. Mistry (1995) 'Financing Imports for Development in Low-Income Africa', Report to SIDA/Danish Foreign Ministry, November, mimeo.

Mathieson, D. J. and L. Rojas-Suarez (1993) 'Liberalisation of the Capital Account: Experiences and Issues', *IMF Occasional Paper*, no. 103.

Montiel, P. (1995) 'The New Wave of Capital Inflows: Country Policy Chronologies', World Bank, Washington, DC, April, mimeo.

Ncube, M., P. Collier, J. Gunning and K. Mlambo (1996) 'Trade Liberalisation and Regional Integration in Zimbabwe' in A. Oyejide, B. Ndulu, and J. Gunning (eds), *Regional Integration and Trade Liberalisation in Sub-Saharan Africa, Vol. 2: Country Case Studies*, AERC Collaborative Project, forthcoming.

Niehans, J. (1994) 'Elusive Capital Flows: Recent Literature in Perspective', *Journal of International and Comparative Economics*, vol. 3, no. 1, pp. 21–43.

OECD (1994, 1995) *Financing and External Debt of Developing Countries* (Paris).

OECD (1994, 1995) *Financial Market Trends* (Paris).

OECD (1994, 1995) *Geographical Distribution of Financial Flows to Developing Countries* (Paris).

Reinhart, C. M. and V. Reinhart (1995) 'On the Use of Reserve Requirements in Dealing with Capital Flow Problems', October, International Monetary Fund, mimeo.

Reisen, H. (1993a) 'The Case for Sterilised Intervention in Latin America', OECD/mimeo.

Reisen, H. (1993b) 'Capital Flows and their Effect on the Monetary Base', *CEPAL Review*, no. 51.

Roe, A. and N. K. Sowa (1994) 'From Direct to Indirect Monetary Control in Sub-Saharan Africa', plenary paper for the African Economic Research Consortium, Nairobi, December, mimeo.

Rojas-Suarez, L. and S. R. Weisbrod (1995) 'Financial Fragilities in Latin America: The 1980s and 1990s', *IMF Occasional Paper*, no. 132 (Washington, DC).

Schadler, S., M. Carkovic, A. Bennett and R. Kahn (1993) 'Recent Experiences with Surges in Capital Inflows', *IMF Occasional Paper*, no. 108.

Turner, P. (1995) 'Capital Flows in Latin America: a New Phase', *BIS Economic Paper*, no. 44, May (Basle).

UNCTAD (1994) *Trade and Development Report 1994* (New York and Geneva: United Nations).

UNCTAD (1995) *Trade and Development Report 1995* (New York and Geneva: United Nations).

United Nations Economic Commission for Africa, *Economic and Social Statistics on Africa*, various issues.

Williamson, J. (1994) 'The Management of Capital Inflows', paper for International Finance Corporation IFC and the Government of India, December, mimeo.

Williamson, J. (1995) 'Exchange Rate Policy and Development Strategy', plenary paper for the African Economic Research Consortium, Johannesburg, December, mimeo.

World Bank (1993) *World Debt Tables 1993–4* (Washington, DC).

World Bank (1993–5) *Financial Flows to Developing Countries* (Washington, DC, quarterly), various issues.

World Bank (1994) *World Debt Tables 1994–5* (Washington, DC).

World Bank (1994–5) *Global Economic Prospects* (Washington, DC, quarterly), various issues.

Younger, S. (1992) 'Aid and the Dutch Disease: Macroeconomic Management When Everybody Loves You', *World Development*, vol. 20, no. 11, pp. 1587–97.

5 A New Facility for the IMF?

John Williamson

This chapter[1] offers an assessment of the interests of developing countries in the proposal to create a new, fast-disbursing financing facility within the IMF. The idea of creating an 'emergency' facility to counter capital flows judged to be speculative and destabilizing harks back to an idea that was discussed in the Committee of Twenty (on international monetary reform) in the early 1970s. It was revived by Michel Camdessus in speeches in May and June 1994, and subsequent IMF Executive Board papers.

I PURPOSE OF THE PROPOSAL

Under conditions of high capital mobility, countries that receive capital inflows are vulnerable to swings of sentiment in the capital markets. If expectations were always rational, in the technical sense of being based upon the best possible forecasts of fundamentals using available information, and were independent of the opinions of other market participants, then there would be no case for having the official sector second-guess the conclusions of the market. But to the extent that markets are prone to speculative swings of mood (the phenomenon that justifies the quip that a country is creditworthy as long as others are lending to it), it may be useful to have an official presence in the market. Note that there is a convincing institutional reason that can explain why markets may behave in a herd manner rather than act on longer-term, rational considerations, in that the managers of mutual funds are rewarded on a quarterly basis by comparison with their peers: a manager who missed out on the Mexican boom would have been penalized for it, while he would not necessarily have suffered from the Mexican collapse, provided that his peers were caught as well.

One conception of what a new facility should attempt to do is to provide a backstop to resist speculative pressures that are not justified by the fundamentals. However, it may be argued that this would give it an unnecessarily broad brief, since the Fund's existing facilities are capable of handling many of the cases in which capital moves in what is judged to be a perverse direction. If one asks under what situations the Fund's existing arrangements are clearly inadequate, it is to deal with those cases where the need is for action so immediate that the normal operations of the IMF could not be effective. There are two, and only two, types of situation where this holds: (*a*) where a country is trying to defend an exchange-rate peg; and (*b*) where a country is so illiquid that without international help it will have no alternative but to default. In both of those situations help has to be immediate if it is to be of any use at all.

Enthusiasts for floating exchange rates naturally oppose the idea of giving countries extra help in defending pegged exchange rates. It follows that they would seek to restrict the scope of any new facility to helping indebted 'emergent borrowers'. Others seek to limit the scope of a new facility to countries that pose a systemic threat, on the grounds that a case for international action can be justified only if there is some type of international spillover. In practice this would tend to restrict the availability of the facility to large countries.

Hence there are a variety of purposes that might be served by a new facility. At the broadest level, it might be charged with helping countries to finance, and therefore ride out, capital flows that were judged to be unjustified by the fundamentals and therefore destabilizing. A more restricted mandate would limit it to occasions when immediate access was vital, either to defend a pegged exchange rate or to avoid a default. A still more restricted mandate would preclude use of the facility to defend an exchange rate peg. A further limit to the mandate would involve restricting access to countries whose default was judged to pose a systemic threat. Most of the discussion that follows focuses on the broad version of the proposal.

Given that the IMF was conceived with the aim of providing a lender of last resort, it is a natural candidate for the role of providing a backstop facility to deal with disequilibrating capital flows. Of course, the original purpose of the IMF was to lend to cover deficits in the current account, and Article VI specifically precluded lending to finance a capital outflow. But this Article has for long been something of a dead letter: at the very least, many of the current-account deficits for which the IMF has lent have been amplified by capital outflows ('capital flight'). It is many years, if indeed it ever occurred, since the Fund exercised the right given to it by Article VI, Section 1(a), to 'request a member to exercise controls to prevent ... use of the general resources of the Fund' to meet a large or sustained outflow of capital. For some years now the Fund's policy has rather been to encourage liberalization of the capital as well as the current account.

II DEVELOPING-COUNTRY INTERESTS IN THE PROPOSAL

Clearly, developing countries will need to evaluate their interests differently depending on whether or not they could expect to be eligible to draw from a new facility in the next few years. I shall consider first the interests of those countries that could expect to be eligible, and subsequently of other countries.

Interests of Potential Participants

The dominant consideration for potential participants would presumably be whether an IMF facility of the type proposed would work. It would clearly have a limited role: it could not be expected to save a country that has a serious balance-of-payments problem, and indeed its availability to a country in that situation could make things worse rather than better. This is because aid is a two-edged sword: while it can be enormously valuable in giving adjustment measures time to take effect, thus mitigating the need that would otherwise arise to resort to unnecessarily savage deflationary actions, it can also provide an unfortunate opportunity to delay adjustment if it is provided before adequate measures have been adopted. Similarly, if a country were given access to the facility when its balance-of-payments position was unsustainable and before it had implemented adequate adjustment measures, the facility could simply provide it with the leeway to perpetuate the unsustainable for rather longer, intensifying the ultimate pain when adjustment could no longer be delayed. Thus a key requirement for the facility to function effectively is that the IMF be able to diagnose whether or not the balance-of-payments position is sustainable.

Unfortunately, it is clear that the Fund's recent analysis has not been up to the mark in this respect. Many economists outside the IMF were on record as being concerned about the unsustainability of Mexico's policies in 1993–4, and the threat posed by rising United States interest rates. Yet, apparently, the IMF was complacent about the size of the current-account deficit that had developed there, despite an anaemic growth rate, and the absence of any reason for expecting that the deficit would decline substantially without a real devaluation. The only obvious reason for imagining Mexico's policy stance to have been sustainable was the belief that its fiscal accounts were in surplus, coupled with acceptance of the 'Lawson thesis' that current-account deficits do not matter if they are the counterpart to a deficit by the private rather than the public sector. But both elements of that argument were wrong. The Lawson thesis is erroneous in emphasizing the public/private counterpart to a deficit rather than whether it is being used to finance investment rather than consumption. Note that the thesis has failed every time it has been advanced: in Chile in 1981, in the United Kingdom in 1988, and in Mexico in 1994. Second, it turned out that Mexico actually had a less solid fiscal position than appeared, since public sector capital spending had been moved off-budget into the Development Bank several years before, when it was so compressed that no one noticed, but it had grown again to 4.1 per cent of GDP by 1994, without the IMF objecting.

However, it now seems that the IMF has learned from the Mexican débâcle that current-account deficits do matter. While any rule of prudence limiting the size of current account deficits judged sustainable is bound to be somewhat arbitrary, it would be better to have an arbitrary limit of, say, 3 per cent of GDP than to have no specific limit at all. There should be some scope for making such a rule a little more sophisticated than a flat limit applicable to all countries, e.g. by allowing a larger current account deficit where it is financed by inflows of direct investment, by allowing a higher limit for a country with a rapid underlying rate of growth, and/or by allowing a larger deficit for a country with a low stock of debt or a high level of exports relative to GDP. But one should certainly demand that the IMF incorporate some reasonable limits on current account deficits into its judgements about sustainability before giving it the authority to approve automatic access to lines of credit to meet a speculative outflow. Unless and until a country had adopted adjustment measures designed to reduce the deficit to the sustainable range, a country with an excessive deficit should be ineligible. Mexico should not have been pre-approved in 1994 when its current account deficit was unsustainable and there were no policy measures in place to reduce it.

Within the limited range of cases for which such a facility might be relevant, its usefulness would depend on the answers to the following questions:

(1) Would it be possible to provide funds fast enough to nip a crisis in the bud?
(2) Would the facility be large enough?
(3) Would the maturity of loans be long enough to nurture the re-establishment of confidence?

The question of the speed with which funds are provided is crucial. In order to be useful, a special facility would need to be able to provide funds considerably more rapidly than has been traditional. This could be accomplished by pre-establishing access, or potential access, to a line of credit at the time of an Article IV consultation, provided that the IMF were satisfied that the country's policies merited support. Subsequent access to that line of credit in the event of need might be automatic or might require Fund approval.

Automatic access would clearly be an advantage in terms of permitting timely access when market pressures develop. Indeed, in the cases that some argue provide the only rationale for creating a new facility, where speed is crucial if assistance is to be of any use at all, automatic access would seem to be essential. This is because it seems inevitable that a requirement that the Fund approve a drawing on a line of credit would involve a significant delay before a drawing were possible. Admittedly, there is no very obvious reason why IMF procedures need be as slow as they are, and the speed with which the IMF moved in the Mexican case reinforces doubts as to whether it would not be possible to do better. Macroeconomic management is by now pretty familiar intellectual terrain. On the other hand, the Managing Director's commitment in advance of consultations with the Executive Board provoked strong protests from some of the European countries. It would seem difficult to envisage a drawing taking place in much less than a month from the time a country recognizes that it faces a need, unless that right is automatic. And a delay of a month gives a lot of time for financial markets to magnify a crisis.

It will be objected that a requirement of prior authorization would impose great demands on the Fund's analytical capacity to judge whether or not a country's policies are sustainable. Had the Fund erred by giving Mexico an automatic right to draw prior to 20 December 1994, it is entirely likely that the crisis would have been postponed a few weeks and would subsequently have proved even more intractable because the inherited stock of indebtedness would have been bigger. In fact, however, the difference in analytical requirements is quite limited. If the IMF had to make a quick decision at the time that a country needed to draw, it would still need to make judgements about whether policies were adequate and the balance of payments was sustainable: it would simply avoid the potential embarrassment of seeing a country that it had declared to be sound being judged by the markets to be risky, without having the chance to think again before it provided support. But if one believes that the IMF is capable of making sound judgements, and leading rather than following the markets, then it is really not obvious that it will be in a markedly better position to make such judgements at the time the country needs to draw than a few months before. If the country is required to provide the Fund with key financial statistics which give assurance that its policy stance is indeed that which was endorsed at the time the line of credit was approved, the risks in automatic access ought not to be significantly greater than those involved in a decision at the time a drawing is made. It would be a tragedy if the Fund's blindness to the unsustainability of Mexico's policies, which easily could be and hopefully already has been remedied, were to preclude the facility being designed in such a way as to be useful.

The second question is that of the size of the facility. The Mexican experience made it transparently clear that in order to address this type of need the resources to be made available have to be much larger than those that have traditionally been provided by the Fund. The additional resources that would be needed might come from several sources: from an expansion in the size of the Fund's regular resources; from an expansion in the size of commitments to the GAB, and/or an increase in the number of countries that contribute to the GAB; from an alternative GAB-like facility that might be created for this specific purpose; or from a decision to borrow in the financial markets. It would make little difference to borrowers as to where the funds came from, except in so far as potential participants might be expected to contribute relatively more under some proposals than others, with the presumption being that they would contribute the most if the facility were financed by a tailor-made GAB-like arrangement. But even this would not be a matter of much consequence to them, since the borrowings would doubtless remain liquid and the IMF pays market interest rates on its borrowing comparable to what a country can earn by holding reserves in other forms.

The final question is that of maturity. The Mexican experience shows that a short-term facility would not be very useful. A longer-term facility could, of course, have a requirement for early repayment keyed to the reflow of reserves, so that the average expected maturity might be quite short, but any facility that has an unconditional requirement of repayment in a very short time-frame seems unlikely to be able to help restore confidence except in the easy cases where this awaits some exogenous event (like the approval of NAFTA in November 1993).

Interests of Non-Participants

The interests of countries that would not participate in the new facility involve largely different issues. Of course, a facility that permitted countries that borrowed from it to ride out unjustified speculative pressures would also have some spillover benefits for non-participants, inasmuch as avoidance of unnecessary deflationary adjustment in those countries would help to maintain higher demand for imports (and thus of exports from other developing countries). But there are at least two other issues that seem likely to be of greater significance to those that would not themselves expect to participate.

The first of these issues is whether the new facility would crowd out other lending activities of the IMF. Clearly, this is much more likely if it were financed from the Fund's regular resources than if special arrangements were made to borrow from some other source, either the GAB, the potential participants in the facility in a separate GAB-like arrangement, or the market. This would be of special importance if the maturity were longer, which was argued above to be essential if the facility is to be effective. Thus other developing countries would seem to have a very clear interest in ensuring that, if such a facility comes into being, it be provided with its own distinctive source of finance rather than draw on the Fund's regular resources, and that it be financed in a way that does not require non-participating developing countries to contribute.

In his speech to the Social Summit in Copenhagen on 7 March 1995, the Managing Director of the IMF mentioned study of 'the role the SDR could play in putting in place a last-resort financial safety net for the world'. The intellectual antecedents of this idea go a long way back. In the 1970s the then Research Director of the Fund, Jacques Polak, pointed out the simplification in the Fund's operations that could be effectuated if the General Account were to operate exclusively in SDRs. Before that, the proposals of Robert Triffin to reform the IMF so as to allow it to increase liquidity (1959) had envisaged this being done partly by open-market operations in which the IMF would buy securities in the money markets of major members and partly by allowing the Fund to extend loans to countries that needed to borrow from it. Earlier still, the Keynes Plan for an International Clearing Union had envisaged that 'bancor' would be created automatically as credits on the books of surplus countries as deficit countries drew on their credit lines.

Given that the world has a fiduciary reserve asset created by the IMF, nothing could be more natural, or technically more simple, than to use it to finance lender-of-last-resort activities by a backstop facility of the character here discussed. This way of financing the facility might also overcome the possible objection from some members that it would crowd out the normal lending activities of the IMF by competing for the limited pool of the Fund's financial resources. On the contrary, a decision to finance a new facility by the creation of additional SDRs might lead on in due course to a funding of all the Fund's lending by SDR creation, with the possibility this would offer of expansion in the resources available for other activities. (Of course, the fear of this effect may induce the financially conservative members of the Fund to oppose the proposal.)

The question arises as to whether such a proposal is consistent with the IMF Articles of Agreement. The principle for allocating SDRs that is enshrined in Article XVIII, Section 2(b), reads: 'The rates at which allocations are to be made shall be expressed as percentages of quotas on the date of each decision to allocate ... The percentage shall be the same for all participants.'

No alternative basis for allocation is provided for in the Articles. It is therefore clear that a facility of indeterminate size would not be compatible with Article XVIII. What might be legal would be to create, once and for all, a new facility of significant size by having every member, or all the members that would be eligible to draw, assign their share of an allocation to the facility. Obviously those members that do not expect to draw would have an interest in ensuring that only countries that did expect to draw would be required to assign their share of the allocation: under such a formula they might even receive an allocation that otherwise would not happen.

This formulation recalls the many ingenious proposals that have been advanced over the years for enabling deserving groups of countries to receive new SDR allocations in the absence of a general allocation. The basic idea has always been that some countries should pass on their new allocations to the group that it was desired to favour. None of these proposals has ever won approval: they require not only the willingness of 85 per cent of the IMF voting power to approve an allocation, but unanimous consent on the part of the members expected to assign their allocations.

The alternative to achieving such unanimity would be to amend the Articles of Agreement, which is an equally daunting task.

The other issue that surely impinges on non-participants is whether the creation of such a facility might provide a mechanism for reinvigorating the IMF. It is a weakness of the IMF that since the mid-1970s it has provided rather little in the way of services that its major shareholders find of any direct value: they have not borrowed from it, nor has there been any effective IMF input into producing mutual consistency among their macroeconomic policies. The main benefits that they perceive themselves to derive from their participation in the IMF are to have an institution to deal cooperatively with systemic problems like debt and the transition and to provide a collective international response to countries that require international support in order to get back on their feet. Having the IMF meet a systemic need for a backstop facility to stabilize the process of investment in emergent markets, or even more to help fulfil agreed exchange-rate commitments on the part of industrial countries, might help maintain their support for the institution. Such support would seem to be in the interest of developing countries, inasmuch as they are now the borrowers from the Fund and the recipients of its technical assistance.

The adoption of a backstop facility might even provide an occasion for extending the scope of effective surveillance beyond the countries that borrow from the IMF. This is because it would introduce the Fund into the business of asking whether its members' policies are sustainable even when they are not seeking to borrow immediately. Essentially the same principles that are needed to evaluate whether a country can safely be given access to a line of credit could be used to evaluate the policies of the major industrial countries. It might therefore be a relatively small additional step to introduce effective surveillance over the countries of major systemic significance, with the hope that might offer of improving their macroeconomic management.

If there is felt to be a need for backstop finance and the IMF is not chosen as the vehicle for providing it, one would assume that the BIS or the G-7 would be called on to fulfil that role. The BIS has in the past provided only bridging finance, so that its acceptance of this role would be a major departure. In either event, developing countries would be deprived of any input into the determination of how much help is provided and on what conditions. Individual countries that sought help would have to negotiate bilaterally with the G-7 or the BIS, neither of which have any developing-country participation, such as one hopes provides a relatively sympathetic environment within the IMF.

V CONCLUSIONS

The role envisaged for a backstop facility of the character discussed in this chapter is necessarily limited to cases where the balance-of-payments position is sustainable but not so solid as to preclude the emergence of speculative pressures in response to unexpected developments. This will typically mean countries with current-account deficits in the range of 1 to perhaps 4 per cent of GDP, or with larger deficits but where remedial adjustment measures have already been implemented and the Fund is satisfied that the deficit is in the course of declining to a sustainable level. If the facility were also used to provide resources to help defend pegged exchange rates, it would similarly be crucial to develop and utilize techniques for estimating equilibrium exchange rates, and avoid lending to defend disequilibrium rates. Given the uncertainty involved in such estimations, this would imply restricting support to countries operating with a wide band for their exchange rates.

Quite a large number of developing countries, including many of the larger ones, might be eligible to draw on such a facility. Their interest is primarily in judging whether such a facility could work. This depends upon the IMF learning the lesson of the Mexican crisis, that large current-account deficits are presumptively dangerous, and showing greater awareness of that in the future than it has done in the immediate past. It also requires that any facility be automatically available once a line of credit has been approved, upon the finance made available being on a scale substantially greater than the IMF has been providing in recent years, and upon maturities being sufficiently long.

The interests of the remaining developing countries, those that still have little access to the international capital market and that accordingly are unlikely to be candidates for drawing on any such facility for the foreseeable future, are different. They certainly have a strong interest in ensuring that, if such a facility is developed, it has its own source of financing and does not lead to a squeeze on the funds available to them under the Fund's existing facilities. Provided that condition is met, however, it might be advantageous to them to have such a facility developed within the context of the IMF, since this would help to keep the institution alive and might help to increase its role in areas such as surveillance of the larger countries. The larger scale on which such a facility would have to operate in order to be effective might even create precedents to which non-participants could subsequently appeal in arguing for larger access limits under the Fund's existing facilities.

However, even if one does not take the traditional concerns about moral hazard very seriously,[2] it may seem unlikely that the industrial countries will be willing to endorse the conditions that have been suggested above as being essential in order to allow such a facility to operate effectively. Most problems of capital flows can probably be addressed through the Fund's existing facilities, and it may be judged an over-reaction to create a new facility to deal with the occasional case where a threat of default could arise in the absence of immediate disbursement. Perhaps it would be better to think of some other way of containing that particular threat.

The most promising alternative approach would seem to be that being urged by Jeffrey Sachs, who has recently been developing proposals for giving the IMF a duty and a capacity to respond to debt difficulties by operating an international analogue to the Chapter 11 proceedings in the United States bankruptcy code. To prevent a government that has decided to undertake reforms from being pushed into a vicious circle, in which the erosion of the state's fiscal capacity emasculates its ability to supply basic services which in turn undermines the willingness of the populace to respect the authority of the state and pay their taxes, Sachs argues that it needs the same elements as in a financial restructuring under Chapter 11. These involve 'a debt service standstill at the outset of reforms; fresh working capital during restructuring, so that critical governmental functions don't collapse; and (usually) some debt reduction at the culmination of reforms, to help reestablish the Government's solvency' (Sachs, 1995).

It can be argued that the IMF already has the legal authority to impose a debt-service standstill, by invoking the provisions of Article VI of the IMF. The fresh working capital during restructuring is already in principle provided by the Fund's lending programmes (although, Sachs argues, typically on too modest a scale). Extensive debt reconstruction, involving both debt reduction and a stretching of maturities, was negotiated for a number of countries under the Brady Plan, albeit without the assurance that a legal basis would have provided for enforcing acceptance by recalcitrant creditors. Thus the idea of turning the IMF into an agency responsible for administering bankruptcy-style proceedings where countries find themselves impossibly illiquid does not appear entirely fanciful. Moreover, market knowledge that this was likely to happen if a country overborrowed might provide a useful discipline discouraging the markets from pouring excessive funds into emergent markets as has tended to happen in recent years.

Notes

1. The author is indebted to William Cline, Jeffrey Frankel and Morris Goldstein for helpful comments on a previous draft.
2. What country would deliberately risk getting itself into a situation like that in which Mexico found itself because of a belief that this would entitle it to some bailout finance?

References

Sachs, Jeffrey (1995) 'The IMF and Economies in Crisis', Harvard Institute for International Development, mimeo.

Triffin, Robert (1959) *Gold and the Dollar Crisis* (New Haven: Yale University Press).

6 Cross-Border Payments Taxes and Alternative Capital Account Regimes

Rudi Dornbusch

I INTRODUCTION

This chapter reports on the scope for managing international capital flows by means of explicit taxes or restrictions. This has been an area of hot debate ever since the Mexican crisis, and the resulting contagion spread to other emerging market economies. At the same time, it is a topic left over from the 1992 collapse of European economies. The IMF has already issued a verdict: there is a problem, something ought to be done, nothing can be done (IMF, 1995). But the question stays on the agenda simply because it is implausible that countries otherwise well managed should become exposed to excess capital flows or the accompanying volatility.

Specifically, several points are to be made:

- First, capital controls are in no way a panacea. In fact, they are undesirable if their purpose is to support and sustain mismanagement of exchange rates (see Dornbusch *et al.*, 1995).
- Second, while a near-perfect system of managing capital flows would be desirable, something that falls even far short may still do the job much better than doing nothing.
- Third, experience with the management of capital flows is not uniformly negative – Chile is an outstanding example of stellar performance and managed capital flows.
- Fourth, a Tobin tax is a plausible measure for any individual country even if there is no global move to such a scheme. We advocate here a specific variant, a cross-border payments tax.
- Fifth, there are other ways of segmenting capital markets, ranging from strict exchange control to reserve deposits on selected or all cross-border transactions.
- Finally, no system is effective unless it is comprehensive in its coverage and moderate in its ambitions. Failure on either count

will lead to troublesome distortions. Managing the capital account decidedly does not provide coverage for bad macroeconomic policies. It may, however, provide a window for sequencing the opening of domestic financial markets or trade in a way that is not dominated or even swamped by cross-border capital flows.

II THE CAPITAL-FLOW PROBLEM

To prepare the ground, consider the capital-flow problem of developing countries. Stated simply, there is either too much capital or too little, and it is mostly hot rather than cold.

Table 6.1 shows the size and composition of capital flows. Across sub-periods – the build-up of the first debt crisis, the period of involuntary lending, the new boom – the amounts vary sharply across periods and even in sign. In composition, direct investment is always small and portfolio investment large.

More strikingly, the number of emerging market funds increased almost tenfold in the period 1988–94. For Latin America, the increase in the number of funds was by a factor of more than twenty.

Of course, the capital-flow issue is not just one of emerging economies and perhaps not even dominantly so. The large swings in the exchange rates of the United States dollar and the yen clearly have their counterpart in capital flows that are largely unrelated to the financing of current-account balances or the real exchange rate consistent with full employment. Little rhyme or reason can be found, for example, for the strong dollar in 1985 or the superstrong yen in early 1995.

Table 6.1 Net capital inflows to developing countries (period average, $ billion)

	1977–82	*1983–9*	*1990–4*
All developing countries	30.5	8.8	104.9
Asia	15.8	16.7	52.1
Net direct investment	2.7	5.2	23.4
Latin America	26.3	−16.6	40.1
Net direct investment	5.3	4.4	11.9
Other	−11.6	8.7	12.7
Net direct investment	3.2	3.7	3.8

Source: International Monetary Fund.

In what follows we concentrate on issues raised for emerging economies where the management of capital flows is a problem in several different ways.

- First, as an individual country opens up, how can it avoid the fact that large capital inflows lead to excessive currency appreciation? The smaller the country, the larger the risk.
- Second, in the course of the waves of lending and credit rationing, what is a regime that helps stabilize capital flows?
- Third, what is a good capital account regime to deal with the ebb and flow of capital movements driven by country-specific news, good or bad?
- Fourth, what is appropriate advice to countries receiving too little capital?

The last issue can be dealt with quickly. Clearly, a country has to offer attractive, plausible returns to investors. If not, why should capital come? Often it may be difficult in terms of social, economic and political trade-offs to offer such returns. It may also be short-sighted because capital flows can potentially make a lot of difference. For countries receiving too little capital, the issue of managing the capital account is just as significant as for those receiving too much. In all likelihood, poor policies towards capital flows are one of the reasons why capital is unwilling to come. These policies might involve, for instance, measures that raise serious questions about property rights or apparently random behaviour towards convertibility or other issues bearing on the quality of an investment. Predictability and stability of the regime are key aspects of good policy. They may not be enough to attract capital, but they certainly are preconditions. Any capital that comes even in the absence of these basics is also likely to leave without much notice.

But the focus today is much more on countries receiving either too much capital or capital that is too erratic, resulting in excess volatility throughout the macroeconomy. Consider then countries receiving too much capital. The most obvious case is a situation of initial opening-up. Or consider a country exposed to volatile capital – say Brazil, as a bystander of Argentine and Mexican instability, or Asian countries faced with a Latin-driven sell-off. A financial transactions tax may be a remedy or at least a shock-absorber for these problems. We state the case, elaborate some points of cost:benefit and then return to the application.

III A TRADING TAX

It is useful to state at the outset that the economic contribution of capital inflows varies directly with the commitment of investors. The more the lenders have the mind-set of investors rather than traders, the longer the horizon with which they approach a proposition and the more stabilizing and growth-enhancing their contribution. By contrast, the shorter the maturity of loans, the more they are out of tune with development needs and the more risky they are in the perspective of a bank-run syndrome. A financial transactions tax, or more narrowly a foreign-exchange transactions tax, is designed to lengthen horizons and shift agents from trading to investing; if there is too much trading at short horizon, trading should be taxed.

Such a tax has been advocated by Nobel Laureate James Tobin, but has also attracted vigorous support from the present Deputy Secretary of the United States Treasury, Larry Summers, in his former academic incarnation. Among industrial countries, it was on the G-7 Halifax menu and enjoys official interest, if not support, in Canada and France. Among emerging economies it has attracted interest in the aftermath of the Mexican crisis or in the context of excessive capital inflows and resulting sterilization problems. Finally, among NGOs it is of interest as a source of world revenue for good causes.

A financial transactions tax heavily penalizes short-run trading but puts virtually zero penalty on the long-term profitability of investment. The reason is that payment of, say, 0.25 per cent tax on a ten-year investment represents a negligible fraction of the principal earnings. By contrast, on an overnight round trip it would eat up the profits except on investments with extremely high returns. With this tax, the hurdle rate of return for short-term transactions is inversely related to the holding period. A one-night stand would require an annualized rate of return of more than 470 per cent just to pay the tax. For a half-year round trip the hurdle rate is down to almost 1 per cent, and for a three-year investment the burden falls to less than 0.2 per cent.

Clearly, the tax is not an obstacle to long-term investment. Investors will look for assets that promise serious returns in the long term, not for a way to get overnight returns from the negative-sum game of volatility. Predictably, the round-trip industry will disappear, and good riddance.

The scheme might sound populist – 'tax the trader' – but it is, in fact, in the best tradition of the Chicago School. The economy needs a favourable environment for capital accumulation. Often, chief executives of non-financial businesses divide their time between litigation and speculation, rather than focusing on investment in research and development of technology, products and markets. Capitalism blossoms when business takes the long view, unimpeded by insecurity of property rights or financial fragility. Innovation and competition have undermined the blessings of capitalism by turning financial markets into overly trigger-happy institutions with an emphasis on debt-leverage, capital gains and the short horizon. Liquidity is the buzzword; the fallacy is that in liquid markets 'one can get out' before the curtain goes down.

Keynes, in the *General Theory*, offers a description of the difference between 'speculation' – which is geared to making capital gains from uncovering the shifting psychological moods of the market – and 'enterprise'– which seeks to earn income from the long-term holding of an asset. He notes the markets' pursuit of short-term capital gains rather than long-term holding yields:

> When capital development of a country becomes a by-product of the activities of a casino, the job is likely to be ill-done. The measure of success attained by Wall Street, regarded as an institution of which the proper social purpose is to direct new investment into the most profitable channels in terms of future yield, cannot be claimed as one of the outstanding triumphs of laissez-faire capitalism – which is not surprising, if I am right in thinking that the best brains of Wall Street have been in fact directed toward a different object.

Keynes concludes with the recommendation of: 'a substantial transfer tax on all transaction ... to mitigate the dominance of speculation over enterprise in the United States'.

That advice of 1934 is even more appropriate today. In fact, as already noted, James Tobin has advocated a variant of this scheme to curb excessive zest for speculation in international capital markets. In Tobin's scheme, a tax on international currency purchases should 'throw some sand in the wheels' of international markets. Others have gone further to argue that if sand is not enough, use rocks.

Why interfere with short-horizon speculations? It could be argued that financial market participants must know what is best for them. Who is to second-guess them to claim that their individual profit maximization does not also lead to the best social use of resources? The answer is that short-run focus creates a negative externality in the form of excessive liquidity. An analogy helps build the case. Most sane people agree that gun control is desirable because an uncomfortably large number of people carry guns. Whatever they may be maximizing, it surely is not social welfare. Gun control disarms an unduly trigger-happy world, just as speed-limits cool unduly aggressive driving. Liquidity is of the same nature: it cries out for a tax that curbs the excess. We all want to be totally liquid, all the time; yet the economy's capital must be held. Too sharp a focus on the short run means that the capital stock will adjust; there will be too little, and what there is will be short-lived and not the most productive.

If most trading takes a short focus, most actors in the economy cannot but follow the same pattern. If everybody speaks loudly, we have to shout to be heard; if everybody carries revolvers, we have to carry submachine guns to be safe. And if everybody trades by the minute, we have to trade by the second to get ahead. The economy converges to a bad equilibrium, totally focused on minute capital gains, and far away from the investment in productive ventures and the building of businesses. Nobody stops us from taking the long view, but that would be a lonely life made far more precarious by the high volatility created by the market's short horizon. Excess liquidity produces an abnormal and counter-productive shortening of the economic horizon; it spreads from financial markets to corporate suites and the shop floor.

A financial transactions tax is no panacea, just as gun control would not stop all murder; poison and knives would make a comeback. And speed-limits have not done away with traffic accidents (and not even altogether with speeding). A financial transactions tax will not stop speculation altogether. But it certainly will help lengthen the horizon and focus the mind of capital markets on enterprise and investment rather than trading.

The notion of a financial transactions tax involves a much broader ambition to refocus financial markets – it would apply to all financial assets rather than only foreign exchange. Here our concern is a much narrower one of lengthening the horizon for cross-border flows. That makes effectiveness much stronger and limits the costs. Let us consider how such a foreign-exchange tax might work.

Implementation

Suppose every purchase or sale of foreign exchange and every cross-border payment is taxed in a particular country at the rate of, say, 0.25

per cent, irrespective of whether it is a goods transaction, a service deal or a financial operation. Whatever sale or purchase of foreign exchange occurs, participants are required to remit to the government 0.25 per cent and are jointly liable. (Much like a stamp tax of old. Of course, the payment would only be made by one party, exporter or importer.) Thus, clearly an exporter on receipt of his proceeds will have to pay; an importer will pay as she acquires foreign exchange for payment. The same is true for tourist operators or insurance brokers, recipients of interest or dividends, buyers of stocks or bonds or real estate.

The point of the Tobin tax is that the amount paid is independent of the maturity of the project – it is a fixed cost incurred for making cross-border transactions. The profitability of the transactions, however, depends on the maturity. The tax achieves two desirable outcomes: first, unlike in the case of quotas or administrative procedures, investors can self-select as to who wants to invest in what. Thus, a maximum of market choice and discipline is maintained and a minimum of bureaucratic control intrudes. Second, the incentive structure of the tax is such as to discourage investors who are unwilling to commit. The tax makes it very expensive to stay only for a brief period and thus discriminates against investors who *ex ante* feel they only want to stay for a short period. This self-selection process lengthens the implicit maturity of the investment.

A Tobin tax does not take investors hostage. In the face of a fundamental and lasting deterioration of prospects they would sell off. But if the deterioration is only temporary, they would weigh hanging in against the extra cost of a round trip. If the uncertainty is limited and the adversity short-lived, on balance they might choose to stay. This discussion highlights the fact that a Tobin tax in no way is a panacea permitting a government to get by with bad policies; it merely makes capital somewhat less liquid.

Effectiveness

The focus of the proposed tax is on cross-border payments which lead to reserve losses or gains, exchange-rate movements, inflation or deflation. The focus is not on whether, offshore, someone buys from someone else a claim on domestic assets. Here is a critical difference from financial transactions taxes. Our purpose is not to reduce the volatility of stock or bond prices but rather to manage the pace of cross-border flows. The prospects of accomplishing this are far better than those of stabilizing asset prices. Hence much of the discussion of why financial transactions taxes cannot work is irrelevant to a foreign-exchange tax. (For a forceful statement of why a financial transactions tax might not work and is definitely undesirable, see Hakkio, 1994.)

How effective would the tax be? Consider implementation in a single country. Can it work? The immediate temptation, not surprisingly, is to ask how the tax can be avoided. It is obvious that unless it applies to all and any cross-border transaction, the untaxed transactions will become vehicles for under-or over- invoicing. Once it is comprehensive, avoidance is difficult, much more difficult than in the case of financial transactions taxes. The latter can be avoided by trading outside the jurisdiction where the tax is levied.

A tax that applies solely to cross-border transactions falls fully within the jurisdiction of the levying country. Consider the example of a securities transactions tax designed to reduce short-term speculation in stocks and the resulting volatility. Levying the tax forces the business offshore and leaves the volatility unchanged. By contrast, cross-border payments by definition cannot be forced offshore. This difference takes away the central criticism of financial transactions taxes, namely that they cannot work unless they are practised at the world level.

This is an important aspect of my proposal. Suppose cross-border investments in stocks and bonds are taxed as is bank borrowing abroad. That obviously forces large corporations into borrowing abroad. That does not make a difference because they, too, are taxed upon repatriating their borrowing. If the tax is administered in a comprehensive way, by registration of capital transactions where they do not enter the foreign-exchange market and by stiff penalties, the system can be broadly effective.

No doubt, there will be some transactions that might escape. One possibility is obviously fraud, but that is hard for large corporations or financial institutions and hence will not systematically amount to much. The other is the possibility of offshore transactions by domestic agents: rather than exporting capital at the cost of the tax, a Brazilian firm might borrow in New York to finance an investment in Angola. Again this will be hard for large companies, and for small companies it is difficult and hence unimportant. There is always some leakage in taxation; the point of this system is that it is difficult to circumvent it and not really worthwhile since the tax rate is very low except for round-trip financial agents.

Costs

If the tax is effective, what are the costs of applying the system?. There are obviously two kinds of costs. First, this is a tax on trade in goods, services and assets and as such reduces the level of trade. That is undesirable but also unlikely to be quantitatively of great importance. A tax of 0.25 per cent is so small that, except for the administrative encumbrance, it would practically not matter for any goods or services transactions. And the same is true for long-term investments. For short-term financial transactions, by contrast, it does matter, and in fact is prohibitive; but here is precisely where the effect should be.

There is, of course, the additional question of the administrative bureaucracy required to implement the tax. Since foreign-exchange transactions mostly go through a relatively concentrated market, there is very little cost in levying the tax. As for cross-border payments that do not go through the local foreign-exchange market, they have to be monitored at the level of tax audits of major firms. Again, this does not appear to be an overriding issue. Auditing will, however, be necessary to avoid such possibilities as offshore clearing of inflows and outflows with taxation only applying to the residual. No doubt, schemes of this kind will come up, but in most countries everybody, including the government, knows how they work, and it is just an issue of tax enforcement to assure compliance.

IV IMF ARGUMENTS

In its important report on international capital markets the IMF (1995) has directly addressed the issue of volatility induced by capital flows, the merits in attempting to shield an economy from capital account disturbances, and the effectiveness of alternative strategies of sterilization, regulation or a financial transactions tax. The IMF team was sufficiently impressed with the problems raised by capital flows to recognize the desirability of policies to manage the capital account. Postponing capital account liberalization is specifically recommended – i.e. financial repression should be continued while other measures of reform go ahead.

The IMF concludes with scepticism on the issue of effective policies to limit capital flows. Policies including selective regulations or reserve requirements can be effective, but not on a lasting basis, not fully, not without important side effects or even perverse results. Its judgement on a financial transactions tax is basically negative.

The IMF discussion of financial transactions taxes picks up the wide range of negative reactions to such a measure that have been offered, specifically in the context of taxes on security transactions rather than cross-border transactions taxes. That discussion need not be entered here because it has little bearing, if any, on the question of a tax on cross-border transactions. There is an IMF reference, however, to capital outflow restrictions practised in the United States in the 1960s which were subsequently repealed because of ineffectiveness due to loopholes. This would seem to draw attention to the need for comprehensiveness rather than to ineffectiveness *per se*. The IMF report also specifically mentions reserve requirements, at the margin, on capital inflows such as practised by Chile or proposed in the European context by Eichengreen and Wyplosz (1993). No judgement is offered on these proposals; this might be deemed to mean quiet IMF assent for lack of alternatives.

V WHO SHOULD USE THE CROSS-BORDER TAX?

In the abstract, a cross-border payments tax appears a plausible instrument to domesticate capital flows. But whose problems, specifically, would it solve? To be honest at this point, one has to say that it will do relatively little other than change a bit the temperature of capital flows, and possibly the extent of capital committed to emerging markets.

That the temperature will cool off is not in doubt. By and large, the tax will work and, once in place, it will sort out investments, encouraging those towards the longer end. There will be disappointments and surprises – investors who stay shorter than they had thought or others who stay beyond their expected duration; but on average the maturity is up and that is a stabilizing factor. It is even more stabilizing if governments respond to the opportunity by shifting to more stable policies which help business take a longer view, and if their own financing employs longer maturities.

The question of what happens to the total capital committed to emerging markets is difficult to assess. The first answer is that volatility is what attracts capital, and less volatility means less lending. That is true for some of the trade-oriented capital, but clearly not for all. It might also be true that the drop-off in trade-oriented investment is offset or perhaps even more than compensated for by an increase in longer-term investment, including direct investment. That is not at all excluded. Thus, the presumption that with the tax less capital will be available is simply not warranted. And even if this were warranted, it would still have to be demonstrated that it is harmful.

Consider then specific situations to see how a tax might work or what else is called for. The starting point is a country that has a balanced current account, or some moderate deficit, and experiences recurrent surges and dry-ups of external capital. These would be predominantly reflected in reserves with the accompanying problem of sterilization or of macroeconomic adjustment. When money comes, reserves swell and costly sterilization has to offset the inflows; when money goes, reserves fall and restraint has to be practised. Some of these fluctuations measure the productivity of capital throughout the world and should be reflected in the country's external balance and level of absorption: when elsewhere capital is plentiful, that is the time to invest and spend, and when it is scarce, the country should save. But because, on account of a number of externalities, these swings are expensive, a cross-border payments tax will be useful in mitigating at least the short-term fluctuations in capital availability. This is the cleanest case.

The next case involves a country with intrinsic political and economic instability. It is difficult to look ahead and get a clear picture of what will happen. External money is available on occasion, but only on a short-term basis. Hard as it is, the country should screen out the 'hot' portion of money and deny itself the temptation to spend more. The hot money, more likely than not, exacerbates the instability. A cross-border payments tax is useful in reducing instability. This is a clear-cut case, too.

Consider next the difficult case of a country that is basically closed to foreign capital and is under pressure to open up – OECD membership requires an open current account. Specifically, consider the Republic of Korea. The country practises relatively complete restrictions against the inflow of capital, for three main reasons. First, saving and investment rates are high and hence there is no obvious need for more capital. In fact, how would the country accommodate a major capital inflow other than by an undesired and even troublesome real appreciation? Second, opening-up means exposure to external instability for which there is little need or tolerance. Third, the domestic financial system is only starting to be deregulated. Accordingly, there is a serious risk in too much cross-border finance, as domestic institutions are still learning to practise competition.

The reasons seem highly plausible. Yet, Korean interest rates are far higher than those in the United States and the won has been appreciating. Clearly, opening-up would increase the supply of capital, push down interest rates and increase lending. In the process, spending would rise and the transfer of resources from foreign lenders to home borrowers would occur via an increased external deficit. Where is the problem in going down to world interest rates?

The Republic of Korea would be well served to proceed with its inevitable opening in two directions. First, direct investment should be immediately and fully liberalized in both directions. Restrictions in this area merely hamper the effectiveness of the division of labour within firms and across borders. Second, a cross-border payments tax should be introduced and, at the outset, should be quite substantial. That acts as a significant restraint on any but the longest cross-border investments. Over time that tax should be reduced so that five years later it will be very moderate. At the same time, full liberalization of cross-border portfolio flows should take place. The combination of policies allows a gradual internationalization of the financial sector. It ensures that flows will be at the outset of very substantial maturity and hence fully impervious to short-term events. Once the internationalization is accomplished, a far more moderate tax is appropriate to provide the minor noise reduction that combines the double objective of substantial openness and short-term stabilization.

The strategy will not altogether contain net capital inflows. The Republic of Korea may well find that the net direction of flow is still inward and that either a difficult sterilization task or a current-account deficit results. Here the issue is predominantly how long-term capital should be allocated in the world, and it is neither operational nor desirable to interfere too much in this respect. The purpose of a cross-border tax is to avoid countries having precarious financing for large deficits, not to avoid imbalances.

VI ALTERNATIVE MEASURES

If the issue is to contain capital flows, a broad array of policies can be thought of. At one extreme, there is full financial repression with a heavy exchange-control bureaucracy. A milder form is selective control of capital flows according to stated criteria such as the nature of investment vehicles or maturity or characteristics of financial intermediaries. At the other end of the spectrum, there is a clean, comprehensive, moderate cross-border transactions tax. Controls are strictly undesirable – they involve bureaucracies, corruption and a lack of flexibility in response to economic criteria. The more moderate strategy of selective controls at least allows the prospect of full liberalization for direct investment, possibly the stock market and long-term fixed income. Of course, financial engineering may easily play havoc with such attempted controls.

Then there is the possibility of reserve requirements on cross-border flows, either across the board or at the margin. The trouble here is that these deposits must be fully comprehensive, including not only all forms of inward-bound financial transactions but also reserves on offshore borrowing of non- financial agents. A clean reserve requirement system is effectively the same as a cross-border transactions tax. The only difference is that a cross-border payments tax is more comprehensive and involves less administrative complication. It thus limits from the outset the incentive to invent transactions that could circumvent the tax.

VII A WORLD SYSTEM?

A last set of questions concerns the implementation of such a system. Specifically, would it not be a good idea to do this at the world level? And failing that, can an individual country do it?

Opponents of a cross-border financial tax will be quick to claim that it cannot work. Business will simply move offshore, to the islands where catering to tax evasion is already the chief industry. True, some trading would move offshore. But the risk is easily exaggerated, and in any event it can be checked. As argued above, what is true of a financial transactions tax is much less true of a cross-border tax. Moreover, why not seek international agreement on a world tax since the disease is clearly spreading?

The G-7 has not done anything useful for years. Why not surprise the world with a genuine innovation – an agreement on a world cross-border tax or even the broader concept of a comprehensive financial transactions tax? All governments want revenue; none believes short-horizon speculation does anyone any good. Liberalization of world trade in financial services is the most fiercely lobbied issue of the day; a financial transactions tax can tame resulting capital flows, thus enhancing their productivity, and make the world capital market safe for development finance.

It is clear from the IMF's account (IMF, 1995, pp. 98–9) that this is not about to happen. There is scepticism of the effectiveness and potential comprehensiveness of such a tax, and there is an overriding fear of the vehement backlash from Wall Street. That leaves the question of whether individual countries, against the background of the difficulties of many emerging economies, should not just move ahead individually. The answer is quite clear. A cross-border transactions tax can definitely be administered unilaterally. It gains relatively little from being the system for all. The experience of Chile indicates that prudent, flexible, moderate management of the capital account is an effective strategy in the opening process and beyond. Once capital has become thoroughly accustomed to a country, markets have deepened and the future has stabilized, there is no reason to tamper with international capital flows. Of course, most emerging economies still have a long way to go before reaching that stage.

An entirely different question about the world system is the discriminatory aspect of cross-border payments taxes. Clearly, such a tax discriminates between internal and international transactions and, in that fashion, results in new barriers. International institutions rightly express concern when new measures of discrimination are introduced. But the point here is that the negative externalities associated with too volatile and large capital flows interfere with the process of opening up goods and internal financial markets. There is no theory demonstrating that capital liberalization must be phased in exact parallel with domestic financial deregulation and trade liberalization. In this perspective, cross-border payments taxes, although they are decidedly discriminatory, are an essential instrument in carrying out the successful integration of a country into the world economy. Inability to use such an instrument will be reflected in excess volatility, inefficient controls and financial repression or a reluctance to open up altogether.

References

Dornbusch, R., I. Goldfajn, and R. O. Valdez (1995) 'Currency Crises and Collapses', *Brookings Papers on Economic Activity*, no. 2.

Eichengreen, B., and C. Wyplosz (1993) 'The Unstable EMS', *Brookings Papers on Economic Activity*, no. 1.

Hakkio, C. (1994) 'Should We Throw Sand in the Gears of Financial Markets?', *Federal Reserve Bank of Kansas Economic Review*, no. 2.

IMF (1995) *International Capital Markets* (Washington, DC: International Monetary Fund).

Summers, V., and L. Summers (1989) 'When Financial Markets Work Too Well: A Cautious Case for a Financial Transactions Tax', *Journal of Financial Services Research*, vol. 3, no. 3.

Tobin, J. (1984) 'On the Efficiency of the Financial System', *Lloyds Bank Review* (July).

Tobin, J. (1993) 'International Currency Regimes, Capital Mobility and Macroeconomic Policy', *Greek Economic Review* (Autumn).

Wall Street Journal (1995) 'Backward at the IMF', editorial page, 24 August.

7 Issues Relating to the Treatment of Capital Movements in the IMF

Aziz Ali Mohammed

I INTRODUCTION

The role of the International Monetary Fund in relation to capital movements has been under intensive discussion in 1997. Under the Articles of Agreement, a 'member may not use the Fund's general resources to meet a large or sustained outflow of capital . . . and the Fund may request a member to exercise controls to prevent such use' (Article VI, Section 1(a)). In a world of rapidly growing but volatile capital flows and increasingly integrated capital markets, there is a vast potential for balance-of-payments difficulties emanating from the capital account. The current Article poses an apparent constraint on the ability of the Fund to help member countries whose policies might otherwise merit Fund support. Moreover, the widespread acceptance of the convertibility obligations of Article VIII has made the imposition of capital controls an untenable general prescription for the Fund to recommend, given the practical difficulties of distinguishing current from capital transactions in many developing countries.

The recognition of the many advantages that the growth of cross-border flows of capital have provided to the global economy, and to emerging market countries in particular, has produced a consensus, within the Fund's decision-making circles, that the IMF should be accorded a leading role in promoting freer movement of capital. Its universal membership and its fifty-year experience of helping to manage the balance-of-payments problems of its members makes it *the* international organization with the best credentials for playing such a role in the capital account area. Developing countries have adhered, in the main, to this consensus, as indicated by their approval of the Interim Committee communiqué of 30 April 1997 to the effect that 'the Fund's Articles should be amended to make the promotion of capital account liberalization a specific purpose of the Fund and to give the Fund appropriate jurisdiction over capital movements'.

However, the developing-country position is carefully nuanced, as indicated by the language of the G-24 Ministerial communiqué approved one day earlier:

> [Ministers] underscored the importance of reaching consensus on a wide variety of issues prior to the consideration of a possible amendment of the Articles of Agreement. These include, inter alia, a clear and workable definition of capital account transactions to be covered under such an Amendment; the advantages of permanent price-based controls; the consideration of restrictions introduced for prudential reasons; the need for flexibility to re-impose controls under specific circumstances; and the confidence that IMF assistance would be available to members facing volatile capital flows. Furthermore, Ministers recalled that several conditions need to be in place to ensure the success of liberalization, including a sustainable macroeconomic framework, well-capitalized banking institutions, and clearly defined legal and institutional arrangements.
>
> (Communiqué of the Intergovernmental Group of Twenty-Four on International Monetary Affairs, 29 April 1997)

II IS AN AMENDMENT NEEDED?

The reference in the G-24 communiqué to reaching consensus *prior* to considering an amendment points to a position taken by several developing-country representatives to the effect that the Fund has sufficient scope under the current Articles to promote the liberalization of capital, without the necessity of imposing new obligations on members through an amendment and creating a new jurisdiction for the Fund to administer. The Fund has, in fact, been pursuing the objectives of full convertibility of member currencies through its surveillance activities and the provision of technical assistance. A more proactive role could be undertaken by intensifying these activities. They have also pointed to the fact that the Fund has not been constrained from lending into capital account problems, as illustrated by the Fund's lending to the United Kingdom as far back as the early 1960s or as recently as Mexico (1995) and Thailand (1997). The Fund will, in any event, have to continue dealing with such capital account problems during the period between the adoption of an amendment by the Executive Board, its approval by Governors for submission to national parliaments and meeting the requirement of a double majority for its coming into force (i.e. approval by *three-fifths* of the members, having *85 per cent* of the total voting power).[1]

III DEFINING JURISDICTION

While maintaining a reservation on their eventual position on the need for an amendment, developing-country representatives have participated in the debate on the implications of an amendment with specific reference to prospective IMF jurisdiction over international capital movements. The discussion has tended to proceed on the analogy of the Fund's existing jurisdiction in respect of current transactions. The analogy can be questioned, however, on the ground that there is today a quite widespread recognition among the Fund's members as to the merits of convertibility on capital account, an acceptance that was not extant in respect of current transactions when the rules and obligations with regard to the Fund's jurisdiction were elaborated in the early 1950s. The following discussion should therefore be construed with this caveat in mind:

Span of Jurisdiction

Parallelism with the methodology applying to the Fund's existing jurisdiction suggests that the Fund's jurisdiction should be restricted to payments and transfers on capital account. However, this is regarded as being too narrow, because most restrictions on capital transactions are not applied to payments and transfers (as was commonly the case in the past with exchange controls) but directly to the underlying transactions. Moreover, in the case of current transactions there was another international organization in place (the General Agreement on Tariffs and Trade (GATT)) dealing with underlying transactions in the trade area and transactions in the services area are covered (albeit more recently) under the General Agreement on Trade in Services (GATS) and are administered by the WTO. There is no corresponding set of international institutional arrangements covering underlying transactions in the capital account area, although discussions have been under way in the OECD and the WTO on the subject. Hence there has been a certain willingness to accept, at least for purposes of discussion, that *if* the Fund is to be invested with effective jurisdiction, it should extend over a range of underlying transactions. Developing countries have cautioned, however, that any broadening of coverage beyond those affecting payments and transfers should be confined to transactions that are directly relevant to the Fund's mandate as overseer of the international monetary system and should be carefully dovetailed with the existing or the prospective institutional architecture for dealing with capital movements (see below). Most developing countries have also considered it important to exclude 'receipts' in order to ensure that they maintain discretion in managing capital inflows.

Character of Transactions

Given the macroeconomic focus of Fund surveillance and its responsibilities in the balance-of-payments area, this would argue for restricting jurisdiction to transactions of a strictly financial character; transactions in real estate, intellectual property and other non-financial intangible assets would thus stand excluded. Similarly, most direct investment transactions that are related to *real sector* activities involving long-term commitments would also be excluded. Moreover, codes of conduct have been formulated or are under discussion to deal with *inward* foreign direct investment (FDI) in both a bilateral and multilateral context (e.g. the OECD work on a Multilateral Agreement on Investment or MAI). However, this leaves open the related issue of regulations applied to *outward* direct investment. It is contended by some that restrictions on outflows are more likely to be applied for macroeconomic and balance-of-payments reasons, and there is little or no coverage of them under existing investment treaties or codes, since these are largely designed to protect the interests of foreign investors and are not concerned with the rights of domestic investors to invest abroad.

Definition of Restrictions

In line with the existing practice (as applied to current payments and transfers) the criterion for determining when a measure is a 'restriction' is that of *discrimination* between domestic and international *transactions*. Thus, discrimination would arise if the authorities permitted their residents to enter into transactions with each other but prevented their residents from engaging in the same transactions with non-residents. However, there have been arguments to the effect that the criterion should be applied more broadly so that members would also be precluded from discriminating between local and foreign *assets* and that foreign assets be classified according to their location. The latter interpretation would create Fund jurisdiction even if restrictions were applied, for example, to residents in respect of property located abroad. It has also been argued by those advocating an even broader interpretation that the discrimination could be either explicit or implicit and it would extend to domestic legislation that conferred 'discriminatory authority', even in the absence of any exercise of such authority in practice. In the view of many developing countries, all such extensions of the criterion are unfruitful and discretion should remain with host governments.

IV TRANSITIONAL PROVISIONS

Several additional issues arise if it is accepted that the Fund should be invested with statutory jurisdiction over international capital movements, however broad or restricted the definitions that are eventually agreed. The first relates to the formulation of transitional provisions (on the analogy of those applied to current transactions under Article XIV). Members are bound to be in different initial positions when an amendment comes into force and their regulations on capital movements have evolved individually over many years to deal with particular structures and conditions. In parallel with the practice applying to the Fund's existing jurisdiction, all restrictions on capital transactions should therefore be 'grandfathered' when the amendment comes into effect, and members would have the authority to adapt them to changing circumstances during the transition period. Members would presumably require prior Fund approval for all new restrictions and procedures would have to be devised for granting such approval on a temporary or a longer-term (or even permanent) basis. The issues here are likely to be more complex, given the constant innovations of products and instruments being devised in financial markets. The Fund could easily become overstretched under the burdens of making fine legal and technical judgements on whether a particular change was an adaptation of an existing restriction or the introduction of a new one. In the case of sudden changes in market sentiment, control measures would have to be adopted quickly and procedures would have to be *prespecified* to deal with emergency situations.

Another issue is the identification of criteria for determining when a member is no longer eligible to shelter under the transitional provisions. This raises a whole set of questions as to the necessary preconditions for liberalization and its pace and sequencing. The debate in the professional literature points to the conclusion that capital account liberalization should be the *last* step in overall liberalizing reforms. On preconditions, there is agreement on the existence of at least the following four elements:

(1) Domestic macroeconomic stabilization, not least the establishment of sound fiscal practices and the attainment (or restoration) of fiscal balance;
(2) Domestic financial strength in the sense of strong prudential regulation, solvent and competitive banking and other financial institutions;
(3) Trade liberalization to remove the most egregious of microeconomic 'distortions' to incentive structures;
(4) A reasonably diversified and strengthened export sector, with ability to withstand periodic severe shocks and maintain a viable balance of payments position.

Another issue that has been raised – again following the analogy with the existing Article XIV – is who determines when the country is ready to accept the new obligations for capital account convertibility. The Fund's past record in assisting members to accept the obligations of Article VIII under its existing jurisdiction demonstrates flexibility and moderation. Arguments have been advanced that the Fund should be expected to take a more proactive role to ensure that members do not delay unduly the acceptance of any new obligations. However, given the widespread acceptance of the merits of capital account convertibility among the membership, it is best left up to members to decide when the conditions for fulfilling any new obligations have been met. The experience of many developing country members with large capital flows, whether inward or outward, is of comparatively recent origin and they must attain a degree of comfort before they can be expected to abandon their dependence on regulations, explicit or implicit taxes or other practices in respect of different types of capital. Hence the pace of liberalization should remain a matter for the country's judgement rather than being subjected to externally-imposed deadlines applied within the context of conditionality for the use of Fund resources.

V APPROVAL POLICIES

Any *new* restrictions on capital outflows as well as inflows applied for macroeconomic (i.e. domestic liquidity and/or exchange rate) management and/or balance-of-payments reasons would presumably be approved on the basis of the same requirements as those for restrictions on current international payments and transfers, i.e. that they are necessary for balance of payments reasons, temporary and non-discriminatory. It is also understood that the Fund would have to permit emergency application of new restrictions on capital *outflows* when a member is confronting a crisis situation; some would insist on the emergency procedures being applied to capital inflows as well.

There are differences of view on whether IMF jurisdiction should cover restrictions imposed for reasons other than balance of payments or macroeconomic management. While most measures of a prudential character are considered unlikely to discriminate between residents and non-residents (and would therefore not constitute a 'restriction'), it is important to agree that members could (*i*) have recourse to restrictions for market and institutional evolution reasons (e.g. when a country is establishing a new stock exchange) and (*ii*) maintain restrictions because of institutional constraints on the effectiveness of their monetary policy instruments. The length of period for which approval of measures taken for these and for prudential reasons is to be given could well be of such extended duration as to argue for excluding them altogether from Fund jurisdiction. There is no agreement on how the restrictions applied by sub-national entities are to be treated; in countries where federal constitutional arrangements invest provinces, states or local governments with independent powers, members would have to be permitted to enter reservations of a blanket character. Also to be considered is whether existing IMF procedures for restrictions imposed for national and international security reasons should be extended to capital account restrictions as well.

Many of the problems touched upon in preceding paragraphs could be minimized if an amendment were simply to state that members would be expected to move to convertibility on capital account with all feasible speed. Given that:

there is a broad acceptance in the Fund membership of the importance of avoiding inappropriate regulation of capital transactions;

- there is much experience of the eroding effectiveness with the passage of time of capital controls applied for balance of payments reasons;
- the Fund has a record of success, acting as a truly cooperative institution, in moving countries to Article VIII status and beyond;

it does appear unnecessary to replicate the practices of the early 1950s – to devise a new jurisdiction for the Fund, to elaborate transitional provisions and develop approval policies, all to promote a purpose that most Fund members already accept as being to their benefit in a rapidly integrating global economy.

VI FINANCING ARRANGEMENTS

Regardless of the merits of an amendment, developing countries continue to emphasize the need for the Fund to provide assurances that its resources would be available to support members' macroeconomic stabilization and/or capital liberalization efforts, including the financing of 'large' (though not necessarily of 'large *and* sustained') outflows. This could mean new and potentially larger requirements in individual cases and at particular times because of several factors: (*i*) the supply of market financing is subject to sudden shifts in risk assessments and changes in actual or perceived relative rates of return; (*ii*) debt-creating private market financing could, over time, contribute to a *structural* widening of individual members' current-account deficits and result in larger financing requirements in the event of policy or exogenous shocks; (*iii*) a build-up in the stock of debt through market borrowing could result in contractual obligations which would be difficult to roll over in the event that market perceptions change.

The possibility of the Fund requesting members to impose (or reimpose) controls on a temporary basis on capital outflows has been raised in the context of conditionality and access to Fund resources where a country faces large capital outflows with only limited prospects of regaining access to capital markets within a relatively short time period. Despite the possibility that Fund financing could engender moral hazard for both creditors and debtors, and knowledge that the effectiveness of many controls erodes with time, it has been argued that the extent of adjustment required and the magnitude of financial support needed could be so beyond the ability of the Fund to provide as to require temporary resort to controls, taxes or other measures to deal with capital account problems in some cases.

VI INSTITUTIONAL ARRANGEMENTS

While the recognition of a leading role for the Fund in the area of capital movements is accepted (most readily within the decision-making circles in the Fund itself), there is 'evidently considerable clutter, confusion and overlapping jurisdiction in the international regimes for capital flows and financial transactions' (see Helleiner, Chapter 1 in this volume). It is important before proceeding to an amendment of the Fund treaty to agree on arrangements that avoid duplication and potential conflicts among different agencies, such as the WTO, the BIS and the OECD. In some respects, other agencies might have the advantage of being able to deploy dispute settlement and compensation mechanisms which the Fund is not equipped to deliver.

Note

1. Amendments have taken between 9 and 27 months to come into force *after* approval by Governors. An amendment to permit the agreed 'equity' allocations of SDRs is already required, and there may be other amendments to be dealt with in the near future, e.g. to achieve an increase in basic votes.

Appendices

COMMUNIQUÉ OF THE INTERGOVERNMENTAL GROUP OF TWENTY-FOUR ON INTERNATIONAL MONETARY AFFAIRS, 20 SEPTEMBER 1997, PARAGRAPHS 5 AND 6

II Capital Account Liberalization

5. While recognizing the benefits for the world economy of greater freedom of capital movements, Ministers emphasize that the capital account liberalization process could put additional stress on the economies that are already straining to adjust to globalization. Ministers agree that, in particular circumstances, precautionary and price-based measures could help countries protect economic stability and sound macroeconomic management.

6. Ministers agree to support further work on the orderly liberalization of capital movements as a prelude to any amendment of the Fund's Articles. They emphasize the need for a progressive and flexible approach, even under any transitional arrangements, to enable members to adjust the pace and sequencing of the liberalization of their capital account, in light of their policy, institutional, and financial conditions. While reiterating that the Fund should play the leading role among international organizations in promoting capital account liberalization, Ministers call attention to the need for the Fund to avoid institutional overstretch, as well as duplication and potential conflicts with other relevant agencies and agreements. They also emphasize the need for adequate technical assistance and financing assurances to help countries to move toward capital account convertibility. In addition, they stress that: (*a*) the liberalization of the capital account should not be made a condition for the use of Fund resources; (*b*) restrictions arising from measures taken by members for prudential and financial market development purposes should benefit from flexible approval policies; and (*c*) the treatment of foreign direct investment and restrictions for security reasons should be outside Fund jurisdiction.

COMMUNIQUÉ OF THE INTERIM COMMITTEE OF THE BOARD OF GOVERNORS OF THE INTERNATIONAL MONETARY FUND, 21 SEPTEMBER 1997, PARAGRAPH 7, AND STATEMENT ON THE LIBERALIZATION OF CAPITAL MOVEMENTS UNDER AN AMENDMENT OF THE FUND'S ARTICLES

7. The Committee reiterated its view that an open and liberal system of capital movements, supported by sound macroeconomic policies and

strong financial systems, enhances economic welfare and prosperity in the world economy. The Committee adopted the Statement on 'The Liberalization of Capital Movements Under an Amendment of the Fund's Articles', and considered that an amendment of the Fund's Articles will provide the most effective means of promoting an orderly liberalization of capital movements consistent with the Fund's role in the international monetary system. The Committee requested the Executive Board to accord high priority to completing its work and submitting a report and a proposed draft amendment to the Board of Governors.

STATEMENT OF THE INTERIM COMMITTEE ON THE LIBERALIZATION OF CAPITAL MOVEMENTS UNDER AN AMENDMENT OF THE FUND'S ARTICLES

1. It is time to add a new chapter to the Bretton Woods agreement. Private capital flows have become much more important to the international monetary system, and an increasingly open and liberal system has proved to be highly beneficial to the world economy. By facilitating the flow of savings to their most productive uses, capital movements increase investment, growth, and prosperity. Provided it is introduced in an orderly manner, and backed both by adequate national policies and a solid multilateral system for surveillance and financial support, the liberalization of capital flows is an essential element of an efficient international monetary system in this age of globalization. The IMF's central role in the international monetary system, and its near universal membership, make it uniquely placed to help this process. The Committee sees the Fund's proposed new mandate as bold in its vision, but cautious in implementation.

2. International capital flows are highly sensitive, inter alia, to the stability of the international monetary system, the quality of macroeconomic policies, and the soundness of domestic financial systems. The recent turmoil in financial markets has demonstrated again the importance of underpinning liberalization with a broad range of structural measures, especially in the monetary and financial sector, and within the framework of a solid mix of macroeconomic and exchange policies. Particular importance will need to be attached to establishing an environment conducive to the efficient utilization of capital and to building sound financial systems solid enough to cope with fluctuations in capital flows. This phased but comprehensive approach will tailor capital account liberalization to the circumstances of individual countries, thereby maximizing the chances of success, not only for each country but also for the international monetary system.

3. These efforts should lead to the establishment of a multilateral and nondiscriminatory system to promote the liberalization of capital

movements. The Fund will have the task of assisting in the establishment of such a system and stands ready to support members' efforts in this regard. Its role is also key to the adoption of policies that would facilitate properly sequenced liberalization and reduce the likelihood of financial and balance of payments crises.

4. In light of the foregoing, the Committee invites the Executive Board to complete its work on a proposed amendment of the Fund's Articles that would make the liberalization of capital movements one of the purposes of the Fund, and extend, as needed, the Fund's jurisdiction through the establishment of carefully-defined and consistently-applied obligations regarding the liberalization of such movements. Safeguards and transitional arrangements are necessary for the success of this major endeavor. Flexible approval policies will have to be adopted. In both the preparation of an amendment to its Articles and in its implementation, the members' obligations under other international agreements will be respected. In pursuing this work, the Committee expects the IMF and other institutions to cooperate closely.

5. Sound liberalization and expanded access to capital markets should reduce the frequency of recourse to Fund resources and other exceptional financing. Nevertheless, the Committee recognizes that, in some circumstances, there could be a large need for financing from the Fund and other sources. The Fund will continue to play a critical role in helping to mobilize financial support for members' adjustment programs. In such endeavors, the Fund will continue its central catalytic role while minimizing moral hazard.

6. In view of the importance of moving decisively towards this new worldwide regime of liberalized capital movements, and welcoming the very broad consensus of the membership on these basic guidelines, the Committee invites the Executive Board to give a high priority to the completion of the required amendment of the Fund's Articles of Agreement.

Index